The Marching Band Handbook

THIRD EDITION

The Marching Band Handbook

*Competitions, Instruments, Clinics, Fundraising,
Publicity, Uniforms, Accessories, Trophies,
Drum Corps, Twirling, Color Guard, Indoor Guard,
Music, Travel, Directories, Bibliographies, Index*

THIRD EDITION

Compiled by Kim R. Holston

foreword by Jim Morrison

McFarland & Company, Inc., Publishers

Jefferson, North Carolina, and London

IN MEMORIAM
Albert Holston
James Feeley

ALSO BY KIM R. HOLSTON

Susan Hayward:
Her Films and Life (McFarland, 2002)

ALSO BY KIM R. HOLSTON AND TOM WINCHESTER

Science Fiction, Fantasy and Horror Film Sequels, Series and Remakes:
An Illustrated Filmography, with Plot Synopses
and Critical Commentary (McFarland, 1997)

LIBRARY OF CONGRESS CATALOGUING-IN-PUBLICATION DATA

Holston, Kim R., 1948–
The marching band handbook : competitions, instruments, clinics,
fundraising, publicity, uniforms, accessories, trophies,
drum corps, twirling, color guard, indoor guard, music,
travel, directories, bibliographies, index /
compiled by Kim R. Holston ;
with a foreword by Jim Morrison.—3rd ed.
p.   cm.
Includes bibliographical references and index.

ISBN 0-7864-1650-5 (softcover : 50# alkaline paper)

1. Marching bands—Directories.
I. Title.
MT733.4.H64   2004   784.8'3'02573—dc22   2003024601

British Library cataloguing data are available

On the cover: Helmet provided by Christopher Ferguson, West Wilkes High School
(Photograph by Marty McGee)

Manufactured in the United States of America

McFarland & Company, Inc., Publishers
Box 611, Jefferson, North Carolina 28640
www.mcfarlandpub.

For the greater Delaware Valley's past and present,
aggressive and charismatic, and dedicated and dynamic
marching activity members, including Rebecca Anderson,
Stephanie Barrar, Isabel Bauerlein, Amanda Carosi, Rose Forlano,
Callie Hildreth, Laura Kuhn, Sara LaMonte, Brittany Marihugh,
Kathy O'Connor, Deanna Parisi, Samantha Riley, Holly Russell,
Rachael Spinken, Ashley Williams, Kerri Winters, Aurelia,
and a Black-Eyed Angel.

Acknowledgments

I want to again thank the band directors, contest sponsors, music publishers, instrument manufacturers, and association directors who responded to my queries when I compiled the previous two editions of this book.

For information, confirmation and special insights this time around, appreciation goes to Raul Reyes and Steve Keiser, Apex and Bpex indoor guards, Newark, DE; John Shaw; Irene and Gina Pratt; Everett and Sarah Randall; Annette and Luke Bauerlein; Lynne Feldman; Joan Satchell; Helen McCormick; Kelly Hensley, instructor, Springfield High School (PA) Indoor Guard; Tammy Lynn Russell, Russell's Allstars Baton and Dance Academy, Coatesville, PA; Jeremy of Trinity High School, NC; Susan Oliver, Arizona State University; Melinda Wemhoff, North Texas Color Guard Association; Tom Britanyak, D.C. Everest High School, WI; Brad Simon, Judges Association of Mid-America; George Hopkins and Deb Rogerson, Crossmen Drum & Bugle Corps; Bluecoats Drum & Bugle Corps chefs and support staff Aunt Buff, Chris Coale, Deenie Werkmeister; Shanon Pollock, communication director of the Auxiliary Dance Alliance; Joey Fortino, Gilroy High School, CA; Kay, American Baton/National Baton Twirling Association; James South, Southwestern Oklahoma State Director of Bands; Tim Redmon, GIA Publications; Jim Saker, Director of University Bands, University of Nebraska–Omaha; Steven Moser, Associate Director of Bands, University of Southern Mississippi; Jeff Weir, U.S. Naval Academy; Elizabeth Z. Barnette, U.S. Air Force Heartland of America Band; Lisa Scheiber, Chesterton (IN) High School; Nichola Stokes, Festival Director, Shrewsbury International Music Festival; Lynn W. England, Air National Guard Band of the Smoky Mountains; W. D. "Bill" Smith, Director, USAF Academy Drum & Bugle Corps; Mitch Dissinger, New Holland (PA) Spectacle of Bands; Karissa Read, Alfred Publishing Company; Sandy Lee and Myra McShane, St. Petersburg Festival of States; Tracy Veglahn, Marshall High School, MN; Glen Buckalew, Gulfport High School, MS; Tony Christofano, Winter Guard International; Todd Zimbelman, Northwest Marching Band Circuit; Allen Henderson, Associate Professor, Department of Music, Austin Peay State University; Rudy Gilbert, Band Director, Norcross High School, GA; Ed Baker, Rome (GA) City Schools Band Booster Association; Roger Wolfe, Rockdale County High School, GA; Woody

Leonard, Band Director, Tift County (GA) High School Band; Joseph Hasty, Assistant Director of Bands, Effingham County (GA) High School; John Mashburn, Forsyth Central High School, Cumming, GA; Jarrett Farrell, Band Director, Worth County (GA) High School; Josh Johnson, Mid-East Performance Association; Sally Romonowski, Miss America Organization; Stephen Cannedy, Pinckneyville (IL) Community High School; Paul Lemen, Director of Bands, Orem (UT) High School; Michelle Howe and Steve Park, Ogden (UT) High School; Kevin Stockman, midwestmarching@yahoo.com; Judy Mitchell, Putnam (OK) City Schools; Debbie Arehart, St. Louis Convention & Visitors Commission; Stephen McCarthy, Band Director, Stockbridge (GA) High School; Adam Albright, Brouhaha Youth Organization; Joseph Lerch, Washington Township (NJ) Schools; and Jim Morrison, Henderson High School, West Chester, PA.

As always, my wife Nancy's advice on the selection of photographs was invaluable.

Contents

Foreword

by Jim Morrison

(Band Director, Henderson High School, West Chester, Pennsylvania*)

Anyone fortunate enough to be entering the job world as a high school marching band director is coming into one of the most potentially enjoyable and gratifying vocations that exist today. That may sound overly dramatic, but I truly believe it. Unfortunately the position can also be one of the most intimidating, confusing, frustrating, and even humiliating experiences you can go through. A new band director needs resources to navigate a sea of decisions, many of which may be scrutinized by administration, band parents, and the tax paying public. Some decisions will be made for you, dictated by the community, the parents, the administration, and perhaps even the students.

One of the most daunting decisions is whether or not to compete. Marching band competitions are held all over the country with as many philosophies and styles as there are bands. Entering a program which is already competitive will require a level of expertise and experience often not available from the college that was supposed to prepare you. Student, parent, and administrative expectations may be high, even if the band was not particularly successful in the past. In some areas, your job security may depend on the band's competitive success.

The drum and bugle corps world has contributed greatly to the evolution of marching band style and has increased the level of challenge well beyond what most band students were asked to do even ten years ago. Imagine showing a football team a play book with only one play, possibly over one hundred pages in length, with each page showing a different route and assignment every four or eight steps. Now tell them to memorize eight to ten minutes of Shakespeare and recite it precisely during the play. Now teach them to do so with the emotion and articulation of professional Shakespearean actors. Then add choreography to each of the four or

*The Henderson Marching Warriors are three-time Atlantic Coast Champions in the Tournament of Bands.

eight step routes, and expect them to achieve it with the poise and grace of experienced dancers. Your team room is probably empty by now—and yet I, like many other band directors around the country, ask my students to do something just this difficult every August. And they do. And they love it. And they do it very well. No other activity or subject utilizes the cognitive, aesthetic, and physical domains of learning to this extent. Not even close. I believe the benefits are life long.

I live next door to several school districts whose bands are noncompetitive, or who compete only in several parades each fall. Some don't even have football programs! Are their jobs any easier? Absolutely! Do they have any less of a need for accurate resources? No. Many of the entries in Kim Holston's book will be useful to any band director, regardless of the philosophy of their program or its level of achievement. Just page through the contents and see the wealth of information he has provided, from buying equipment to hiring show designers to traveling and participating in festivals, parades, and contests.

This book does not seek to rate or judge the information. Directors should do their own research, asking colleagues and veterans for support and guidance on which company to order from or which festival to attend. What it does is present the raw material for all those decisions in a very organized, easy to use, and complete format. I can't think of any area Holston hasn't covered.

It has taken me a long time, with a lot of help and a lot of failure, to get my students to achieve at their current level. This book could very well have made that journey a much shorter one. I plan to use it for the rest of my career.

Preface

There is no lengthy, definitive history of the marching band. And no wonder: It's a big subject with a problem of definition. What is a marching band? When did it originate? A traditional brass band may not qualify. The Gilmore, Sousa, and Goldman bands were primarily concert units. Do percussionists and horn players celebrating a Roman triumph qualify? Eighteenth-century fife and drum? How about Civil War drummers and buglers? Mummers? For this book a broad definition applies: any group that plays instruments or performs to live or recorded music and on numerous occasions marches in parades or performs in indoor or outdoor contests. The primary focus is on the marching band, drum corps, indoor guard and twirling. (Note: The marching activity continues to evolve, and some urban drill teams, heretofore specializing in precision "stepping" or foot stomping, have been seen of late spinning rifles in parades.)

Today there are many types of marching units that incorporate music: high school and college marching bands, drum corps, fife and drum corps, military bands, string bands, twirling units, indoor color guards, and indoor drumlines. High school bands, if they so choose, supplement their football halftime shows and local parades by competing in contests each autumn and during spring trips. Most competitive units include woodwinds, percussion and brass, with a "pit" of electronic instruments, marimba, timpani, gongs and bells gracing the sidelines. The "band front" of rifle squad, silk flag squad, sometimes twirlers, less often these days pom-pom squads, adds to the color and general effect.

More so than in high school, the college student has demands that hinder practice time and thus preclude more than the occasional contest. College bands do, however, maintain an active performance schedule via football halftime shows, community parades, and exhibitions during high school marching contests. For the past three decades, drum corps—independent, non-scholastic units relying on brass and percussion—have traveled and competed each spring and summer.

Strangely, all this activity involving thousands of participants nationwide and internationally goes unnoticed by most citizens. Much of the public thinks of marching bands as "just high school" and associates them with parades and football halftime shows. Meanwhile, over the last several decades the marching band "field show" has evolved into an art form. Shows are often designed by a professional clinician—a drill designer—to best use the band members, the music, and the field or gymnasium for maximum visual and aural effect. Many bands belong to competition circuits for weekly contests each autumn. This movement continues to grow and—although publicity is often an afterthought—attracts more and more spectators and more and more students accompanied by parents and enthusiastic supporters.

Students need not put their instruments, flags, batons, rifles, sabers, or drums aside after Thanksgiving, because marching band affiliated activities take place year-round. In the winter, color guards, indoor percussion units and twirlers participate in gymnasium contests. In the spring, bands participate in festivals throughout the country. Nor is it necessary for a marching band member to retire after college. Senior drum corps are an amalgam of young and old, and instructors in all the activities are in demand.

There is a wealth of information about the marching activity, even if it's hidden from the general public. Virtually every aspect of the activity is covered via magazines for band directors, drum corps members, judges, and twirlers. Music publishing houses print catalogs especially for marching bands. Instructional monographs and videos on how to play instruments, how to twirl a baton, or how to write a show are part of the existing information. The Internet has become an avenue through which marching activity members may purchase supplies and share information. Through consolidation and indexing of this information, *The Marching Band Handbook* aims to provide comprehensive lists for the director, drill designer, booster, musician, guard member and twirler. Information includes sources for instruments or batons, lists of spring and fall competitions, contact information for judging organizations and fund-raising organizations, clinic locations, names and addresses of marching band music publishers, and lists of magazines covering drum corps, twirling or band.

The photos accompanying the text sample, in all its variety, the exciting world of the musical marching activity.

Part 1
Clinicians, Clinics, Workshops, and Drill Design

A symbiotic relationship can exist between high school bands, college bands, and drum corps. High school bands located in the vicinity of DCI or DCA drum corps often can obtain brass, percussion and auxiliary unit instruction. Many colleges sponsor summer clinics. In turn, college band and corps recruitment is facilitated.

Clinicians, Clinics and Workshops

1 American Band College for Directors
Southern Oregon University
1250 Siskiyou Blvd.
Ashland, OR 97520
541-552-7672
www.sou.edu
http://bandworld.jeffnet.org

2 Angelo State University Band Camp
Department of Art & Music
Angelo State University
San Angelo, TX 76909
915-942-2341, x233
http://asubandcamp.com
email: David.Scott@angelo.edu

Arizona State University Band Leadership
Training *see* Educational Programs Network

3 Arkansas State University Band Auxiliary
Camp
Music Department
Box 779
State University, AR 72467

4 Auxiliary JanFest Clinic
University of Georgia School of Music
250 River Road
Athens, GA 30602-3153
706-542-1505
www.uga.edu/~ugabands/aux/main.html
email: ugabands@arches.uga.edu

5 Ball State University Band High School
Band Camps
Ball State University
Office of Conferences and Special Events
Student Center, SC 309
Muncie, IN 47306

765-285-1396
Fax 765-285-5457
www.bsu.edu/provost/confs/about.html

6 Bands of America Summer Band Symposium (site: Illinois State University, Normal, IL)
Bands of America, Inc.
526 Pratt Avenue, North
Schaumburg, IL 60193
800-848-BAND
www.bands.org

7 Brigham Young University Band Leadership Training
c/o Educational Programs
1784 Schuylkill Road
Douglassville, PA 19518

Camp Crescendo *see* Lions Camp Crescendo

8 Central Connecticut State University
Summer Music Institute (brass, instrument repair)
1615 Stanley Street
New Britain, CT 06050
860-832-CCSU
www.ccsu.edu/SummerMusic/Courses.
html

9 Central Michigan University Marching
Band Auxiliary Clinics
College of Extended Learning
School of Music
Mt. Pleasant, MI 48859
800-950-1144, x7137
www.music.cmich.edu

10 The Citadel Summer Camp (drill team,
drum & bugle, guard)

MSC 53
The Citadel
Charleston, SC 29409
www.citadel.edu/summercamp/index.
html

11 Dixie Band Camp (flags, twirling; site:
University of Central Arkansas, Con-
way, AR))
P.O. Box 19004
Jonesboro, AR 72402
870-933-9004
www.geocities.com/dixiebandcamp
email: dixie@inet-direct.com

12 Domaine Forget Music and Dance Academy (brass, woodwinds)
Le Domaine Forget De Charlevoix Inc.
398 chemin les Bains
St. Irenee, Quebec
Canada
www.domaineforget.com/indexang.html

The Drum Club.com *see* Mark Wessels Publications

Drum Set Workshops *see* Sounds of Summer

13 East Carolina University Band Camp
School of Music
A. J. Fletcher Music Center
Greenville, NC 27858-4353
252-328-6331
www.music.ecu.edu/summer/summer_
02.html

East Texas State University Summer Camps
see Texas A&M University-Commerce Summer Music Camps

14 Eastern Trombone Workshop (hosted by
U.S. Army Band)
703-696-3644
www.easterntromboneworkshop.org

15 Department of Music
East Texas State University
Commerce, TX 75428

16 Educational Programs Network
1784 West Schuylkill Road
Douglassville, PA 19518
800-323-0974 (East Coast)
800-305-7565 (West Coast)
www.educationalprograms.com
email: info@edprog.com

17 Ferrito Education, Inc.
545 Ellm Grove Road, Suite 4
Elm Grove, WI 53122
262-786-3140 (Fax same)
www.ferrito.com
email: peter@ferrito.com

18 Florida A&M University Marching 100
Band Camp
FAMU Box 425
Martin Luther King, Jr. Blvd.
Tallahassee, FL 32307-0000
www.famu.edu/acad/colleges

19 Florida State University Marching Band
Leadership Camp
Center for Professional Development
Florida State University
Tallahassee, FL 32306-1640
850-644-2508
Fax 850-644-9934
www.music.fsu.edu
email: rawillia@mailer.fsu.edu

20 Fred J. Miller Inc.
118 Westpark Road
Dayton, OH 45459
800-444-FLAG

George N. Parks Drum Major Academy *see*
Vivace Productions, Inc.

21 High Plains Band Camp
Department of Music
Fort Hays State University
600 Park Street
Hays, KS 67601-4099
785-628-4226
www.fhsu.edu/bandcamp
email: brown1@ruraltel.net

Illinois State University Marching Band Camp
see Bands of America Summer Band Symposium

22 Indiana University Summer Music Clinic
(leadership, brass, woodwind)
c/o Stephen W. Pratt, Director
Indiana University
School of Music—Merrill Hall
Bloomington, IN 47405-0000

23 Indianhead Arts & Education Center
(brass and woodwind repair)
Box 315
Shell Lake, WI 54871
715-468-2414
www.indianheadartscenter.com
email: pelloqaj@uwec.edu
includes instrumental Brass and Woodwind Repair Workshops

24 International Music Camp (includes drumming, piping)
1725 11th Street SW
Minot, ND 58701
Fax 701-838-8472
www.internationalmusiccamp.com

International Peace Gardens Music Camp *see* Sounds of Summer

International Percussion Workshops & Festival *see* KoSA International Percussion Workshops & Festival

25 James Madison University Summer Band
Camp
School of Music
James Madison University
800 S. Main Street
Harrisonburg, VA 22807
540-568-6656
www.jmu.edu/music/mrd/band_camp.
html

26 KoSA International Percussion Workshops & Festival

c/o KoSA Communication
Box 889
Lawton, OK 73502
www.kosamusic.com

27 Leadership Training (directors)
c/o Vivace Productions, Inc.
882 S. Matlack Street, Ste. 202
West Chester, PA 19382
800-264-1121
www.vivaceproductions.com
Sites: Lafayette College (PA), West
Chester University (PA), Lincoln High
School (Sioux Falls, ID), Overton
High School (Memphis, TN), Azle
High School (Azle, TX), Houston
(TX), Timpview High School (Provo,
UT), Tallwood High School (VA)

28 Lions Camp Crescendo
1480 Pine Tavern Road
Lebanon Junction, KY 40150
502-833-4427
Fax 502-833-4249
www.travelbullitt.org/accommodations.
html

29 Lutton Music Personnel Services
732-40 terrace NW
Gainesville, FL 32607
904-376-9055

30 M.A. Dance
P.O. Box 940605
Plano, TX 75094
800-977-7933
Fax 972-633-9737
www.madance.com

31 Marching Auxiliary Camps
800-977-7933
www.maux.com/training.htm
www.MADANCE.com (for dance/drill)

32 Marching Band Drill Designing Workshops
c/o Dan Ryder, Field Drills
12325 Hymeadow, Bldg. 3, Suite 100

Austin, TX 78750
800-727-7889
Fax 512-258-8918
www.danryderfielddrills.com
email: ryderdrill@aol.com

Marching Band Workshop *see* Vivace Productions, Inc.

33 Mark Wessels Publications
8501 Loomis Drive
Plano, TX 75024
972-335-1537
www.thedrumclub.com
email: mwessels@aol.com

34 Mid-America Jr. High Music Camps (drill team, flags, marching)
3541 N. 2nd Street
Lincoln, NE 68521
402-474-4023
www.midamericamusic.com/supercamp.htm
email: dehly@lps.org

35 Mid-Atlantic Band Camps (marching band and band front camps held at Ferrum College, Roanoke, VA)
6223 Lakeside Avenue
Richmond, VA 23228
804-264-9681
www.fiestaval.com/midatlantic/marching_band_camps.htm

36 The Midwest Clinic (site: Chicago)
1920 Waukegan Road, Suite 2
Glenview, IL 60025
www.midwestclinic.com

37 Mobile Percussion Seminar (Thom Hannum's)
8 Sylvia Heights
Hadley, MA 01035
www.percussion.org

38 Motions, LLC (marching auxiliaries)
www.motionsonline.net/home.html

39 New England Music Camp
549 Spring Street

Manchester, CT 06040
860-646-1642

Percussion One/Yamaha "SOS" Series *see* Sounds of Summer

40 Skidmore Jazz Institute
Skidmore College
Office of the Dean of Special Programs
Saratoga Springs, NY 12866-0000

41 Smith Walbridge Clinics (site: Eastern Illinois University)
11 Magnolia Court
Savoy, IL 61874
217-352-4262
Fax 217-352-1656
www.swclinics.com
email: swclinics@swclinics.com

42 Sounds of Summer
c/o Yamaha Corporation of America
3445 East Paris S.E.
Grand Rapids, MI 49512
www.yamaha.com/band/news/nevent/sos.htm
Camps: Texas A&M University (Commerce, TX), Midwest Percussion Camp (Lebanon, IL), Iowa All-State/Yamaha "SOS" Percussion Camp (Iowa City, IA), International Peace Gardens Music Camp (Dunseith, ND), Columbus Pro Percussion (Columbus, OH), University of Nevada (Las Vegas, NV), Percussion One/Yamaha "SOS" Series (Donna, TX), Percussion One/Yamaha "SOS" Series, Del Mar College (Corpus Christi, TX), University of Kentucky (Lexington, KY), Conrad Music Service, Floyd Central High School (Corydon, IN), Oakland University (Rochester, MI), Alma College (Alma, MI), Stephen F. Austin University (Nacogdoches, TX), Percussion One/Yamaha "SOS" Series, Shoemaker High School (Killeen, TX), Bands of America Summer Symposium (Normal, IL), Texas Christian University (Fort Worth, TX), James Madison University (Harrisonburg, VA), Rutgers University (New Brunswick, NJ),

Lafayette College (Easton, PA), Pecknel Music SOS Camp, Furman University (Greenville, SC), Rush's Music Camp (Knoxville, TN), Central Washington University (Ellensburg, WA), Saied Music "SOS" Camp, Broken Arrow High School (Tulsa, OK), Duncan Music Summer Camp, Wake Forest (Winston-Salem, NC), Louisiana State University (Baton Rouge, LA), Midwestern State University (Wichita Falls, TX), Percussion one/Yamaha "SOS" Series, Memorial High School (San Antonio, TX), University of Wisconsin "SOS" Camp (Whitewater, WI), West Chester University (West Chester, PA), Nick Rail Music "SOS" Camp, Monrovia High School (Monrovia, IN)

43 Sounds of Summer Percussion Clinic
    (site: Furman University, SC)
    800-868-2275
    www.pecknelmusic.com/sounds.html

44 Southeast Missouri State University Summer Music Camps (includes auxiliaries)
    One University Plaza
    Southeast Missouri State University
    Cape Girardeau, MO 63701
    573-651-2335
    www6.semo.edu/camps
    email: tclark@semo.edu

45 Southwest Texas State University Marching Camp (drum major, drumline, colorguard)
    Southwest Texas State University
    601 University Drive
    San Marcos, TX 78666-0000
    512-245-2111
    www.swt.edu/bobcatband/camps

46 Southwestern Oklahoma State University Marching Auxiliary Camp (directors, guard, percussion)
    Southwestern Oklahoma State University
    Department of Music
    100 Campus Drive
    Weatherford, OK 73096
    580-772-6611

Fax 580-774-3795
www.swosu.edu/depts/music
email: jsouth@itlnet.net

47 Superior Marching Band Enterprises, Inc.
    13549 Lake Vining Drive
    Suite 11201
    Orlando, FL 32821
    888-825-6650
    Fax 407-827-0471
    www.superiorcamps.com/rescamps.htm
    email: info@superiorcamps.com
    North Carolina Camp

        University of North Carolina
        Greensboro, NC

        Virginia Beach Camp
        Virginia Wesleyan College
        Norfolk, VA

48 Texas A&M University-Commerce-Summer Camps (directors, drum major, guard, percussion)
    P.O. Box 3011
    Commerce, TX 75429
    903-886-7478
    Fax 903-468-6010
    www7.tamu-commerce.edu/music/
        SummerCamps

49 Texas Christian University Summer Band Camp
    TCU Bands—School of Music
    TCU Box 297500
    Fort Worth, TX 76129
    817-257-7640
    www.music.tcu.edu/Band/bandcamp.
        htm
    email: t.parker@tcu.edu

50 Texas Tech Band/Orchestra Camp
    School of Music
    Box 42033
    Texas Tech University
    Lubbock, TX 79409-2033
    806-742-2225
    Fax 806-742-4193
    www.orgs.ttu.edu/bandorchestraand
        choircamps/contact.htm
    email: Anna.MW.Henry@ttu.edu

Henderson High School Warrior Marching Band (West Chester, PA)

51 Tigerland Auxiliary and Leadership Camp
Department of Bands
Louisiana State University
Baton Rouge, LA 70803
225-578-2384
Fax 225-578-4693
www.music.lsu.edu

52 United States Percussion Camp
Eastern Music Camp
Eastern Illinois University
Charleston, IL 61920-0000

53 United States Scholastic Band Association/Jeff Queen (percussion clinics)
www.yea.org

54 University of Akron Summer Camps and Workshops (brass, directors, percussion, junior high)
School of Music, Summer Workshops
The University of Akron
Akron, OH 44325-1002
330-972-6919
www3.uakron.edu/music/Resources/Pages%20Folder/Workshops.html

55 University of Alabama Band Camp
School of Music
University of Alabama
Box 870366
Tuscaloosa, AL 35487
205-348-7110
Fax 205-348-1473
www.music.ua.edu

56 University of Florida Band Camps (color guard, drum major, majorette, percussion)
The School of Music
University of Florida
P.O. Box 117900
Gainesville, FL 32611-0000
352-392-0223
Fax 352-392-0461
www.arts.ufl.edu/music

57 University of Georgia Redcoat Summer Camps (drum major. guard, leadership, percussion, twirlers)
University of Georgia School of Music
250 River Road
Athens, GA 30602-3153

706-542-1505
www.uga.edu/~ugabands/aux/auditions.
   html
email: ugabands@www.uga.edu

58 University of Houston Cougar Band Camp
    (flags, leadership, marching band dance,
    percussion)
    Attn: John Benzer
    120F School of Music Building
    Houston, TX 77204-4017
    www.uh.edu/music/band_camp_reg.html

59 University of Iowa All-State Music Camp
    (includes percussion)
    The University of Iowa
    1064 Voxman Music Building
    Iowa City, IA 52242-1795
    800-553-IOWA
    Fax 319-353-2555
    www.uiowa.edu/~bands/asmc
    email: kevin-kastens@uiowa.edu

60 University of Kansas Marching Band Camp
    (band, drum major, color guard, lead-
    ership)
    c/o David Bushouse, Director
    University of Kansas Music Summer
    Events
    452 Murphy Hall
    1530 Naismith Drive #452
    Lawrence, KS 66045-5023
    785-864-4730
    Fax 785-864-5023
    www.ku.edu/~mad/summer/guardweb.
       guardweb.htm
    email: musicamp@ku.edu

61 University of Kentucky Marching Band
    Auxiliaries and Percussion Camp
    University of Kentucky Band Office
    105 Fine Arts
    Lexington, KY 40506-0001

62 University of Lousiana at Lafayette
    School of Music
    University of Southwestern Louisiana
    P.O. Drawer 41207
    Lafayette, LA 70504-0400

63 University of Memphis Marching Band
    Clinics (directors)
    Rudi E. Scheidt School of Music
    Music Building, Room 121
    University of Memphis
    3775 Central Avenue
    Memphis, TN 38152-3160
    901-678-2541
    Fax 901-678-3096
    http://music.memphis.edu

64 University of Nebraska-Lincoln Summer
    Marching Camp
    University of Nebraska
    113 Westbrook Music Building
    Lincoln, NE 68588-0102
    402-472-2505
    www.unl.edu/band

65 University of Nebraska-Omaha Summer
    Flag Camp
    Department of Music
    PAC University of Nebraska at Omaha
    Omaha, NE 681182-0245
    402-554-3446
    Fax 402-554-2252
    email: jsaker@mail.unomaha.edu

66 University of Oregon Summer Band
    Camp (brass, percussion, woodwind)
    School of Music
    1225 University of Oregon
    Eugene, OR 97403-1225
    541-346-2138
    Fax 541-346-6188
    http://music1.uoregon.edu/EventsNews/
       Camps/band.html
    email: cjhansen@darkwing.uoregon.edu

67 University of South Carolina Summer
    Music Camp (color guard, drum major,
    percussion)
    University of South Carolina
    School of Music
    813 Assembly Street
    Columbia, SC 29208
    803-777-4278
    Fax 803-777-6508
    www.music.sc.edu/EventsWorkshops/

bandcamp.html
email: USCBands@mozart.sc.edu

68 University of Southern Mississippi Summer Camps (drum major, guard, leadership, percussion)
College of the Arts
University of Southern Mississippi
2701 Hardy Street
Hattiesburg, MS 39406-5166
www.usm.edu/band
email: Steven.Moser@usm.edu

69 University of Texas at Austin Summer Clinics
College of Fine Arts
School of Music
25th and East Campus Drive
Austin, TX 78712
www.utexas.edu/cofa/music

70 University of Washington Summer Program
Office of Graduate and Undergraduate Advising
University of Washington
School of Music, DN-10
Seattle, WA 98195

71 VanderCook College of Music M.E.C.A. Program (instrument and percussion repair)
3140 Federal Street
Chicago, IL 60616-3731
800-448-2655
Fax 312-225-5211
www.vandercook.edu/internetEx/index.html

72 Villanova University Summer Studies (includes instrument repair, silks, twirlers)
Office of Music Activities
Villanova University
800 East Lancaster Avenue
Villanova, PA 19085
610-519-7214
www.music.villanova.edu

73 Virginia Wesleyan College
1584 Wesleyan Drive
Norfolk/Virginia Beach, VA 23502
757-455-3200
www.vwc.edu/contact.php

74 Vivace Productions, Inc.
882 S. Matlack Street, Ste. 202
West Chester, PA 19382
800-264-1121
www.vivaceproductions.com
Sites: Amherst, MA; Atlanta, GA; Charlotte, NC; Dallas/Ft. Worth, TX; Delaware, OH; Des Moines, IA; Detroit, MI; Easton, PA; Fayetteville, AR; Fresno, CA; Greeley, CO; Huntsville, TX; Indianapolis, IN; Kent, OH; Memphis, TN; Provo, UT; Richmond, KY; Sacramento, CA; Sioux Falls, SD; Tulsa, OK; Tuscaloosa, AL; Virginia Beach, VA; West Chester, PA

West Chester University see Sounds of Summer and Vivace Productions, Inc.

75 Western Illinois University Senior High Drum Major Camp
Western Illinois University
1 University Circle
Macomb, IL 61455
www.wiu.edu/musiccamp

Products, Aids, Drill Design and Software

76 Accent on Achievement (band method)
Alfred Los Angeles
P.O. Box 10003
Van Nuys, CA 91410-0003
818-891-5999
Fax 818-891-2369

www.alfred.com
email: customerservice@alfred.com

77 AdkiSong Publications (arrangements for marching band)
Harry R. Adkins

989 Meadow Lane
Barnwell, SC 29812
803-259-1128
http://singnring.tripod.com/adkisong
    publications
email: harry@barnwellsc.com

78 Advantage Showare (drill design software)
239 Southland Drive, Suite B
Lexington, KY 40503

79 Alfred Publishing Company (software)
P.O. Box 10003
Van Nuys, CA 91410

80 AZ-South Musical Enterprises
http://azsouth.com

81 BandArranger.com (Rob Sigler)
www.bandarranger.com

82 BVP Marching Videos (videos of march-
    ing band contests)
790 W. Main Street
Newark, OH 43055

83 Caprock Drill Design
2400 44th Street #243
Lubbock, TX 79412
806-785-9638
Fax 806-785-9641
www.caprockdrilldesign.com
email: info@CaprockDrillDesign.com

84 Choreography Central
310-477-2118
www.choreographycentral.com
email: info@morezap.com

85 Coda Music Software
Wenger Music Learning Division
1401 E. 79th Street
Minneapolis, MN 55425-1126

86 COHO Company (video for trombone
    students)
2904 Branch Hollow
Flower Mound, TX 75028

Columbia Pictures Publications *see* CPP/
Belwin, Inc.

87 Cordwainer Systems (HalfTime)
2525 Buckelew Drive
Falls Church, VA 22046
703-849-0855
www.cordwainer.com/halftime_order_
    form.htm
email: sales@cordwainer.com

88 Coverdown Productions (musical arrange-
    ments and show design)
PMB 63
420 West Emmaus Avenue
Allentown, PA 18103
610-791-9238
Fax 610-797-1848
www.coverdown.com
email: cdp@coverdown.com

89 CPP/Belwin, Inc. (marching band, rifles
    and flags video tapes)
15800 Northwest 48th Avenue
P.O. Box 4340
Miami, FL 33014

90 Creative Solutions
P.O. Box 394
Meridian, ID 83680-0394
877-895-6744
Fax 208-895-6749
www.crsolutions.biz
email: info@crsolutions.biz

91 Dan Ryder Field Drills
12325 Hymeadow, Suite 100, Building 3
Austin, TX 78750
800-727-7889
Fax 512-258-8918
www.danryderfielddrills.com
email: ryderdrill@aol.com

DCI Music Video *see* CPP/Belwin, Inc.

92 DCI Recordings (compact discs and audio
    cassettes of drum corps shows)
P.O. Box 548
Lombard, IL 60148

The Light Brigade Color Guard (Philadelphia, PA)

93 Dr. T's (publishes software)
220 Boylston Street
Chestnut Hill, MA 02167

330-417-2117
www.drillquest.com
email: info@drillquest.com

94 Drill Quest
P.O. Box 268
Middlebranch, OH 44652

95 Drillcomp (show design plus footwear, headgear, podiums, rifles, sabres, uniforms)

P.O. Box 668
New Hope, PA 18938
866-Drillcomp
www.drillcomp.com/companyinfo.html

96 Drilldesign.com
Fax 845-369-1337
www.drilldesign.com/contact.htm

97 DrillPro for Windows
www.cadence.org.uk/drillpro.htm

98 800 Video Express, Inc. (Bands of America shows, etc.)
P.O. Box 142
Palatine, IL 60078
800-848-8433
Fax 847-891-8230
www.800videoexpress.com
email: Mail@800videoexpress.com

99 Electronic Arts (publishes software)
1820 Gateway Drive
San Mateo, CA 94404

100 Elite Designs
P.O. Box 1622
Bayonne, NJ 07002
201-339-2227
www.elite-designs.org/contact.html
email: Admin@elite-designs.org

101 Gamble Music Company (software, videos)
Dept. 0997
1313 W. Randolph Street
Chicago, IL 60607
800-621-4290
Fax 312-421-7979
www.gamblemusic.com
email: custserv@gamblemusic.com

102 G-Vox
P.O. Box 2755
Westfield, NJ 07091-2755
Fax 973-828-0412
www.gvox.com
email: support@gvox.com

103 Lutton Music Personnel Service, Inc.
P.O. Box 13985
Gainesville, FL 32604

MacDrums *see* Coda Music Software

104 Maestro Music, Inc. (publishes software)
2403 San Mateo N.E., Suite P-1
Albuquerque, NM 87110
505-881-9181 (Fax same)
www.wrldcon.com/maestro
email: slkunitz@aol.com

105 Marching Concepts Online
423 Pine Ridge Road
Bluff City, TN 37618
877-299-4387
Fax 276-328-6105
www.marchingconcepts.com
email: sales@marchingconcepts.com

106 Marching Show Concepts
829 Lawrence Drive
Fort Wayne, IN 46804
800-356-4381
Fax 260-459-0615
www.msconcepts.com
email: msc@mscconcepts.com

107 MarchMaker Show Concepts
P.O. Box 37
Atkinson, NH 03811-0037
www.marchmaker.com/contact.html
email: mikec@marchmaker.com

108 The Music Mart Inc. (books, handbell accessories, manuscript paper, notation software)
3301 Carlisle Blvd. NE
Albuquerque, NM 87110
800-545-6204/505-889-9777
Fax 505-889-9070
www.musicmart.com

109 Opcode (subsidiary of Gibson Guitar Corporation; publishes software)
1024 Hamilton Court
Menlo Park, CA 94025
www.opcode.com

Passport Designs *see* G-Vox

Crossmen Drum & Bugle Corps rehearsal (Bergenfield, NJ)

110 Pathway Productions
640 Linwood Street
Abington, MA 02351
781-857-2951
email: pathwayp@yahoo.com

111 Peterson Electro-Musical Products, Inc.
(strobe tuners/ear training devices)
11601 South Mayfield Avenue
Alsip, IL 60803
708-388-3311
www.petersonemp.com

112 Pyware Music Products (drill design
software)
P.O. Box 399
Argyle, TX 76226
800-222-7536
Fax 940-464-0573
www.pyware.com
email: pyware@pyware.com

113 Raven Labs (drill design software)
1365 Sugarwood Lane

Norcross, GA 30093
770-806-9621
email: info@ravenlabsinc.com

114 RolandCorp US (publishes software)
7200 Dominion Circle
Los Angeles, CA 90040

115 Shuey Drill Design
613 North Lancaster Street
Jonestown, PA 17038
717-865-0456
www.shueydrilldesign.com/contact.html
email: admin@shueydrilldesign.com

116 Sibelius USA Inc. (music writing software)
1407 Oakland Blvd., Suite 300
Walnut Creek, CA 94596
888-474-2354
www.sibelius.com
email: infoUSA@sibelius.com

117 Silver Burdett & Ginn (publishes software)

Bluecoats Drum & Bugle Corps rehearsal (Canton, OH)

250 James Street
Morristown, NJ 07960
800-552-2259
Fax 800-841-8939
www.scottforesman.com/products/pdf
/music.pdf

118 SoftwareDP (band data management
and accounting software)
128 Wolfe Road
Copperas Cove, TX 76522
email: sdp@softwaredp.com

119 TOA Electronics, Inc. (amplifiers, microphones, speakers)
601 Gateway Blvd., Suite 300
South San Francisco, CA 94080
800-733-7088
Fax 650-588-3349
www.toaelectronics.com
email: info@toaelectronics.com

120 Under the Sun Productions (marching
band, indoor guard and parade show
design)

882 South Matlack Street, Ste. 202
West Chester, PA 19382
800-264-1121/610-431-1121
www.utsp.com
e-mail: UnderSunPr@aol.com

121 Warren Creative Designs (show design
for band, drum corps, indoor guard,
percussion, dance)
223 Claremont Circle
P.O. Box 32
Brooklyn, MI 49230
800-947-5877
Fax 517-592-5115
www.warren-creative-design.com/main.
html
email: ewarren@voyager.net

122 Yamaha Band Student (band method)
Yamaha Corporation of America
Band & Orchestral Division
Alfred Publishing Company, Inc.
PO Box 10003
Van Nuys, CA 91410-0003

Associations

123 American Bandmasters Association
2221 Morgan Drive
Norman, OK 73069
405-321-3373
Fax 405-321-4117
www.americanbandmasters.org
email: thurston3@juno.com

124 American School Band Directors' Association
P.O. Box 696
Guttenberg, IA 52052-0696
319-252-2500
www.asbda.com
email: asbda@netins.net

125 Canadian Band Association
Jim Forde, President
17 Coronet Avenue
Halifax, NS B3N 1L4
Canada
902-427-7501
Fax 902-427-7498
www3.sk.sympatico.ca/skband/cba.html
email: jimforde@psphalifax.ns.ca

126 College Band Directors National Association
823 College Avenue, Ste. 1300
Austin, TX 78701
512-479-0425
Fax 512-495-9031
www.cbdna.org

127 MENC: The National Association for Music Education
1806 Robert Fulton Drive
Reston, VA 20191

800-336-3768
Fax 703-860-1531
www.menc.org or www.musicfriends.org

Music Educators National Conference *see* MENC: The National Association for Music Education

128 Music Teachers National Association
441 Vine Street, Suite 505
Cincinnati, OH 45202-2811
888-512-5278/513-421-1420
Fax 513-421-2503
www.mtna.org
email: mtnanet@mtna.org

129 National Band Association
P.O. Box 121292
Nashville, TN 37212
615-385-2650
Fax 615-385-2650
email: nbassoc@bellsouth.net

130 National Catholic Band Association
3334 N. Normandy Avenue
Chicago, IL 60634
773-282-9153
www.thencba.org
email: ncbamail@aol.com

131 Women Band Directors National Association
345 Overlook Drive
West Lafayette, IN 47906-1210
765-463-1738
www.music.acu.edu
email: cornetpat@aol.com

Selected Bibliography

Articles

132 Bailey, Wayne A. "Marching Tips for the Small Band." *Instrumentalist* (June 1982): 12.

133 Batcheller, James. "Excellence on the Field Comes with Good Fundamentals." *Instrumentalist* (August 2002): 18–21.

134 Berg, Ron. "Fit to March." *Music Educators Journal* (May 1981): 44–45.

135 Cappio, Arthur L. "Marching Percussion Drum Corps Style." *School Musician, Director & Teacher* (August / September 1977): 62, 65.

136 Clements, Phillip. "Marching with a Method." *Instrumentalist* (June 1999): 40, 42, 44.

137 _____. "Saving Time During Marching Rehearsals." *Instrumentalist* (August 1998): 50, 52, 54.

138 DeJournett, William. "Planning Marching Rehearsals." *Instrumentalist* (July 1997): 38, 40–42.

139 Dunnigan, Patrick. "Field Perspectives in Charting a Show." *Instrumentalist* (June 1997): 12–17.

140 _____. "The Growing Complexity of Marching Bands." *Instrumentalist* (August 1995): 74–77, 193–194.

141 _____. "Simplicity in Marching for Inexperienced Bands." *Instrumentalist* (June 1998): 50, 52–54, 56, 58, 60.

142 Dvorak, Raymond. "Marching Maneuvers: Music and Pageantry." *Instrumentalist* (September-October 1946): 6–7.

143 Dye, Ken. "Marching Band Films and Tapes." *Instrumentalist* (October 1980): 96–99.

144 Farnsworth, Roger W. "A 'Do-It-Yourself' Summer Music Camp for Your Entire Organization." *School Musician, Director & Teacher* (March 1978): 50–51.

145 Follett, Richard J. "The Drum Major Camp." *Instrumentalist* (March 1978): 40–43.

146 Green, Gary, and Donald E. Cury. "The Percussion Session Field Solo." *School Musician, Director & Teacher* (May 1981): 12–14.

147 Hammer, Rusty. "From Battlefield to Concert Hall: The Career of Patrick S. Gilmore." *Instrumentalist* (June 1992): 46–47, 49.

148 Hejl, James G. "Marching Band Warm-Ups." *Instrumentalist* (August 1983): 26–28.

149 Holmes, Charles. "Snare Drum Tips." *Instrumentalist* (August 1987): 48, 50, 52.

150 Holston, Kim. "West Chester, Pennsylvania: A Lively Place for Marching." *Music and Pageantry Journal* (January 1982: 23.

151 Hong, Sherman. "Common Sense in Marching Percussion." *Percussive Notes* (Spring / Summer 1980): 42–45.

152 _____. "Judging Marching Percussion." *Instrumentalist* (September 1989): 44, 46, 48.

153 Hosler, Mark. "Adding Variety to Halftime Shows." *Instrumentalist* (August 1996): 34, 36, 38, 40, 42.

154 Kastens, L. Kevin. "From Paper to Field Drills: Clear Instructions Improve Marching Band Rehearsals." *Instrumentalist* (July 1999): 34, 36, 38, 40.

155 Kuzmich, John, Jr. "Field Show Design: Drill Design Options." *School Band and Orchestra* (May 2002): 54–61.

156 Lange, Sam. "Sam Lange Talks About Drum Majoring and Field Generalship." *Drum Major* (January 1982): 8.

157 Laudermilch, Kenneth. "Brass Clinic: More Air, Less Lip, and Good Tone." *Instrumentalist* (June 2002): 40, 42, 44, 46.

158 Lautzenheiser, Tim. "Today's Marching Band Percussion Section." *School Musician, Director & Teacher* (August/September 1980): 14–16.

159 LeCroy, Hoyt F. "Section Solos for the Marching Percussion Section." *School Musician, Director & Teacher* (April 1979): 48, 67.

160 Lenzini, Catherine Sell. "Veteran Drill Writers Cite Common Pitfalls." *Instrumentalist* (July 2000): 12–16.

161 Mahin, Bruce P. "Business Uses of Computers." *Instrumentalist* (February 1987): 52, 54, 56.

162 Mallen, James K. "Arranging Rudimental Training Technique." *Percussive Notes* (Fall 1980)): 44–45.

163 "Marching Band Rehearsal Techniques." *Instrumentalist* (August 1997): 24–26, 28, 30, 32, 77.

164 Mazur, Ken. "Advanced Rudimental Training Technique." *Percussive Notes* (Spring/Summer 1980): 45–49.

165 Michalski, Stanley, Jr. "The Upcoming Gridiron Extravaganza (A Band Directors Comments and Laments)." *School Musician, Director & Teacher* (June 1984): 8–9.

166 Miller, Richard A. "Intensity Designs: Guidelines for Show Planning." *Instrumentalist* (June 1984): 14–15.

167 Montgomery, Timothy. "The Rotation Concept." *Instrumentalist* (June 1981): 10–13.

168 Neiman, Marcus. "If You Can't Find It—Write It!" *Instrumentalist* (September 1987): 80, 82.

169 Nelson, Judy Ruppel. "Gene Thrailkill—Guiding the Pride." [University of Oklahoma] *Instrumentalist* (September 1987): 16–19.

170 Pratt, Stephen W. "The Music Newsletter: An Effective Tool for Music Education." *Instrumentalist* (September 1987): 106, 108.

171 Prentice-Lambrecht, Barbara. "Preparing for Marching Contests." *Instrumentalist* (August 1996): 76–77, 79. [tips on busing, field configuration, stretching, posture, etc.]

172 Province, Martin. "Marching Band Warm-Ups for Stiff Chops." *Instrumentalist* (August 1988): 18–20.

173 _____. "Marching Voluntarily." *Instrumentalist* (September 1998): 112, 111.

174 Rideout, Roger R. "Summer Tasks for the First-Year Band Director." *Instrumentalist* (July 1987): 50, 52, 54.

175 Rohrer, Thomas P. "Marching Handbook for Students." *Instrumentalist* (August 1994): 78–79.

176 Ryder, Dan. "Drill Design: Exciting Field Shows for Small Bands." *School Band and Orchestra* (May 2002): 23–28.

177 Schoettle, David Allen. "Composing on a Computer." *Flute Talk* (September 1992): 21–23.

178 Sherry, Heather Rakauskas. "Fundamental Colorguard Techniques: Adding Flair to the Marching Band." *Instrumentalist* (September 1999): 30–33.

179 Smith, Joseph T. "Time-Saving Techniques for the Marching Band Rehearsal." *Instrumentalist* (October 1979): 20–21.

180 Thulien, James W. "So Now You Want to March Corps Style?" *School Musician, Director & Teacher* (May 1980): 10–11.

181 Trytten, Kim. "The Benefits of Marching Camp." *Instrumentalist* (June 1993): 33–34, 36, 38, 40.

182 Vogel, Lauren. "Marching Mallet Percussion." *Instrumentalist* (May 1981): 48–51.

183 Wanamaker, Jay A. "Visual Effects." *Percussive Notes* (Fall 1979): 46.

184 Zotti, Gina. "WCU Holds Marching Band Leadership Camp." *Daily Local News* [West Chester, PA], July 29, 2001, pp. A1, A5.

Books and Monographs

185 Bailey, Wayne, and Thomas Caneva. *The Complete Marching Band Resource Manual: Techniques and Materials for Teaching, Drill Design, and Music Arranging.* Philadelphia: University of Pennsylvania Press, 1994.

186 Beckham, Rick. *The Beckham Book: Rudimental Competition Solos.* Princeton, TX: Ruff Notes Publishing (405 Christi Lane, 75407), 2001.

187 _____. *The Rudimental Drummer.* Princeton, TX: Ruff Notes Publishing (405 Christi Lane, 75407), 2001.

188 Bennett, George T. *The In and Out of 26 Letter Formations.* Marching Maneuver Series, Vol. IX. Chicago, IL: Gamble Hinged Music Company, 1939.

189 _____. *New and Novel Formations for Marching Bands and Drum Corps.* Marching Maneuver Series, Vol. VII. Chicago, IL: Gamble Hinged Music Company, 1938.

190 Blades, James. *Percussion Instruments and Their History.* reprint ed. Westport, CT: Bold Strummer Ltd., 1997.

191 Butts, Carrol M. *High School Band Clinic: Drills & Exercises That Improve Performance.* Englewood Cliffs, NJ: Prentice-Hall, 1978.

192 _____. *Illustrated Handbook of Band Formations: 200 Models with Recommended Music Selections.* Englewood Cliffs, NJ: Prentice-Hall, 1975.

193 *Camp Kit.* Colgate, WI (631 Violet Ct., 53017).

194 Casavant, Albert R. *Block Formation Drill.* San Antonio, TX: Southern Music Company, n.d.

195 _____. *Block Progressions.* San Antonio, TX: Southern Music Company, 1965.

196 _____. *Block Specials.* San Antonio, TX: Southern Music Company, 1968.

197 _____. *Corner Drill Movements.* San Antonio, TX: Southern Music Company, 1967.

198 _____. *Double Gait.* San Antonio, TX: Southern Music Company, 1968.

199 _____. *The Fast Break.* San Antonio, TX: Southern Music Company, 1962.

200 _____. *Field Entrances.* San Antonio, TX: Southern Music Company, 1959.

201 _____. *Field Routines: Book 1: Five Complete Precision Drill Routines with Suggested Music.* Grade 3. For: Football Halftime, Field Exhibition, Marching Contest. San Antonio, TX: Southern Music Company, n.d.

202 _____. *Manual of Drill*. San Antonio, TX: Southern Music Company, 1960.

203 _____. *Marching Routines*. 2 v. Book 1: Five Complete Precision Drill Field Routins (Grade 1) Company Front Drill, End Zone Entrances and Exits, 1963. Book 2: Five Precision Drill Routines with Company Front End Zone and Side Entrances and Exits (Grade 1), 1964. San Antonio, TX: Southern Music Company, c1963-64.

204 _____. *Phalanx Drill Movements*. San Antonio, TX: Southern Music Company, 1959.

205 _____. *Precision Drill*. San Antonio, TX: Southern Music Company, 1957.

206 _____. *Precision Drill Line Movements*. San Antonio, TX: Southern Music Company, 1958.

207 _____. *The Precision Drill Squad*. San Antonio, TX: Southern Music Company, 1960.

208 _____. *The Precision Drill Team*. San Antonio, TX: Southern Music Company, 1961.

209 _____. *Precision Flash*. San Antonio, TX: Southern Music Company, 1962.

210 _____. *Progression Drill Line Movements*. San Antonio, TX: Southern Music Company, 1963.

211 _____. *Rhythmic Arm Movements for Marching*. San Antonio, TX: Southern Music Company, 1962.

212 _____. *Six to Five*. San Antonio, TX: Southern Music Company, 1962.

213 _____. *Staggered Block Drill Movements*. San Antonio, TX: Southern Music Company, 1961.

214 _____. *Wrapping the Block*. San Antonio, TX: Southern Music Company, 1968.

215 Combs, F. Michael. *Percussion Manual*. 2nd ed. Prospect Heights, IL: Waveland Press, 2000.

216 Cook, Gary D. *Teaching Percussion*. 2nd ed. Florence, KY: Wadsworth Publishing Company, 1997.

217 Dale, Carroll R. *Fundamentals of Drill*. Chicago, IL: Gamble Hinged Music Company, 1940.

218 Davila, Lalo. *Contemporary Rudimental Studies and Solos*. Nashville, TN: Vision Publications (P.O. Box 17066, Nashville, TN 37217). Book plus CDs.

219 Dietz, William. *Teaching Woodwinds: A Method and Resource Handbook for Music Educators*. Florence, KY: Wadsworth Publishing Company, 1997.

220 Foster, Robert E. *Multiple-Option Marching Band Techniques*. 3rd ed. Van Nuys, CA: Alfred Publishing Company, 1991.

221 Garofalo, Robert. *Blueprint for Band: A Guide to Teaching Comprehensive Musicianship Through School Band Performance*. Portland, ME: J. Weston Walch, 1976.

222 Glasgow, William. *Exhibition Drills*. Harrisburg, PA: Military Service Publishing Company, 1958.

223 Hal Leonard Music. *Band Shows Can Be Easy*. Winona, MN, 1948.

224 Hal Leonard Publishing. *Marching Band Director*. Milwaukee, WI.

225 Hal Leonard Publishing. *Marching Band Drill Design*. Milwaukee, WI.

226 Hindsley, Mark H. *Band-at-ten-tion! A Manual for the Marching Band*. Drill

masters and drum majors ed. New York: Remick Music Corporation, 1932.

227 _____. *How to Twirl a Baton*. Chicago, IL: Ludwig and Ludwig, 1928.

228 _____. *24 Formations, Designs, and Entrances for the Marching Band*. Marching Maneuver Series, Vol. I. Chicago, IL: Gamble Hinged Music Company, 1935.

229 Hopper, Dale F. *Corps Style Marching*. Oskaloosa, IA: C.L. Barnhouse, 1977.

230 _____. *The Drill Designer's Idea Book*. Macomb, IL: Dale Hopper Music, 1988.

231 Jones, Stefan. *Band Shows Dance Drill Book*. New York, NY: Charles H. Hansen Music Corporation, 1953.

232 Lautzenheiser, Tim. *The Art of Successful Teaching: A Blend of Content & Context*. Chicago: GIA Publications, 1992.

233 _____. *The Joy of Inspired Teaching*. Chicago: GIA Publications, 1993.

234 _____, and Charlie Menghini. *Band Director's Communication Kit*. Milwaukee, WI: Hal Leonard Publishing, 2000.

235 Lee, Jack. *Modern Marching Band Techniques*. Winona, MN: Hal Leonard Music Company, 1955.

236 Lentz, Bernard. *Cadence System of Teaching Close Order Drill and Exhibition Drills*. 8th ed. Harrisburg, PA: Military Service Publishing Company, 1957.

237 Long, A.H. *Marching to the Yard Lines*. Ponca City, OK: Luther Music Company, 1952.

238 Lyon, Muriel J., and Marcia M. Peterson. *Fundamental Drill Team and Marching Percussion*. Dubuque, IA: William C. Brown, 1964.

239 McCormick, Robert. *Percussion for Musicians*. Miami, FL: Warner Bros., 2000.

240 Mahan, Jack. *Quick Steps to Marching*. New York: Carl Fischer, 1953.

241 Malstrom, George N. *The Drum Major's Manual*. Chicago, IL: Ludwig and Ludwig, 1928.

242 Marcouiller, Don R. *Marching for Marching Bands*. Dubuque, IA: William C. Brown, 1958.

243 Mazur, Ken. *The Technique & Mechanics of Competitive Rudimental Snare Drumming*. St. Claire Shores, MI (21600 Englehardt, 48080): 1979.

244 Meaux, Robert. *Contemporary Field Designs for Marching Band*. San Antonio, TX: Southern Music Company, 1990.

245 _____. *Teaching Marching Band Techniques for Preparation Through Performance*. San Antonio, TX: Southern Music Company, 1991.

246 Oldfield, Willis P. *Twenty and Seven Drill Band Maneuvers*. Mansfield, PA: Swain's Music House, 1938.

247 *Opportunities in Music Careers 1991*. Saddle Brook, NJ: Regent Book Company, Wholesale Booksellers (101A Route 46, 07662). $10.95.

248 Parks, George. *The Dynamic Drum Major*. Oskaloosa, IA: C.L. Barnhouse, 1984.

249 Perkins, Phil. *The Logical Approach to Rudimental Snare Drum*. Cincinnati, OH: Logical Publications, 1980.

250 Peters, Mitchell. *Fundamental Method for Timpani*. Van Nuys, CA: Alfred Publishing Company, 1993.

251 Raxsdale, Bill. *Contemporary Color Guard Manual*. New Berlin, WI: Jenson Publications, 1980.

252 Regent Book Company. *Opportunities in Music Careers 1991*. Saddle Brook, NJ.

253 Revelli, William D., and George Cavender. *Marching Fundamentals and Techniques for the School Bandsman*. Ann Arbor, MI: LesStrang Publishing Company, 1961.

254 Reynolds, R.B. *Drill and Evolutions of the Band*. Annapolis, MD: National Service Publishing Company, 1928.

255 Schilling, Richard Lee. *Marching Band Maneuvers*. Evanston, IL: Instrumentalist Company, 1961.

256 Scuro, Vincent. *Presenting the Marching Band*. New York: Dodd Mead, 1974.

257 Shellahamer, Bentley; Swearingen, James; and Woods, Jon. *The Marching Band Program: Principles and Practices*. Oskaloosa, IA: C.L. Barnhouse, 1986.

258 Smith, Claude B., and Wallace Capel. *Practical Stunts and Evolutions*. Marching Maneuver Series, Vol. II. Chicago, IL: Gamble Hinged Music Company, 1935.

259 Snider, Larry. *Developing the Corps Style Percussion Section*. Oskaloosa, IA: C.L. Barnhouse, 1979.

260 _____. *Total Marching Percussion*. Oskaloosa, IA: C.L. Barnhouse. Book 1: 1976. Book 2: 1978. Book 3: 1983.

261 Weaver, Max, and Carrol M. Butts. *Field-Color Entrances for Marching Band*. Oskaloosa, IA: C.L. Barnhouse, 1975.

262 _____, and _____. *Field-Color Shows for Marching Band*. Oskaloosa, IA: C.L. Barnhouse, 1979.

263 Wessels, Mark. *A Fresh Approach to Mallet Percussion*. Plano, TX: Mark Wessels Publications.

264 _____. *A Fresh Approach to the Snare Drum*. Plano, TX: Mark Wessels Publications.

265 West, Adam. *Marching Class Method*. San Antonio, TX: Southern Music Company, 1953.

266 Whitener, Scott. *A Complete Guide to Brass Instruments and Techniques*. 2nd ed. Florence, KY: Wadsworth Publishing Company, 1997.

267 Winter Guard International. *Contemporary Marching Band Concepts*. Wheat Ridge, CO.

268 World Rhythm. *Mastering the Rudiments*. Colorado Springs, CO, 1993.

269 Wright, Al G. *Marching Band Fundamentals*. New York: Carl Fischer, 1963.

270 _____. *The Show Band*. Evanston, IL: Instrumentalist Company, 1957.

271 Wyand, Alan. *Band Training Camps*. York, PA, 1962.

Videos

272 Buckner, Bob. *Band Excellence Video*. Ft. Wayne, IN: Marching Show Concepts.

273   Clark, Larry, ed. *Marching Fundamentals.*
Miami, FL: Warner Bros.

274   _____. *Rifle Fundamentals.* Performed by
Karl Lowe. Miami, FL: Warner Bros.

Websites

275   www.blackcollegebandvideos.com

276   www.rudimentaldrumming.com

Part 2
Competitions

To compete or not to compete? The question has bedeviled directors for half a century. Even though they often recognize the public relations importance of a marching band, some directors feel contests or even football halftime shows debilitate concert band and orchestra. Nevertheless, schools with the best marching bands usually have the best indoor ensembles. As Paul Dobson, Jr., director of bands at Hardee County Junior High School in Wauchula, Florida, said, "So what if it [marching band] is not the greatest single achievement of musical development in history? The kids love it, and I love to watch them as they develop and succeed. 'Ten-hut!'" (in "Marching Bands at the Middle School Level?" Music Educators Journal, *October 1990, p. 48).*

Before engaging in competition, questions must be asked. Will the unit be traveling far afield? Outside the county? Outside the state? Saturday or Sunday? Who will provide and pay for buses—the school administration or the boosters? Do the students want to compete every Saturday night in addition to performing Saturday afternoon at a football game? Will they engage in all the practices necessary? Will there be a rooting section on the road? Will it be only the hardcore of boosters or most of the parents? Publicity—letting the parents know what they and their students get out of competing—is a high priority.

It is often easier to win away from home on a spring trip, especially if your region has an established competition circuit. There are probably more bands in the circuit than will be encountered on the trip. Of course, if you have good musicians and a 190-member unit, you may do well anywhere. On the other hand, even a large unit may need some experience in the circuit. Do not expect to win the championships the first year. (Note that many springtime festivals seem to have dispensed with field show contests in favor of parades but have added indoor guard and percussion competitions.)

In your first season, it may be wise to go slow. Traveling 40, 60, or 80 miles away every Saturday night may exhaust everyone, especially if you don't do well. Winning, obviously, will make the excursions seem shorter. A reasonable policy is to shoot for more points each outing. Even if you don't win, you will have improved—and there's the proof on the score sheet.

Be sure to know the rules for competing in the championships. You may not qualify. Case in point: A band director, dissatisfied with average showings in his circuit, begins a new season in a different circuit. The band does fairly well but must travel to the next state for wide exposure. Then come the area playoffs. The band must win or place high in the playoffs to compete in the championships. The trouble is, the band from this area that must be beaten is the perennial winner of not only the area but the championships as well! The new band does not overcome this handicap and thus does not attend the championships. If the band had remained in the other circuit, it would not have encountered this situation because every member band that chooses may compete in the finals. Note: Membership in one contest circuit does not prevent membership in other circuits nor the remittance of a small fee to compete in a single contest.

Because competition is for trophies, not money, funding is important. Some competition associations provide travel reimbursement depending on the number of advance tickets sold.

College and university bands rarely compete. In addition to the issues of time away from studies and the expense of traveling, the disparate styles (corps, Midwest high step, precision) would leave judges in a quandary.

Competitive scholastic bands are usually members of one or more competitive circuits. True invitationals are rare because most contest bands are locked into contests well before each autumn. A college may sponsor an invitational for bands that aren't circuit members or have a date free. If the college has a noteworthy band that performs in exhibition before awards are presented, this can serve to recruit future college band members.

Some parents are never fully apprised of judging criteria or exactly what sort of contest their children are involved in. There are independent contests which may be judged by people in the stadium pressbox. If a marching band circuit is involved, judges are generally on the field as well. Circuit judging usually involves number scores. Independent competitions may rank with word scores like "Good," "Excellent," "Superior," or "Outstanding." Directors will invariably receive in-depth analysis via audiocassettes the judges have utilized while observing the performance.

Is there a national marching band championship? No. Bands of America, with its regional contests and championship site, comes closest. Remember that competitive high school bands usually belong to home circuits with their own championships. Plus, a West or East Coast band will probably not be able to raise money for a trip to a Midwest autumn championship site if it is also planning a major spring trip to a sunny southern clime.

Spring and Summer Competitions

Some spring competitions involve parades only while others consist of parades, field shows, jazz band, chorus, orchestra, indoor guard and twirling.

277 All American Festivals
1130 West Center Street
North Salt Lake, UT 84054
877-328-2583
Fax 806-763-7637
http://dcfestivals.com

278 All American Music Festival of Orlando
8651 Commodity Circle
Orlando, FL 32819
800-243-4365
Fax 407-352-2962
www.bandfest.com

America's Youth on Parade (AYOP) *see* National Baton Twirling Association

279 Association of Scottish Games and Festivals
5010 Mayfield Road, #206
Lyndhurst, OH 44124

280 Competition for Marching Show Bands
(July; Calgary Stampede, Canada)
www.csmarchingbands.com

281 Dakota Days Band Festival and Patriotic Parade
Box 747
Rapid City, SD 57709

282 DC Festivals
2020 50th St.
Lubbock, TX 79412

283 De Soto Band Contest
c/o The Spanish Manor House
910 Third Avenue West
Bradenton, FL 34205

284 Dixie Classic Festivals
4964 Warwick Road
Richmond, VA 23224
    Sites: Richmond, VA; Virginia Beach, VA; Washington, D.C.

285 Dogwood Arts Festival
Department of Parks and Recreation
P.O. Box 1631
Knoxville, TN 37917

286 Educational Programs Network
1784 West Schuylkill Road
Douglassville, PA 19518-9100
800-323-0974 (East Coast)
800-305-7565 (West Coast)
Fax 888-305-7565
www.educationalprograms.com
email: info@edprog.com
    See also Festivals of Music, Music in the Parks

287 Festival
1701 East Parham Road, Suite 203
Richmond, VA 23228

288 Fiesta-Val
Spectrum of Richmond, Inc.
6223 Lakeside Avenue
Richmond, VA 23228
800-222-6862
Fax 804-264-6302
www.fiestaval.com
email: info@fiestaval.com
　　Sites: Atlanta, GA; Dallas, TX; Gatlin-
　　burg/Pigeon Forge, TN; Myrtle
　　Beach, SC; St. Louis, MO; Toronto,
　　Ontario; Virginia Beach, VA;
　　Williamsburg, VA

289 Festival of States
P.O. Box 1731
St. Petersburg, FL 33731
727-898-3654
www.festivalofstates.com
email: festivalofstates@ij.net

290 Festivals of Music
1784 W. Schuylkill Road
Douglassville, PA 19518-9100
800-305-7565
Fax 610-327-2562
www.festivalsofmusic.com
　　Sites: Anaheim, CA; Atlanta, GA;
　　Boston, MA; Branson, MO; Chicago,
　　IL; Dallas, TX; Las Vegas, NV; Mon-
　　treal, Canada; Myrtle Beach, SC;
　　Nashville, TN; New Orleans, LA;
　　New York, NY; Ocean City, MD; Or-
　　lando, FL; Philadelphia, PA; St. Louis,
　　MO; Toronto, Canada; Virginia
　　Beach, VA; Washington, D.C.;
　　Williamsburg, VA

291 Gateway Music Festivals & Tours
P.O. Box 1165
Monticello, MN 55362
800-331-8579
Fax 612-295-6029
www.musicfestivals.com
　　Sites include: Bristol, England; Limer-
　　ick, Ireland; Honolulu, HI; San Fran-
cisco, CA; Chicago, IL; New York,
NY; Harrlemmermeer, Holland; New
Orleans, LA; Toronto, Canada; At-
lanta, GA; Denver, CO

292 Great Lakes Band Championships
Kenosha Band Boosters, Inc.
c/o Larry Simons
3600 52nd Street
Kenosha, WI 53144

293 Hawaii Invitational International Music
　　Festival
c/o World of Pageantry/Coastline
P.O. Box 2961
Anaheim, CA 92804
714-952-2263/800-448-2374
www.worldofpageantry.com/hawaiinv.
php

294 Heritage Festivals
P.O. Box 571187
Salt Lake City, UT 84157-1187
800-223-4367
www.heritagefestivals.com
　　Sites: Anaheim, Atlanta, Boston,
　　Chicago, Colorado Springs, Dallas,
　　Gatlinburg, Hawaii, Las Vegas, Lon-
　　don (International Festival), Mon-
　　treal, Myrtle Beach, New Orleans,
　　New York City, Orlando, Quebec
　　City, Salt Lake City, San Diego, San
　　Francisco, St. Louis, Seattle, Toronto,
　　Vancouver (Cloverdale Rodeo Parade,
　　Hyack Parade), Virginia Beach, Wash-
　　ington (D.C.), Williamsburg

295 Homestead Travel
7 West Main Street
P.O. Box 304
Hummelstown, PA 17036
800-635-8749
www.homesteadtravel.vacation.com
email: book@homesteadtravel.com

296 International Band Festival
Red River Exhibition Association
876 St. James Street
Winnipeg, Manitoba R3G 3J7
Canada

297   International Marching Band Festival
Present Australia
P.O. Box A1126
Sydney South, New South Wales 1235
Australia
+61 2 9212 7299
Fax +61 2 9212 5399
www.presentaustralia.com

298   International Music Festivals
P.O. Box 41
Parchment, MI 49004
299 Invitational Music Festivals
6219 Lakeside Avenue
Richmond, VA 23228
    Sites: Atlanta, GA; Lakeland/Or-
    lando, FL; Myrtle Beach, SC; Nash-
    ville, TN; Pigeon Forge/Gatlinburg,
    TN; Richmond, VA; Toronto,
    Canada; Virginia Beach, VA; Wash-
    ington, D.C.; Williamsburg, VA

299   Mid-America Competing Band Direc-
    tors Association Championship Band
    Classic Field Show
(field show and parade during National
Cherry Festival)
608-241-9366 (Ken Paris)
www.marching.com/events/macbda.ht
ml or www.cherryfestival.org
email: kenneth.paris@att.net

300   Music in the Parks
1784 West Schuylkill Road
Douglassville, PA 19518-9100
800-305-7565 (West Coast), 800-323-
0974 (East Coast)
www.musicintheparks.com   (and/or
    www.educationalprograms.com)
email: info@ed.prog.com
    Sites: Busch Gardens (Tampa, FL and
    Williamsburg, VA), Cedar Point (San-
    dusky, OH), Disneyland (Anaheim,
    CA), Dorney Park (Allentown, PA),
    Frontier City (Oklahoma City), Her-
    sheypark (PA), Jazzland (New Or-
    leans, LA), Kennywood (Pittsburgh,
    PA), Knott's Berry Farm (Anaheim,
    CA), Lagoon (Salt Lake City, UT),
    Lake Compounce (Bristol, CT), Para-

mount Canada's Wonderland (To-
ronto), Paramount's Great America
(Santa Clara, CA), Paramount's Kings
Dominion (Richmond, VA), Sea
World, Paramount's Kings Island
(Cincinnati, OH), Silverwood (Coeur
d'Alene, ID), Six Flags America
(Washington, D.C.), Six Flags Astro-
world (Houston, TX), Six Flags Dar-
ien Lake (Buffalo/Rochester, NY), Six
Flags Elitch Gardens (Denver, CO),
Six Flags Fiesta Texas (San Antonio),
Six Flags Great Adventure and Wild
Safari (Jackson, NJ), Six Flags Great
America (Chicago), Six Flags Ken-
tucky Kingdom (Louisville), Six Flags
Magic Mountain (Los Angeles), Six
Flags Marine World (Vallejo, CA), Six
Flags New England (Agawam, MA),
Six Flags Worlds of Adventure (Au-
rora, OH), Six Flags Over Georgia
(Atlanta), Six Flags Over Texas (Dal-
las), Six Flags St. Louis, Universal Or-
lando (FL), Valleyfair (Minneapolis,
MN)

301   Music Maestro Please, Inc.
2006 Swede Road
Norristown, PA 19401-9930
800-228-1668
Fax 610-272-3998
http://mmpfestivals.com
email: musmaestro@aol.com
    Sites include: Montreal, Canada; To-
    ronto, Canada; Colorado Springs,
    CO; Orlando, FL; Atlanta, GA; Chi-
    cago, IL; New Orleans, LA; Balti-
    more, MD; Boston, MA; Philadelphia,
    PA; Hawaii, Italy

Music Showcase Festivals see Music Tours
    Unlimited, Inc.

302   Music Tours Unlimited, Inc.
P.O. Box 533
321 North Furnace Street, Suite 90
Birdsboro, PA 19508
800-545-0935
www.musfestivals.com/mtctc.htm
    Spring/summer contest site: Dallas,
    TX (Southwest Invitational)

303 Musicfest (sites: Orlando, FL, Anaheim, CA)
771 Kirkman Road, Suite 107
Orlando, FL 32811
800-734-0482
Fax 407-296-8587
www.musicfestorlando.com
email: info@musicfestorlando.com

National Association of Music Festivals *see* Gateway Festivals and Performing Arts Consultants Music Festivals

304 National Baton Twirling Association
Box 266
Janesville, WI 53545
America's Youth on Parade annual competition held at Notre Dame University, IN

305 National Events
9672 South 700 East, Ste. 200
Sandy, UT 84070
800-333-4700
Contest sites: Boston, Chicago, Las Vegas, Minneapolis, New Orleans, New York City, Orlando, San Antonio, San Francisco, Toronto, Vancouver, Williamsburg. Bowl games: Chick-fil-a Peach Bowl (Atlanta), Culligan Holiday (San Diego), Houston (TX), Mobile Alabama (Mobile), Motor City (Detroit), Outback (Tampa)

306 North American Music Festivals & Custom Tours
P.O. Box 36
50 Brookwood Drive, Suite 1
Carlisle, PA 17013
800-533-6263
Fax 717-245-9060
www.greatfestivals.com
email: info@greatfestivals.com
Parade band sites: Myrtle Beach, SC; New York City, NY; Toronto, Ontario; Virginia Beach, VA; Washington, D.C.; Williamsburg, VA

307 Oahu Music Festival (Hawaii)
1033 Shive Lane
Bowling Green, KY 42103

308 Performing Arts Consultants Music Festivals (includes International Azalea Festival, Norfolk, VA)
88 West Front Street
Keyport, NJ 07735
800-872-3378
www.usafest.org

Prestige Festivals *see* "World of Music" Festivals

309 St. Louis Music Festival (indoor guard, team twirling, parade)
800-445-2297
Fax 973-492-5572
www.festivalswcaws.org
email: info@festivalswcaws.org

310 Six Flags Festivals
c/o Educational Tour Consultants, Inc.
934 Baker Lane, Suite A
Winchester, VA 22603

311 Smoky Mountain Music Festival (street parade, indoor guard, indoor percussion; site: Gatlinburg, TN)
c/o Dr. W.J. Julian
601 Westborough Road
Knoxville, TN 37909
800-553-1032
Fax 865-938-0246
www.smmfestival.com
email: HunterSMMF@aol.com

Southwest Invitational (site: Dallas, TX; marching band, parade, percussion, indoor guard) *see* Music Tours Unlimited, Inc.

312 West Virginia Strawberry Festival (indoor guard, parade)
P.O. Box 117
24 Riley Heights, Suite 1
Buckhannon, WV 26201
304-472-9036
Fax 304-472-9037
www.wvstrawberryfestival.com

313 WMC (World Music Contest) Foundation Kerkrade
P.O. Box 133

6460 AC Kerkrade
The Netherlands

314 World of Music Festivals (band on review, auxiliary, drum line)
Don Caneva, National Director
3651 Mount Ashmun Court

San Diego, CA 92111
800-748-5579
Fax 858-292-9951
www.worldofmusic.com
   Sites: Anaheim, CA; San Jose, CA;
   San Diego, CA; Denver, CO; Chicago,
   IL; Minneapolis, MN; Las Vegas, NV

Fall and Winter Competitions

315 A.A. Stagg Marching Band Jamboree
A.A. Stagg High School
111 Street and Roberts Road
Palos Hills, IL 60465
708-974-7400
Fax 708-974-0803

316 Alamance Band Jamboree (exhibitions)
Eastern Alamance High School
4040 Mebane Rogers Road
Mebane, NC 27302
www.ehsmarchingeagles.com

317 Albemarle Showcase of Bands
Albemarle High School
311 Park Ridge Road
Albemarle, NC 28001
http://ahs.scs.k12.nc.us/Mr._%20
   Hedrick.htm

318 Amherst Tournament of Bands
Amherst High School
139 Lancer Lane
Amherst, VA 24521
434-946-9855
email: akarudd@earthlink.net

319 Ancient City Presentation of Bands
(FMBT)
St. Augustine High School
3205 Varella Avenue
St. Augustine, FL 32095
904-829-3471
Fax 904-824-1940
www-sahs.stjohns.k12.fl.us/info/schinfo.
   html
email: dodds@sahs.stjohns.k12.fl.us

320 Anoka Field Show
Anoka High School
3939 7th Avenue North
Anoka, MN 55304
763-506-6200

321 Apollo High School Marching Classic
Apollo High School
2280 Tamarack Road
Owensboro, KY 42301
270-852-7100
Fax 270-852-7120

322 Appalachian Marching Band Festival
c/o Phi Mu Alpha Sinfonia, Rho Tau
   Chapter
School of Music
Appalachian State University
Boone, NC 28608
www.acs.appstate.edu/dept/music

323 Arcadia Festival of Bands (site: Citrus
   College, Glendora, CA)
P.O. Box 660-131
Arcadia, CA 91066-0131
www.arcadiamusic.org

324 Arizona State Marching Band Festival
c/o Arizona Music Educators Association
   and Arizona Band and Orchestra
   Directors Association
Dobson High School
1501 W. Guadalupe Road
Mesa, AZ 85202

325 Arizona State University Band Day (exhibition)

School of Music
Arizona State University
Tempe, AZ 85287-0405
480-965-4392
http://music.asu.edu/performance/
   marching.htm
email: susan.oliver@asu.edu

326 Art in Motion (OMEA)
Norton High School
4128 S. Cleve-Mass Road
Norton, OH 44203
330-825-7277
Fax 330-825-4275
email: psante432@aol.com

327 Artistry in Motion (Western Band Association)
Etiwanda High School
13500 Victoria
Rancho Cucamonga, CA 91739
909-899-2531
www.etiwandahighschool.com

328 Atascadero Colony Days Parade and
   Field Show Competition
Atascadero High School
One High School Hill
Atascadero, CA 93422
805-462-4212
http://ahsband.freehomepage.com/con
   tact.html
email: ahsband@thegrid.net

329 Athens Marching Invitational Festival
   (OMEA)
Athens High School
One High School Road
The Plains, OH 45780
740-797-4521, x243
Fax 740-797-1421

330 Aurora Houn' Dawg Marching Festival
Aurora High School
101 South Roosevelt Avenue
Aurora, MO 65605
417-678-3355
Fax 417-678-2905

331 Avon Invitational
Avon High School
7575 E. Co. Rd. 150 South
Avon, IN 46123
317-272-2586
www.avonband.org

332 Azalea Marching Festival (FMBT)
Palatka High School
302 Mellon Road
Palatka, FL 32177
904-329-0577

333 Baldwin Park High School Invitational
Baldwin Park High School
3900 North Puente Avenue
Baldwin Park, CA 91706
626-960-5431

334 Band Expo (OMEA)
Anderson/Turpin High School
7560 Forest Road
Cincinnati, OH 45255
513-232-2772, x2910
Fax 513-232-3146

335 Band of Bears Classic
Pisgah High School
1 Black Bear Drive
Canton, NC 28716
828-646-3440

336 Band of Gold Marching Classic
Hazard High School
157 Bulldog Lane
Hazard, KY 41701

337 "Band of Pride" Invitational Marching
   Band Contest
Daviess County High School
4255 New Hartford Road
Owensboro, KY 42303
270-852-7300
Fax 270-852-7310
www.daviess.k12.ky.us/dchs

338 Bandmasters Championship (site: Liberty Bowl)
c/o University of Memphis Band Alumni

University of Memphis
Memphis, TN 38152-3370
901-681-9538
cdarr@paritech.com

339 Band-O-Rama (OMEA)
Hamilton High School
1165 Eaton Avenue
Hamilton, OH 45013
513-868-7700
Fax 513-887-4506

340 Band-O-Rama (OMEA)
Marietta High School
208 Davis Avenue
Marietta, OH 45750
740-374-6540, x37
Fax 740-374-6531

341 Bands of America (September-November)
526 Pratt Avenue North
Schaumburg, IL 60193
800-848-BAND
Fax 847-891-1812
www.bands.org
email: boainfo@bands.org
Sites: Daytona, FL; Atlanta, GA; Louisville, KY; St. Louis, MO; Hempstead, NY; Massillon, OH; Toledo, OH; Youngstown, OH; Johnson City, TN; Arlington, TX; Huntsville, TX. Championships: Indianapolis, IN.

342 BC Classic (OMEA)
Bloom Carroll High School
69 S. Beaver Street
Carroll, OH 43112
614-837-0786
Fax 740-756-9525

343 Beddingfield Band Classic
Beddingfield High School
4510 Old Stantonsburg Road
Wilson, NC 27893
252-399-7880

344 Beechwood Festival of Bands
Beechwood High School

54 Beechwood Road
Fort Mitchell, KY 41017

345 Bellbrook Marching Band Invitational (MSBA)
Bellbrook High School
3737 Upper Bellbrook Road
Bellbrook, OH 45305
937-848-6233
Fax 937-848-5016
www.sugarcreek.k12.oh.us/HighSchool/index2.htm
email: Director@marching-eagles.org

346 Bellwood Tournament of Bands (TOB)
Bellwood-Antis High School
400 Martin Street
Bellwood, PA 16617
www.bellwoodfootball.com/band.html

347 Bermuda Invitational Marching Band Competition
Bermuda Dept. of Tourism
310 Madison Avenue, 2nd Floor
New York, NY 10021

348 Big Apple Tournament of Bands
Musselman High School
126 Excellence Way
Inwood, WV 25428
304-229-1950
Fax 304-229-1959
http://boe.berk.k12

349 Billerica Invitational Marching Band Competition (MAC)
Billerica Memorial High School
35 River Street
Billerica, MA 01821
978-436-9300

350 Bishop McDevitt Cavalcade of Bands (CBA)
Bishop McDevitt High School
125 Royal Avenue
Wyncote, PA 19095-1198
215-887-5575
Fax 215-887-1371
www.mcdevitths.org
email: info@mcdevitths.org

351 Blaine Field Show
Blaine High School
12555 University Avenue, N.E.
Blaine, MN 55434-2199
763-506-6500
www.anoka.k12.mn.us/education/
    school/school.php?sectionid=10300

352 Blue and Gold Festival
Morehead State University
150 University Blvd.
Morehead, KY 40351

353 Blue and White Invitational (OMEA)
East High School
224 Marshall Avenue
Sciotoville, OH 45662
740-776-6777
Fax 740-776-6812

354 Blue Devil Classic
Mooresville Senior High School
659 East Center Avenue
Mooresville, NC 28115
www.geocities.com/prideinmotion

355 Blue Ridge Classic Marching Band Festival
Mars Hill College
NC Highway 213 West
Mars Hill, NC 28754
www.geocities.com/mhcbands

356 Blue Springs Marching Invitational
Blue Springs High School
901 Northwest Ashton Drive
Blue Springs, MO 64015
816-229-3459

357 Blue Valley Tiger Marching Festival
Blue Valley High School
6001 West 159th Street
Stilwell, KS 66085-8808
913-239-4800

358 Bluegrass Invitational Band Festival
West Jessamine High School

2101 Wilmore Road
Nicholasville, KY 40356

359 Bluegrass Pageant of the Bands
Bryan Station High School
1866 Edgeworth Drive
Lexington, KY 40505-2010

360 Bonanza of Bands Marching Competition (OMEA)
Zanesville High School
Zanesville, OH 43701
740-588-4029
Fax 740-455-4329

361 Bowl Games of America
P.O. Box 571187
Salt Lake City, UT 84157-1187
888-242-7597
www.bgaskys.com
    Sites: Jacksonville, FL (Toyota Gator
    Bowl); Memphis, TN (Axa Liberty
    Bowl); Miami, FL (Fedex Orange
    Bowl); New Orleans, LA (Nokia
    Sugar Bowl); San Antonio, TX (Sylva-
    nia Alamo Bowl); San Jose, CA (Sili-
    con Valley Football Classic)

362 Boyertown Cavalcade of Bands
Boyertown High School
120 N. Monroe Street
Boyertown, PA 19512-1299
610-369-7435
Fax 610-369-7533

363 Bradford Area High School (Lakeshore
    Marching Band Association/Pennsyl-
    vania Federation of Contest Judges)
81 Interstate Parkway
Bradford, PA 16701-1011
814-362-3845
www.bradfordareaschools.org/bahs

364 Brandywine Classic (TOB)
Brandywine High School
1400 Foulk Road
Wilmington, DE 19803
302-479-1600
Fax 302-479-1604
www.bsd.k12.de.us

365 Brick Capital Classic
     Lee County Senior High School
     1708 Nash Street
     Sanford, NC 27330
     http://www.ls.lee.k12.nc.us/lee_senior_
       webpage.html

366 Brick Township Memorial High School
       (USSBA)
     2001 Lanes Mill Road
     Brick, NJ 68724
     732-785-3090

367 Bronco Marching Classic
     Brookwood High School
     1259 Dogwood Road
     Snellville, GA 30078
     770-972-7642

368 Brunswick Sound Spectacular (OMEA)
     Brunswick High School
     3581 Center Road
     Brunswick, OH 44212
     330-273-0268
     Fax 330-273-0268

369 Buckeye Classic (OMEA)
     Ironton High School
     1701 S. 6th Street
     Ironton, OH 45638
     740-532-0110
     Fax 740-533-6067

370 Buckeye Classic Band Invitational
       (OMEA)
     Nelsonville-York High School
     One Buckeye Drive
     Nelsonville, OH 45764
     740-753-1963
     Fax 740-824-3760

371 Bunnell High School (USSBA)
     1 Bulldog Blvd.
     Stratford, CT 06614

372 Butler County Contest
     Butler County High School
     1147 S. Main Street
     Morgantown, KY 42261-9409

California State University-Fresno *see* Sierra
  Cup Classic

373 Cambridge Cavalcade of Bands (OMEA)
     Cambridge High School
     1201 Claremont Avenue
     Troy, OH 43725
     740-439-3653
     Fax 740-439-3314
     email: twoodman@jadeinc.com

374 Capital City Expo
     J. O. Sanderson High School
     5500 Dixon Drive
     Raleigh, NC 27609
     http://www.rtpnet.org/shsband

375 Cardinal Classic
     East Surry High School
     801 W. Main Street
     Pilot Mountain, NC 27041
     http://surry.k12.nc.us/EastSurry/index
       htm

376 Cardinal Fall Classic Field Show
     Coon Rapids High School
     CRHS Marching Band Boosters
     P.O. Box 48272
     Coon Rapids, MN 55448-0272

377 Cardinal Marching Band Invitational
       (OMEA)
     New Bremen High School
     901 E. Monroe Street
     New Bremen, OH 45869
     419-629-8606, x1330
     Fax 419-629-0115

378 Carmel Invitational
     Carmel High School
     520 East Main Street
     Carmel, IN 46032
     317-846-7721
     Fax 317-571-4066
     www.ccs.k12.in.us/chsPA/padhome.htm

379 Carolina Cavalcade of Bands (BOA)
     Central Cabarrus High School
     505 NC Highway 49 South

Concord, NC 28025
http://www.cabarrus.k12.nc.us/central/
index.html

380 Carolina Classic
East Lincoln High School
6471 NC Highway 73
Denver, NC 28037
http://www.elhsband.org

381 Carroll County Marching Band Festival
(KMEA)
Carroll County High School
1706 Highland Avenue
Carrollton, KY 41008

382 Carrollton Band Day
Carrollton R-7 School District
300 East 9th Street
Carrollton, MO 64633

383 Carthage Maple Leaf Marching Festival
Carthage Senior High School
714 South Main Street
Carthage, MO 64836
417-359-7020

384 Cary Band Day
Cary High School Band
638 Walnut Street
Cary, NC 27511
http://www.caryband.org

385 Casey County Marching Classic
Casey County High School
1841 E. KY 70
Liberty, KY 42539-6718

386 Castle Invitational
Castle Band Boosters
Castle High School
3344 Highway 261
Newburgh, IN 47630
www.simplyinstrumental.com/bands/
band_castle02.shtml

387 Catoosa Tournament of Bands
Catoosa High School
2000 South Cherokee Street

Catoosa, OK 74015-3232
918-266-1631

388 Cavalcade of Bands
Western Michigan University
Kalamazoo, MI 49001

389 Cavalcade of Bands (CBA)
Annville-Cleona Secondary School
South White Oak
Annville, PA 17003
717-867-7700, x4094

390 Cavalcade of Bands (CBA)
J. P. McCaskey High School
445 Reservoir Street
Lancaster, PA 17602
717-291-6219

391 Cavalcade of Bands Association (NJ, PA)
High school members include: An-
nville-Cleona (Annville, PA); Bishop
McDevitt (Harrisburg, PA); Burling-
ton City (Burlington, NJ); Coatesville,
PA; Collingswood, NJ; Conestoga Val-
ley (Lancaster, PA); Conrad Weiser
(Robesonia, PA); James M. Coughlin
(Wilkes-Barre, PA); Daniel Boone
(Birdsboro, PA); Eastern York
(Wrightsville, PA); Greencastle-
Antrim (Greencastle, PA); Hempfield
(Landisville, PA); J. P. McCaskey
(Lancaster, PA); Lampeter-Strasburg
(Lampeter, PA), Lebanon Catholic,
PA; Manheim Township (Lancaster,
PA); Marple Newtown (Newtown
Square, PA); Northern Lebanon
(Fredericksburg, PA); Owen J. Rob-
erts (Pottstown, PA); Palisades (Kin-
tersville, PA); Pennsville, NJ; Phoe-
nixville, PA; Plymouth-Whitemarsh
(Plymouth Meeting, PA); Pottstown
(PA); Reading, PA; Red Lion, PA;
Shawnee (Medford, NJ); South West-
ern, (Hanover, PA); Spring Grove, PA;
Susquehannock (Glen Rock, PA);
Unionville (Kennett Square, PA);
Upper Dauphin (Elizabethville, PA);
Upper Dublin (Ft. Washington, PA);
Upper Moreland (Willow Grove, PA);
West Chester-East (West Chester,

McLean High School Indoor Guard (McLean, VA)

PA); William Penn (York, PA); Wissahickon (Ambler, PA); Wyomissing, PA; York Catholic, PA; York Suburban, PA. One of the competitions is held at West Chester University. Championships normally held in Millersville or Hershey, PA.

392   Cavalier Classic
Hugh M. Cummings High School
2200 North Mebane Street
Burlington, NC 27217
http://geocities.com/cummingsband
email: cummingsband@yahoo.com

393   Caverna Colonel's Marching Band Festival
Caverna High School
2276 S. Dixie Street
Horse Cave, KY 42749-1460

394   Cecil County Parade of Bands (TOB)
Elkton High School
110 James Street
Elkton, MD 21921
410-996-5000

395   Centennial High School Music in Motion
Centennial High School
8601 Hageman Road
Bakersfield, CA 93312-3957
661-588-8601
Fax 661-558-8608
www.kernhigh.org/centennial

396   Center Grove Invitational
Center Grove High School
2717 South Morgantown Road
Greenwood, IN 46143
317-881-0581
Fax 317-885-4509
www.centergrove.k12.in.us/cghs

397   Central California Band Review (NCBA)
Merced High School
205 West Olive Avenue
Merced, CA 95340
209-722-4466
www.mhs.muhsd.k12.ca.us

398   Central North Carolina Band Festival
Western Alamance High School
1731 Highway 87 North
Elon, NC 27244
http://www.wazbb.org

399   Chamberlain Invitational Marching Band Festival (FMBT)
Chamberlain High School
9401 North Blvd.
Tampa, FL 33612
813-975-7677
Fax 813-975-7687
www.sdhc.k12.fl.us/~chamberlain.high
email: GansemerP@AOL.COM

400   Champlin Park Field Show
Champlin Park High School
6025 109th Avenue North
Champlin Park, MN 55316-3488
763-506-6800
Fax 763-506-6803
http://rebelweb.anoka.k12.mn.us/rebel/champlin.html

401   Charlestown Invitational
Charlestown High School
#1 Pirate Place
Charlestown, IN 47111
812-256-3328

402   Charlottesville Cavalcade Marching Band Contest
Charlottesville High School
1400 Melbourne Road
Charlottesville, VA 22901
804-295-8453
email: chsb@avenue.org

403   Cherokee High School Classic (USSBA)
Cherokee High School
120 Tomlinson Mill Road
Marlton, NJ 08053
856-983-5140

404   Cheshire High School (USSBA)
525 South Main Street
Cheshire, CT 06410-3146
www.cheshirect.org/chs
email: jkuhner@ramband.com

405 Chesterton ISSMA Regional (ISSMA)
     Chesterton High School
     2125 S. 11th Street
     Chesterton, IN 46304
     219-983-3730
     Fax 219-983-3772
     www.duneland.k12.in.us/chs/perform.
     html

406 Chicagoland Marching Band Festival
     Wheeling High School
     900 South Elmhurst Road
     Wheeling, IL 60090
     847-718-7000

407 Chippewa Falls Field Show (WSMA)
     735 Terrill Street
     Chippewa Falls, WI 54729
     715-726-2406
     Fax 715-726-2792
     http://cfsd.chipfalls.k12.wi.us/HS/HS
     index.htm

408 City of Palms Tournament of Bands
     (FMBT)
     Cypress Lake High School Center for
     the Arts
     6750 Panther Lane
     Fort Myers, FL 33919
     941-481-4850
     www.lee.k12.fl.us/schools/cyh
     email: IvanW@Lee.k12.fl.us

409 Clarkston Invitational
     Clarkston High School
     6093 Flemings Lake Road
     Clarkston, MI 48346
     248-623-3600

410 Clay County Contest
     Clay County High School
     128 Richmond Road
     Manchester, KY 40962
     606-598-2168
     Fax 606-598-7829
     email: username@clay.k12.us

411 Claymont Band Round Up (OMEA)
     Claymont High School

4205 Indian Hill Road
Uhrichsville, OH 44683
740-922-3471
Fax 740-922-1031

412 Clayton High School Marching Band
     Festival
     Clayton High School
     600 S. Fayetteville St.
     Clayton, NC 27520
     http://www.johnston.k12.nc.us/web/
     SCHOOLS/s324/index.htm

413 Clinton Band Day
     Clinton High School
     1201 West Elizabeth Street
     Clinton, NC 28328
     http://www.clinton.k12.nc.us/clinton/
     programs/band/marching/index.htm

414 Cloverleaf Cavalcade of Sound (OMEA)
     Cloverleaf High School
     8525 Friendsville Road
     Lodi, OH 44254
     330-948-2500, x3538
     Fax 330-948-4068
     email: c.carasea@worldnet.att.net

415 Clovis Schools Field Tournament (West-
     ern Band)
     Buchanan High School
     1560 N. Minnewawa Avenue
     Clovis, CA 93611
     559-327-3000

416 Coastal Empire Classic (GMEA)
     Effingham County High School Band
     Boosters
     Effingham County High School
     1589 Highway 119 North
     Springfield, GA 31329

417 Cocoa Beach (FMBT)
     Cocoa Beach Jr./Sr. High School
     1500 Minutemen Causeway
     Cocoa Beach, FL 32931
     321-783-1776
     Fax 321-868-6602
     www.cbhs.brevard.k12.fl.us

418 Coliseum Classic Marching Festival
(site: Lindenwood University)
Francis Howell Central High School
4545 Central School Road
St. Charles, MO 63304
636-441-0088
www.fhsd.k12.mo.us/parents/schools/
central-high.asp

419 Collegiate Band Festival (site: J. Birney
Crum Stadium, Allentown, PA)
c/o Vivace Productions, Inc.
882 S. Matlack Street, Suite 202
West Chester, PA 19383
610-431-1121

420 Collins Hill Eagles Nest Invitational Festival
Collins Hill High School
50 Taylor Road
Suwanee, GA 30024
770-682-4100
Fax 770-682-4105
www.gwinnett.k12.ga.us/CollinsHillHS

421 Colonial Band Classic
Washington High School
400 Slatestone Road
Washington, NC 27889
www.beaufort.k12.nc.us/whs

422 Columbia Invitational
Columbia Central High School
Columbia, TN 38401
931-381-2222
Fax 931-381-6434

423 Columbus Grove "Eyes with Pride"
(OMEA)
Columbus Grove High School
201 W. Cross Street
Columbus Grove, OH 45830
419-659-2661
Fax 419-659-5134
email: cg_kuch@cg.noacsc.org

424 Columbus North Invitational
Columbus North High School
1400 25th Street

Columbus, IN 47201
812-376-4431
Fax 812-376-4291

425 Contest of Champions
c/o Lafayette Band Boosters
Lafayette High School
17050 Clayton Road
Wildwood, MO 63011-1794
636-227-5722
Fax 636-458-7219
http://lafayettehighschool.org/band
email: LST89@rockwood.k12.mo.us

426 Contest of Champions Marching Band
Contest
Middle Tennessee State University
1301 E. Main Street
Murfreesboro, TN 37132-0001
615-898-2300

427 Copley High School Marching Band Invitational (OMEA)
Copley High School
3807 Ridgewood Road
Copley, OH 44321
330-668-3242
Fax 330-668-9373

428 Corona del Sol Invitational
Corona del Sol High School
1001 East Knox Road
Tempe, AZ 85284
480-752-8888
www.tuhsd.k12.az.us/Corona_del_Sol_
HS

429 Corydon Central Invitational
Corydon Central High School
Corydon Central Boosters
375 Country Club Road
Corydon, IN 47112
www.simplyinstrumental.com/contests/
contest_corydon02.shtml

430 Covered Bridge Marching Festival
Oneonta City School
27605 State Highway 75
Oneonta, AL 35121

205-625-3801
http://groups.msn.com/theohsredskin
band/coveredbridgemarchingfesti
val.msnw

431 Cross Plains Marching Festival (GMEA)
Dalton High School
1500 Manly Street
Dalton, GA 30720
706-278-8757

Crown Jewel Marching Band Festival *see*
Treasure Coast Crown Jewel Marching Band
Festival

432 Crown of Champions Marching Festival
Weddington High School
4901 Monroe-Weddington Road
Matthews, NC 28104
704-708-5530
www.weddingtonband.org/frontpage.
html

433 Crystal Coast Band Classic
Havelock High Band Boosters
Havelock High School
101 Webb Blvd.
Havelock, NC 28532-1993

434 Cudahy High School (WSMA)
5950 South Lake Drive
Cudahy, WI 53110

435 Cumberland Falls Marching Band Classic
Corbin High School
1901 Snyder Street
Corbin, KY 40701

436 Cumberland Valley Tournament of
Bands (TOB)
Cumberland Valley High School
6746 Carlisle Pike
Mechanicsburg, PA 17050
717-766-0217
www.cvschools.org/cvhs/departments/
music/mband.html

437 Cupertino Band Review (NCBA)
Cupertino High School
10100 Finch Avenue
Cupertino, CA 95014
408-366-7395
Fax 404-255-8466
www.chs.fuhsd.org

438 Curry Marching Band Classic
Curry High School
155 Yellow Jacket Drive
Jasper, AL 35503
205-384-3887
Fax 205-221-7381
www.curryhighschool.net

439 Dacula
Dacula High School
123 Broad Street
Dacula, GA 30019
770-963-6664
www.daculaband.com

440 Danville Invitational Band Contest
Danville High School
E. Lexington Avenue
Danville, KY 40422

441 Davis Cup Marching Invitational (site:
Weber State University, Ogden, UT)
Davis High School
325 South Main Street
Kaysville, UT 84037
801-402-8800
Fax 801-402-8801

Daytona 500 Parade & Festival *see* Music
Tours Unlimited, Inc.

442 Del Oro Band Spectacular (NCBA)
Del Oro High School
3301 Taylor Road
Loomis, CA 95650
916-652-6729

443 DeRidder High School Ambassadors in
Blue Marching Festival
DeRidder High School
732 O'Neal Street

DeRidder, LA 70634
337-463-2522, x28
Fax 337-463-9358
http://deridderbands.tripod.com
email: dhsband@beau.k12.la.us

444 Dixie Classic Band Competition
George Washington High School
701 Broad Street
Danville, VA 24540
www.gwband.org

445 Downers Grove South Marching Mus-
tangs Music Bowl
South High School
1436 Norfolk Avenue
Downers Grove, IL 60516-2632
630-795-8500
Fax 630-795-8599
www.csd99.k12.il.us/south
email: bbaxter3@aol.com

446 Dragon Classic
Warren Central High School
559 Morgantown Road
Bowling Green, KY 42101

447 Drums at Appletime (site: Murphysboro
High School)
c/o Murphysboro Apple Festival
203 South 13th Street
Murphysboro, IL 62966
Fax 618-684-2010
www.murphysboro.com/events/Apple
Fest/Drums.html
email: executive@GlobalEyes.net

448 Drums by the Sea (site: Hull, MA)
New England Scholastic Band Association
c/o Don Vasconcelles, President
17 Elizabeth St.
North Dartmouth, MA 02747

449 Durant High School
4748 Cougar Path
Plant City, FL 33567
813-757-9075
Fax 813-707-7079
www.sdhc.k12.fl.us/~durant.high

450 East Georgia Marching Band Festival
and Championship (GMEA)
Statesboro High School
10 Lester Road
Statesboro, GA 30458

451 East Lincoln High School
6471 Highway 73
Denver, NC 28037
704-483-5681
Fax 704-483-6751
www.lincoln.k12.nc.us/ELHS_Web_
Page/index.htm

452 East Paulding Raider Cup Invitational
Festival
East Paulding High School
3320 East Paulding Drive
Dallas, GA 30157
770-445-5100
Fax 770-443-6357
www.eastpaulding.org/raiderbrigade/
index.html

453 Eastern High School (USSBA)
1401 Laurel Oak Road
Voorhees, NJ 08043

454 Eastern Randolph Wildcat Classic
Eastern Randolph High School
390 Eastern Randolph Road
Ramseur, NC 27316
http://www.randolph.k12.nc.us/schools
/erhs/default.htm

455 Eastview Field Competition
Eastview High School
6200—140th Street West
Apple Valley, MN 55124
952-431-8900

456 Echoes Off the River
Alton High School
2200 College Avenue
Alton, IL 62002
618-474-2700

457 Emerald Coast Marching Band Festival
c/o Randy Nelson, Director of Bands

Choctawhatchee High School
110 Racetrack Road
Ft. Walton Beach, FL 32548

458 Emerald Regime Invitational (Western
Band; site: San Jose State Spartan Stadium)
Live Oak High School
1505 East Main Avenue
Morgan Hill, CA 95037
www.emeraldregime.org

459 Evansville Central Invitational
Evansville Central Band Boosters
Evansville Central High School
5400 1st Avenue
Evansville, IN 47710
www.simplyinstrumental.com/contests/
contest_evvcentral02.shtml

460 Evansville North Invitational
Evansville North High School
Evansville North Band Boosters
2319 Stringtown Avenue
Evansville, IN 47711
812-435-8283
www.simplyinstrumental.com/contests/
contest_evvnorth02.shtml

461 Exhibition of Pride
Elkin High School
334 Elk Spur St.
Elkin, NC 28621
http://www.ncschoolbands.com/elkin.
html

462 F.J. Reitz Invitational
F.J. Reitz High School
350 Dreier Blvd.
Evansville, IN 47712
812-435-8200
Fax 812-435-8517
www.evsc.k12.in.us/schoolzone/schools
/reitz/index.htm

463 Fall Fest Music Show
Franklin Park District
9560 Franklin Avenue
Franklin Park, IL 60131

464 Farmington Invitational Marching Festival
Farmington High School
1 Black Knight Drive
Farmington, MO 63640
573-701-1310
www.farmington.k12.mo.us/school/hs/
organizations

465 Festival of Bands
Fuquay-Varina High School
201 Bengal Blvd.
Fuquay-Varina, NC 27526
919-557-2511
Fax 919-557-2512
http://fvbb.home.mindspring.com

466 Festival of Bands (site: Autzen Stadium)
School of Music
University of Oregon
Eugene, OR 97403
541-346-2138
http://omb.uoregon.edu/Festival%20
of%20Bands/fob.main.page.html
email: cjhansen@darkwing.uoregon.
edu

467 Festival of Bands, USA (includes parade)
P.O. Box 89940
Sioux Falls, SD 57109-1011
605-367-7639
Fax 605-367-7693
www.marching.com/events/siouxfalls.
html

468 Festival of Champions
Central Missouri State University
P.O. Box 800
Warrensburg, MO 64093
800-729-2678
www.cmsu.edu

469 Festival of Champions
Department of Music
Murray State University
1 Murray Street
Murray, KY 42071-3303
800-272-4MSU
www.murraystate.edu
email: webmaster@murraystate.edu

470 Festival of Champions Invitational
      Marching Competition
      Lexington Music Boosters
      103 Clever Lane
      Lexington, OH 44904

471 Festival of Pride
      Caldwell County High School
      350 Beckner Lane
      Princeton, KY 42445-5002

472 Field Competition
      Straughn High School
      Route 10, Box 310
      Andalusia, AL 36420
      334-222-2511
      www.covingtoncountyschools.net/shs/
      band/straughn_sound_of_gold.htm
      #CON

473 Field of Dreams
      Reidland High School
      5349 Benton Road
      Paducah, KY 42003

474 Fiesta Bowl National Band Champion-
      ship (site: Bank One Ballpark, Phoe-
      nix, AZ)
      c/o Blue Cross Blue Shield of Arizona
      480-517-6289
      www.tostitosfiestabowl.com
      email: dickstemple@cox.net (Dick Stem-
      ple, Band Selection Chair)
      also: www.marching.com/events/fies
      tabowl.html (International Travel,
      Inc.)

475 Findlay High School Band Festival
      (OMEA)
      1200 Broad Avenue
      Findlay, OH 45840
      419-425-8318
      Fax 419-420-7051

476 Florida Citrus Sports Holiday Music Fes-
      tival (800) 932-6440
      5850 Lakehurst Drive, Suite 205
      Orlando, FL 32819

477 Florida Marching Band Tournament
      (FMBT)
      High school sites include: Auburndale,
      Cape Coral, Chamberlain, Citrus,
      Cocoa Beach, Cypress Creek, Cypress
      Lake, Deerfield, Durant, G. Holmes
      Braddock, Haines City, Lake Howell,
      Largo, Lely, John I. Leonard, Mariner,
      Miami Coral Park, Olympic Heights,
      Palatka, St. Augustine, Santa Fe, San-
      taluces, Spruce Creek, Tarpon Springs,
      Tate, University High School, Vero
      Beach
        Member schools include: Albany,
      American Heritage, Armwood, At-
      lantic Community, Auburndale, Avon,
      Baker County, Baldwin County, Bar-
      bara Goleman, Bartram Trail, Bay-
      shore, Belleview, Bishop Kenny, Blake,
      Boca Ciega, Boca Raton, Booker,
      Boone, G. Holmes Braddock, Bran-
      don, Brooks County, Cape Coral,
      Centennial, Central, Chamberlain,
      Charlotte, Chiefland, Choctawhat-
      chee, Citrus, Clay, Cocoa Beach, Co-
      lumbia, Cooper City, Coral Shores,
      Coral Springs, Countryside, Crest-
      view, Crystal River, Cypress Lake,
      Daphne, Davidson, Deerfield Beach,
      Deltona, Desota County, Dixie Hol-
      lins, Dr. Phillips, Dunnellon, Durant,
      East Bay, East Ridge, Ed White, Es-
      cambia, Estero, Felix Varela, Fernand-
      ina, Flannagan, Fletcher, Fort Laud-
      erdale, Fort Myers, Fort Walton
      Beach, Frostproof, Gainesville, Gate-
      way, Gibbs, Glynn Academy, Gulf
      Breeze, Haines City, Hardee, Harri-
      son Central, Hernando, Hialeah,
      Hialeah-Miami Lakes, Hollywood
      Hills, Homestead, Hudson, Immoka-
      lee, Indian Rock Christian, Indian
      Rocks, Interlachan, J.P. Taravella,
      Jupiter, Killian, King's Academy, Lake
      Howell, Lake Region, Lakewood
      Ranch, Lake Worth, Land O' Lakes,
      Largo, Lecanto, Leesburg, Lehigh,
      Lely, Lemon Bay, Leto, Lincoln,
      McIntosh, Mainland, Manatee, Mari-
      ner, Martin, Melbourne, Miami,
      Miami Beach, Miami Coral Park,
      Miami Palmetto, Miami Senior,
      Miami Southridge, Miami Springs,

Miami Sunset, Mitchell, Nease, New Smyrna, Northeast, North Fort Myers, North Marion, Northside Christian, Ocala Forest, Okeechobee, Olympic Heights, Orange Park, Osceola, Osceola Meredith, Oviedo, Palatka, Palm Beach Gardens, Palmetto, Pasco, Pedro Menendez, Pensacola, Petal, Pinellas Park, Pine Forest, Pine Ridge, P. K. Yonge D.R.S., Plantation, Plant City, Poinciana, Port Charlotte, Port St. Lucie, Ridgeview, Riverview, Rockledge, Royal Palm Beach, St. Augustine, St. Cloud, St. Petersburg, Santa Fe, Sanderson, Santaluces, Sarasota, Sebastian, Seminole, Southaven, South Broward, Southfork, South Plantation, Southridge, South Sumpter, Southwest Miami, Spanish River, Springstead, Spruce Creek, Stoneman Douglas, Tarpon Springs, Tate, Tavares, Tiff County, Trenton, Trinity, Tuscola, Umatilla, University, Venice, Vero Beach, Wauchula, Wellington, Wesley Chapel, Western, West Orange, West Port, Westwood, Wharton, William Dwyer, Winter Haven

478 Floyd Central Invitational
Floyd Central Junior/Senior High School
6575 Old Vincennes Road
Floyds Knobs, IN 47119
812-923-8811
Fax 812-923-4010
www.venus.net/~fchsadm/index.shtml

479 Foard Band Classic
Fred T. Foard High School
3407 Plateau Road
Newton, NC 28146
www.foardtigerband.org
email: foardband@hotmail.com

480 Food Lion Classic
East Rowan High School
175 St. Luke's Church Road
Salisbury, NC 28146
http://www.eastrowanband.com

481 Foothill Band Review (NCBA)
Foothill High School

230 Pala Avenue
San Jose, CA 95127
925-461-6648

482 Foothills Classic Marching Band Festival and Contest
Seymour High School
c/o Michael Carter, Seymour High Band Boosters
732 Boyds Creek Highway
Seymour, TN 37865

483 Forbush Marching Band Festival
Forbush High School
1525 Falcon Road
East Bend, NC 27018

484 Fort Frye Pageant of Bands (OMEA)
Fort Frye High School
418 Fifth Street
Beverly, OH 45715
740-984-2376
Fax 740-984-4361

485 Francis Howell Invitational
Francis Howell High School
7001 South Highway 94
St. Charles, MO 63304

486 Franklin-Simpson Invitational Marching Contest
Franklin-Simpson High School
400 South College Street
P.O. Box 339
Franklin, KY 42134
270-586-3273

487 Freedom High Patriot Classic
Freedom High School
511 Independence Blvd.
Morgantown, NC 28655
http://members.tripod.com/marching patriots

488 Friendship Cup
c/o Ron Hardin, WGI Marching Band Coordinator
4010 Youngfield Street
Wheat Ridge, CO 80033

303-424-1927
email: ronhardin@aol.com

489 George Wythe Band Festival
George Wythe High School
George Wythe Band Boosters
P.O. Box 411
Wytheville, VA 24382
276-228-3981
http://gwband.wytheville.com/festival

490 Georgia Bandmasters Contest and Festival (GMEA)
Forsyth Central High School
520 Tribble Gap Road
Cumming, GA 30040
770-887-8151
Fax 770-781-2289
www.flashofcrimson.com

491 Georgia Invitational Band Championships (GMEA)
Hiram High School
702 Ballentine Drive
Hiram, GA 30141
770-443-1182
Fax 770-439-5053
www.hiramhigh.org
email: info@hiramhigh.org

492 Georgia Mountain Marching Festival (GMEA)
Habersham Central High School
171 Raider Circle
Mount Airy, GA 30556
http://bandofblue.8m.com

493 Georgia Ridges Marching Festival (GMEA)
Ridgeland High School
2478 Happy Valley Road
Rossville, GA 30741
706-820-9063
Fax 706-820-1342

494 Gilbert Invitational
Gilbert High School
1101 East Elliot Road
Gilbert, AZ 85296

495 Gilroy High School Field Show
Gilroy High School
750 West Tenth Street
Gilroy, CA 95020
408-847-2424
email: Joseph.Fortino@gusd.k12.ca.us

496 Glendale Field Tournament
Glendale Community College
6000 W. Olive Avenue
Glendale, AZ 85302-3090

497 Glenpool Invitational Band Day
Glenpool High School
P.O. Box 1149
Glenpool, OK 74033
918-322-3285

498 Gold Coast Marching Festival (FMBT)
Olympic Heights Community High School
20101 Lyons Road
Boca Raton, FL 33434
561-852-6977
www.palmbeach.k12.fl.us/Olympic
HeightsHS
email: Vega03@AOL.COM

499 Golden Invitational Marching Band Festival (FMBT)
c/o Band of Gold
Largo High School
410 Missouri Avenue
Largo, FL 34640
727-585-4653
Benoit@pcsb.org

500 Golden River Marching Festival (GMEA)
Haralson County High School
1655 GA Highway 120
Tallapoosa, GA 30176
www.goldenriverfest.homestead.com/
index~ns4.html

501 Golden State Tournament of Bands
Championship (Western Band)
Clovis High School
1055 Fowler
Clovis, CA 93611
559-327-1000

502 Governor's Gold Cup Marching Band
     Festival
     Elizabethtown High School
     620 N. Mulberry Street
     Elizabethtown, KY 42701

503 Granada Hills High School
     10535 Zelzah Avenue
     Granada Hills, CA 91344
     818-360-2361

504 Grand Rapids High School Marching
     Band Competition
     Grand Rapids High School
     800 NW Conifer Drive
     Grand Rapids, MN 55744
     218-327-5760

505 Granite City Classic (GMEA)
     Elbert County Comprehensive High
     School
     600 Abernathy Circle
     Elberton, GA 30635
     706-283-3680
     Fax 706-283-1183
     www.elbert.k12.ga.us/~ecchs/music/
     music.htm

506 Grant County Contest
     Grant County High School
     715 Warsaw Road
     Dry Ridge, KY 41035

507 Grape Bowl Classic (NCBA)
     Bear Creek High School
     10555 Thornton Road
     Stockton, CA 95209
     209-953-8298

508 Greater Atlanta Area Marching Festival
     (GMEA)
     Rockdale County High School
     1174 Bulldog Circle
     Conyers, GA 30012
     770-483-8754
     Fax 770-483-8708
     www.rockdale.k12.ga.us/rchs/band

509 Greater St. Louis Marching Band Festival
     (site: Edward Jones Dome, St. Louis)

     C. Herbert Duncan, Festival Director
     257 San Angelo Drive
     Chesterfield, MO 63017
     314-469-9082
     Fax 314-469-1182
     http://greaterstlouis.tripod.com
     email: slfestival@aol.com

510 Green Festival of Bands (OMEA)
     Green High School
     4057 Gallia Pike
     Franklin Furnace, OH 45629
     740-354-9150
     Fax 740-355-4098

511 Greendale High School (WSMA)
     6801 Southway
     Greendale, WI 53129
     414-423-0110

512 Greenwood Band Invitational
     Greenwood High School
     605 W. Smith Valley Road
     Greenwood, IN 46142
     317-889-4060
     Fax 317-889-4069

513 Grove City High School Marching Band
     Invitational (OMEA)
     Grove City High School
     4665 Hoover Road
     Grove City, OH 43123
     614-801-3338
     Fax 614-871-6563

514 Gulf Coast Marching Band Festival
     Gulfport High School
     100 Perry Street
     Gulfport, MS 39507
     228-896-7525
     Fax 228-896-8281

515 Gulf Coast Marching Band Festival
     (FMBT)
     J. M. Tate High School
     1771 Tate Road
     Cantonment, FL 32533
     850-937-2320
     email: tatehigh@escambia.k12.fl.us

www.gulfporthighschool.com/ghs/ind
ex2.html
email: gulfporthigh@gulfport.k12.ms.us

516 Haines City
Haines City High School
2800 Hornet Drive
Haines City, FL 33844
863-422-8566
email: Orpheus_Mu_Eta@yahoo.com

517 Hanahan High School
6015 Murray Avenue
Hanahan, SC 29406
843-820-3710
Fax 843-820-3716
www.berkeley.k12.sc.us/High/HHS/
HHS.htm

518 Hancock County Marching Festival
Hancock County High School
80 State Route 271 S.
Lewisport, KY 42351-6700

519 Harrodsburg Contest
Harrodsburg High School
441 E. Lexington Street
Harrodsburg, KY 40330

520 Harvest Marching Band Festival (site:
Zaepfel Stadium)
Davis and Eisenhower High Schools
c/o Forrest Fisher, Event Co-Chair
Yakima, WA
509-454-3134
www.harvestbands.org
email: forrestf@nwinfo.net

521 Heart of Georgia International Marching Festival (GMEA)
Warner Robins High School
401 South Davis Drive
Warner Robins, GA 31088
478-929-7877

522 Heartland Marching Band Festival
(FMBT)
Hardee Senior High School
830 Altman Road

Wauchula, FL 33873
863-773-3181
BShayman@Hardee.K12.FL.US

523 Hedgesville High School Showcase of
Bands (TOB)
Hedgesville High School
109 Ridge Road North
Hedgesville, WV 25427
304-754-3354
Fax 304-754-7445
http://boe.berk.k12.wv.us/5011marching
page.html

524 Hempfield Area High School Cavalcade
of Bands (CBA)
R.D. 6, Box 77
Greensburg, PA 15601
724-834-9000
www.k12.pa.us/hempfield_area/hs/hs
_base.htm

525 Henderson Heritage Marching Band Invitational
Henderson County High School
2424 Zion Road
Henderson, KY 42420

526 Heritage Hills Invitational
Heritage Hills Boosters
Heritage Hills High School
P.O. Box 1776
Lincoln City, IN 47552

527 Hermitage Classic
Chester Fritz Stadium
8301 Hungary Spring Road
Richmond, VA 23228
804-672-3345

528 Herndon Showcase of Bands
Herndon High School
700 Bennett Street
Herndon, VA 20170
www.herndonband.org

529 Highland Marching Band Festival
(OMEA)
Highland High School

6506 SR 229
Sparta, OH 43350
419-768-3101
Fax 419-768-3560
email: cbrooks98@yahoo.com

530 Highland Senior High School Invitational
1800 Bench Road
Pocatello, ID 83201
208-237-1300
http://hhsf.highwired.com

531 Hilliard Marching Band Invitational (OMEA)
Hilliard Darby High School
4200 Leppert Road
Hilliard, OH 45750
614-527-4200
Fax 614-527-4206

532 Hobbton Marching Festival
Hobbton High School
12201 Hobbton Highway
Newton Grove, NC 28366
910-594-0242

533 Hoover High School Field Show
Hoover High School
Fresno, CA 93706

534 Hoover Marching Invitational
Hoover High School
1000 Buccaneer Drive
Hoover, AL 35244
205-439-1228
Fax 205-439-1348
www.hoover.k12.al.us/hhs/hhsband/festival.htm
email: hmcafee@hoover.k12.al.us

535 Hopkins County Central Contest
Hopkins County Central High School
6625 Hopkinsville Road
Madisonville, KY 42431-7986

536 Hopkinsville High School Marching Band Invitational
Hopkinsville High School

430 Koffman Drive
Hopkinsville, KY 42240

537 Hurricane Pride Invitational (FMBT)
Citrus High School
600 West Highland Blvd.
Inverness, FL 34452
352-621-1418

538 Husky Vanguard Invitational Festival of Bands
Ashe County High School
184 Campus Drive
West Jefferson, NC 28694
http://www.ashe.k12.nc.us/achs/web/band/band.htm

539 Illini Marching Band Festival
University Bands
School of Music
University of Illinois
Urbana-Champaign, IL 61820
217-333-3028
www.bands.uiuc.edu/MI

540 Independence High School Field Show (NCBA)
Independence High School
1776 Educational Park Drive
San Jose, CA 95113
408-923-7363

541 Indiana State School Music Association, Inc.
School and university competition sites: Penn, Northrop, Ft. Wayne, Lewis Cass, Walton, Lawrence Central, Indianapolis, Southport, Columbus East, Jasper, Cloverdale, Chesterton, Carmel, Jeffersonville, Indiana State University, South Bend (Jackson Field)

542 Indiana State University Mid States Marching Contest
Indiana State University Bands
Department of Music
Indiana State University
Terre Haute, IN 47809

812-237-2771
Fax 812-237-3009
www.indstate.edu/music

543 The Invitational Marching Festival &
     Contest
     Worth County High and Middle Schools
     P.O. Box 5441
     Sylvester, GA 31791
     229-776-8625
     Fax 229-776-8614
     www.ram-band.com/invitational.htm
     email: invitational@ram-band.com

544 Iowa High School State Marching Band
     Contests
     c/o Iowa High School Music Association
     Sites: Cedar Rapids, Council Bluffs,
     Des Moines, Eddyville, Fort Dodge,
     Muscatine, Sheldon, Waterloo

545 J.P. McCaskey Cavalcade of Bands
     (CBA)
     J.P. McCaskey High School
     445 N. Reservoir Street
     Lancaster, PA 17602
     717-399-6400

546 James Logan High School Field Show
     (Western Band)
     James Logan High School
     1800 H Street
     Union City, CA 94587

547 James Madison University Parade of
     Champions
     Music Department
     James Madison University
     Harrisonburg, VA 22801
     540-568-6656
     www.jmu.edu/music/mrd

548 Jefferson Classic
     Monticello High School
     1400 Independence Way
     Charlottesville, VA 22902
     434-244-3106
     www.mhsmusicboosters.com
     email: SNothnag@albemarle.org

549 Jefferson High School
     Route 1, Box 83
     Shenandoah Junction, WV 25442
     304-725-8491
     Fax 304-728-6590

550 Jeffersonville Invitational
     Jeffersonville High School
     2315 Allison Lane
     Jeffersonville, IN 47130
     812-282-6601

551 Jenison Invitational
     Jenison Senior High School
     2140 Bauer Road
     Jenison, MI 49428
     616-457-3400
     Fax 616-457-4070
     www.jenisonbands.org

552 John A. Holmes High School Marching
     Band Festival
     John A. Holmes High School
     600 Woodard Street
     Edenton, NC 27932
     http://www.ecps.k12.nc.us/jaholmes.
     htm

553 Johnson Central Contest
     Johnson Central High School
     257 N. Mayo Trail
     Paintsville, KY 41240-1803

554 Kappa Kappa Psi Marching Contest
     Arkansas State University
     Jonesboro, AR 72401

555 Kentucky Marching Band Champion-
     ships
     c/o Kentucky Marching Educators As-
     sociation
     P.O. Box 65
     Calvert City, KY 42029
     270-395-4821
     Fax 270-395-7156
        site: University of Kentucky, Lexington

556 Kettering Classic (OMEA)
     Fairmont High School

3301 Shroyer Road
Kettering, OH 45429
937-296-7750
Fax 937-643-4327

557 Konawa Band Day (parade and field
     show)
     Konawa High School
     Rt. 1, Box 3
     701 W. South Street
     Konawa, OK 74849
     580-925-3244
     www.konawa.k12.ok.us

558 Lake Park Lancer Joust
     Lake Park High School
     500 West Bryn Mawr
     Roselle, IL 60172
     630-529-4500
     http://lancerband.home.mindspring.
     com/index.htm

559 Lancaster Catholic Tournament of
     Bands (TOB)
     Lancaster Catholic High School
     650 Juliette Avenue
     Lancaster, PA 17601
     717-509-0315
     Fax 717-509-0312
     www.lchs-yes.org/about/index.html
     email: lancastercatholic@lchsyes.org

560 Lancaster High School Band of Gold In-
     vitational (OMEA)
     Lancaster High School
     1312 Granville Pike
     Lancaster, OH 43130
     740-681-7523
     Fax 740-681-7505
     email: lahsband@greenapplecom

561 Land of the Sky Marching Band Festival
     Enka Band Boosters
     Enka High School
     475 Enka Lake Road
     Enka, NC 28728
     828-670-5000
     www.enkahigh.net

562 LaRue County Contest
     LaRue County High School
     925 S. Lincoln Blvd.
     Hodgenville, KY 42748

563 Las Plumas Band Festivo (NCBA)
     c/o Jeff Stratton
     Las Plumas High School
     Oroville, CA 95966
     530-538-2310
     Fax 530-534-5974

564 Lawrence Central Marching Band Invi-
     tational
     7300 East 56th Street
     Indianapolis, IN 46226
     317-545-5301
     Fax 317-543-3348

565 Lawton Open Marching Contest
     Eisenhower High School
     5202 West Gore Blvd.
     Lawton, OK 73505
     580-355-9144

566 Ledford Marching Band Festival
     Ledford High School
     140 Jesse Green Road
     Thomasville, NC 27360
     336-769-9671
     www.davidson.k12.nc.us/ledford/led
     ford.htm

567 Lenape Regional (USSBA)
     Lenape Valley Regional High School
     45 Stanhope Road
     Stanhope, NJ 07874
     201-347-7600

568 Lewistown Area High School Tourna-
     ment of Bands (TOB)
     Lewistown Area High School
     2 Manor Drive
     Lewistown, PA 17044
     717-242-1401

569 Lexington Festival of Champions
     (OMEA)
     Lexington High School

103 Clever Lane
Lexington, OH 44904
419-884-1111

570 Licking Valley Band Fest (OMEA)
Licking Valley High School
1379 Licking Valley Road NE
Newark, OH 43055
740-763-2232
Fax 740-763-0471

571 Lincoln County Band Preview
Lincolnton High School
803 N. Aspen Street
Lincolnton, NC 28092
www.lincoln.k12.nc.us/LHS/school.htm

572 Lockland Band Invitational (OMEA)
Lockland High School
249 W. Forrer Street
Cincinnati, OH 45215
513-563-5000, x159
Fax 513-563-9017

573 Logan County Contest
Logan County High School
2200 Bowling Green Road
Russellville, KY 42276

574 Logan Elm Marching Band Classic
(OMEA)
9575 Tarlton Road
Circleville, OH 43113
740-474-7538, x332
Fax 740-477-6525

575 Lone Oak Invitational
Lone Oak High School
260 Bleich Road
Paducah, KY 42003

576 Lone Star Preview
The Woodlands High School
6101 Research Forest Drive
The Woodlands, TX 77381-4902
936-273-4837
Fax 936-273-8599
www.twhsband.org

577 Los Altos High School Field Show Tournament
c/o Southern California School Band
and Orchestra Association
P.O. Box 4706
Anaheim, CA 92803-4706

578 Louisiana Tech Invitational Marching
Band Classic
Louisiana Tech University Bands
P.O. Box 8608
Ruston, LA 71272

579 Louisville Classic
Male High School
4409 Preston Highway
Louisville, KY 40213
www.malehighband.com/classic.htm

580 Louisville Music in Motion
Louisville High School
418 E. Main Street
Louisville, OH 44641
330-875-1042

581 Lowcountry March-a-Rama
Hanahan High School
6015 Murray Avenue
Hanahan, SC 29406
803-820-3710
Fax 803-820-3716
www.berkeley.k12.sc.us/High/HHS/
HHS.htm

582 McAlester High School
200 East Adams
McAlester, OK 74501
918-423-8166
Fax 918-423-8166
www.mcalester.k12.ok.us

583 McKeesport High School (PIMBA)
1960 Eden Park Blvd.
McKeesport, PA 15131
412-664-3650
www.mcktigerband.com

584 McKendree College Preview of Champions (site: Lebanon, IL)

c/o Cavaliers Drum & Bugle Corps
P.O. Box 501
Rosemont, IL 60018
773-281-8737
www.mckendree.edu/bands/pre-
    viewofchampions/POC_letter.html

585 McLean County Green River Marching
    Band Festival
    McLean County High School
    1859 SR-136 E.
    Calhoun, KY 42327

586 McQueen Field Tournament (NCBA)
    c/o Rick Moffitt
    McQueen High School
    6055 Lancer Street
    Reno, NV 89523
    775-746-5818
    Fax 775-747-6883

587 Manchester Township High School
    (USSBA)
    101 South Colonial Drive
    Lakehurst, NJ 08733-3799

588 Manheim Township Cavalcade of Bands
    (CBA)
    Manheim Township High School
    School Road, P.O. Box 5134
    Lancaster, PA 17606-5134
    Fax 717-569-3729
    www.mtwp.k12.pa.us/indexf.html

589 March to Glory (PIMBA)
    Southmoreland High School
    Rt. 981 South
    Alverton, PA 15612
    724-887-2019

590 Marching Band Festival
    East Rutherford High School
    1 Cavalier Drive
    Forest City, NC 28043
    http://www.geocities.com/marching_
        cavaliers/index3band.html

591 Marching Band Festival
    Havelock High School

101 Webb Blvd.
Havelock, NC 28532
http://www.havelockband.com

592 Marching Band Festival
    Mount Airy High School
    1011 N. South Street
    Mount Airy, NC 27030
    http://ww.mahsbears.org

593 Marching Chiefs Invitational (FMBT)
    Santaluces High School
    6880 Lawrence Road
    Lantana, FL 33462
    561-642-6200
    Fax 561-642-6255
    www.palmbeach.k12.fl.us/SantalucesHS

594 Marcos de Niza Tournament of Cham-
    pions
    Marcos de Niza High School
    6000 South Lakeshore Drive
    Tempe, AZ 85283
    480-838-3200, x42520
    Fax 480-730-7665
    www.tuhsd.k12.as.us/Marcos_de_Nisa
        _HS/Index.htm
    email: webmaster@mdn@tuhsd.k12.
        az.us

595 Mardi Gras Field Show Competition
    c/o Stephen Cannedy
    Pinckneyville Band Parents and Pinck-
        neyville Chamber of Commerce
    Pinckneyville Community High School
    600 East Water Street
    Pinckneyville, IL 62274
    618-357-5013
    Fax 618-357-6045
    www.pchs.perry.k12.il.us
    email: scannedy@pchs.perry.k12.il.us

596 Mariner Preview of Champions (FMBT)
    Mariner High School
    701 Chiqiuita Blvd. N.
    Cape Coral, FL 33993
    239-772-9086
    www.lee.k12.fl.us/mrh
    JayH@Lee.K12.FL.US

St. Mark's High School Spartan Marching Band (Wilmington, DE)

597 Maroon Classic
     Madisonville-North Hopkins High
       School
     4515 Hanson Road
     Madisonville, KY 42431-6151

598 Marple Newtown Band-A-Rama (CBA)
     Marple Newtown High School
     120 Media Line Road
     Newtown Square, PA 19073
     610-359-4238
     http://marple.net/schools/MN_Sr_
       High

599 Martinsburg Invitational Band Spectac-
       ular (TOB)
     Martinsburg High School
     c/o Jack & Carolyn Price
     Band Spectacular Chairmen
     118 Cimarron Drive
     Martinsburg, WV 25401
     304-263-5776
     Fax 202-647-1887
     http://members.aol.com/_ht_a/jepcsp/
       invite2.html?mtbrand=AOL_US
     email: jepcsp@aol.com

600 Maryland State Band Championship
       (TOB)
     c/o Towson Rotary Foundation
     www.bcpl.net/~etowner/bandday.html
       Site: Minnegan Stadium, Towson Uni-
       versity, 800 York Road, Towson, MD
       21252-0001; 410-704-2000; www.tow-
       son.edu/bands

601 Mason County Contest
     Mason County High School
     1320 U.S.-68
     Maysville, KY 41056

602 Maumee Music in Motion (OMEA)
     Maumee High School
     1147 Saco Street
     Maumee, OH 43537
     419-893-8778
     Fax 419-893-5621

603 Meadowbrook Festival of Bands (OMEA)
     Meadowbrook High School

58615 Marietta Road
Byesville, OH 43723
740-685-2566
Fax 740-685-2797

604 Medina Fall Festival of Bands (NYSFBC;
       site: Veterans Memorial Park)
     Medina High School
     Two Mustang Drive
     Medina, NY 14103-1845
     585-798-2710

605 Merced Marching 100 Preview of Cham-
       pions (Western Band)
     Atwater High School
     2201 Fruitland Avenue
     Atwater, CA 95301

606 Merrill High School Competition (site:
       Jay Stadium)
     Merrill Senior High School
     Merrill, WI 54452
     715-536-4594, x3042

607 Metro East Marching Band Classic
     O'Fallon Township High School
     600 South Smiley Street
     O'Fallon, IL 62269
     618-632-3507
     www.othsband.com

608 Miami Trace Marching Band Invita-
       tional (OMEA)
     Miami Trace High School
     3722 SR 41 NW
     Washington CH, OH 43160
     740-335-5891
     Fax 740-636-2010

609 Middle Township High School OcTO-
       Berfest (TOB)
     Middle Township High School
     212 Bayberry Drive
     Cape May Court House, NJ 08210
     609-465-1852
     Fax 609-465-9430
     http://middle.capemayschools.com

610 Mid-Iowa Band Championship
     c/o Paul Brizzi, Ankeny High School

1302 N. Ankeny Blvd.
Ankeny, IA 50021
515-965-9630
Fax 515-965-9639
www.marching.com/events/ankeny.
html
email: pbrizzi@ankeny.k12.ia.us

611 Mid-Ohio Classic (OMEA)
Watkins Memorial High School
8868 Watkins Road
Pataskala, OH 43062
740-927-3846
Fax 740-964-0088

Mid-South Invitational *see* Bandmasters Championship

612 Mid-South Marching Band Contest
Austin Peay State University
Department of Music
601 College Street
Clarksville, TN 37044
931-221-7818
Fax 931-221-7529

613 Midwest Ohio Marching Band Festival
Marion Local High School Band
1901 State Route 716
Maria Stein, OH 45860
419-925-4597
Fax 419-925-5111

614 Milan Invitational Marching Festival
Milan High School
7060 Van Hook Street
Milan, TN 38358
731-686-0841
Fax 731-686-9829
www.milanssd.org/MilanHighSchool.
htm

615 Millville Senior High School (USSBA)
200 Wade Blvd.
Millville, NJ 08332
856-327-6040
Fax 856-293-1342

616 Minor High School
2285 Minor Parkway

Adamsville, AL 35005
205-379-4750
Fax 205-791-6202

617 Mission Viejo Field Tournaments (Western Band)
Mission Viejo High School
25025 Christanta Drive
Mission Viejo, CA 92691

618 Mississippi Invitational Marching Band Festival
Tupelo High School
Tupelo, MS 38801

619 Mississippi State Marching Contest
c/o Mississippi High School Activities
Association
P.O. Box 244
Clinton, MS 39060
601-924-6400
Fax 601-924-1725
www.misshsaa.com
email: mhsas@netdoor.com

620 Missouri Day Marching Band Festival
Trenton Senior High School
1415 Oklahoma Avenue
Trenton, MO 64683
660-359-2291
Fax 660-359-4073

621 Modesto Invitational (Western Band)
Peter Johansen High School
641 Norseman Drive
Modesto, CA 95350

622 Mt. Pleasant Knight of Music (USSBA;
site: Frawley Stadium, Wilmington,
DE)
Mt. Pleasant High School
5201 Washington Street Extension
Wilmington, DE 19809
302-762-7125
Fax 302-762-7042
www.bsd.k12.de.us

623 Mount Timpanogos Marching Invitational (site: Mountain View High
School, Orem, UT)

c/o American Fork High School
510 North 600 East
Orem, UT 84003
801-756-8547

624   Mount Vernon Classic
Mount Vernon High School
8515 Old Mount Vernon Road
Alexandria, VA 22309
703-619-3100
Fax 703-619-3197
www.fcps.edu/MtVernonHS

625   Mt. Vernon Invitational
Mt. Vernon High School
Mt. Vernon Band Boosters
Mt. Vernon, IN 47620
www.simplyinstrumental.com/contests/
contest_mtvernon02.shtml

626   Mountain West Marching Competition
(site: Holt Arena)
c/o Idaho State University Marching
Band
Idaho State University
Campus Box 8099
Pocatello, ID 83209
208-282-2748
Fax 208-282-4884
www.isu.edu/departments/bands/isub
ands.htm

627   Music City Invitational Marching Band
Contest
McGavock High School
3150 McGavock Pike
Nashville, TN 37214
615-885-8850

628   Music from the Hart Marching Festival
Hart County High School
1014 South Dixie Highway
Munfordville, KY 42765
270-524-9341

629   Music in Motion
D.C. Everest High School
6500 Alderson Street
Schofield, WI 54476
715-359-6561

630   Music in Motion (OMEA)
Louisville High School
1201 S. Nickelplate Street
Louisville, OH 44641
330-875-7493
Fax 330-875-7671
email: patrick@leps.sparcc.org

631   Music in Motion Festival
Lloyd Memorial High School
450 Bartlett Avenue
Erlanger, KY 41018

632   Music in Motion Marching Competition
c/o Epsilon Kappa Chapter, Phi Mu
Alpha Sinfonia
Southern Illinois University
School of Music
Altgeld Hall
Carbondale, IL 62901-4302
618-453-2776
Fax 618-453-5808
http://siucmandm.tripol.com/Forms/
rules_and_regulations/Rules%20
packet%202001.htm

633   Music in the Mountains
Preston High School
400 Preston Drive
Kingwood, WV 26537
800-759-0747
http://phs.pres.k12.wv.us

634   Music of the Knight Field Show
Irondale High School
2425 Long Lake Road
Irondale, MN 55112

635   Music on the Mountain (site: Lackawanna County Stadium) (TOB)
Pocono Mountain High School Marching Band
Box 200 School Road
Swiftwater, PA 18370-0200
570-839-7121
www.angelfire.com/pa2/motm/letter.
htm

636   Music Tours Unlimited, Inc.
P.O. Box 533

321 North Furnace Street, Suite 90
Birdsboro, PA 19508
800-545-0935
www.musfestivals.com/mtctc.htm
Winter contest sites: Daytona, FL

637 Musical Arts Conference
Connecticut high school sites: Brien McMahon, Bethel, Trumbull, Stamford, Newtown, Naugatuck, Shelton, Masuk, Danbury, Norwalk. Massachusetts high school site: Billerica. New Jersey high school site: Ramsey. New York high school site: Arlington.

638 Nelson County Pageant of Bands
Nelson County High School
1070 Bloomfield Road
Bardstown, KY 40004

639 New Albany High School Marching Band Invitational
New Albany High School
1020 Vincennes Street
New Albany, IN 47150
812-949-4272
Fax 812-949-6910
http://nahs.nafcs.k12.in.us

640 New Castle County Field Band Festival
Newark High School
Newark, DE 19711
302-454-2151

641 New England Scholastic Band Association
High school contest sites: Case (Swansea, MA), Dartmouth (MA), East Bridgewater (MA), Melrose (MA), New Bedford (MA), Westbrook (ME), Weymouth (MA)

642 New Mexico Tournament of Bands
New Mexico State University
Las Cruces, NM 88003-8001
505-646-0111
www.nmsu.edu

643 New Philadelphia Field Competition (OMEA)

New Philadelphia High School
343 Ray Avenue NW
New Philadelphia, OH 44663
330-364-0651
Fax 330-364-0633

644 New York State Field Band Conference
High school contest sites: Jamestown, Cortland, Cicero-North Syracuse, Homer, Oswego, Medina, Norwich, Baldwinsville, West Genesee, Southwestern, Victor, Liverpool, Orchard Park, Webster, New Hartford, East Syracuse Minoa, Jordan-Elbridge, Mohonasen, Falconer, Mahopac
Member high schools: Arlington (LaGrangeville), Auburn, Binghamton, Brentwood, Central Square, Cicero-North Syracuse (Cicero), Copiague, Corning East, C. W. Baker (Baldwinsville), Deer Park, Division Avenue (Levittown), Eastridge Jr./Sr. (Rochester), Eastridge Junior-Senior (Rochester), East Ramapo (Bailey Cottage), East Syracuse-Minoa (Syracuse), Falconer Central (Falconer), Floral Park, Frewsburg Central, Gates Chili (Rochester), Girard (Girard, PA), Homer, Horseheads, Jamestown, Johnstown, Jordan Elbridge (Jordan), Lancaster, Lindenhurst, Liverpool, Mahopac, Marcus Whitman (Rushville), Medina, Mineola (Garden City Park), Mohonasen (Rotterdam), New Hartford, Newtown (Sandy Hook, CT), North Tonawanda, Northwestern (Albion, PA), Norwich, Orchard Park, Oswego, Penn Yan, Phoenix (JCB H.S., Phoenix), Sachem (Lake Ronkonkoma), Union-Endicott (Endicott), Victor, Walt Whitman (Huntington Station), Webster, Wellsville (Westville), West Genesee (Camillus), West Seneca

645 Newark Marching Band Invitational (OMEA)
Newark High School
314 Granville Street
Newark, OH 43055
740-328-2268
Fax 740-328-2284

646 Nordonia Festival of Bands (OMEA)
     Nordonia High School
     8006 S. Bedford Road
     Macedonia, OH 44056
     330-908-6029
     Fax 330-468-0045

647 North Coast Marching Band Festival
       (OMEA)
     Perkins High School
     3714 Campbell Street
     Sandusky, OH 44870
     419-625-1252
     Fax 419-621-2057

648 North Harrison Invitational
     North Harrison High School
     North Harrison Band Boosters
     1070 Highway 64 NW
     Ramsey, IN 47166
     www.simplyinstrumental.com/con-
     tests/contest_nharrison02.shtml

649 North Laurel Invitational
     North Laurel High School
     1300 Daniel Boone Parkway
     London, KY 40741

650 North Penn Knight of Sound (USSBA)
     North Penn High School
     1340 Valley Forge Road
     Lansdale, PA 19446
     215-368-980
     Fax 215-855-0632
     www.marchingknights.com

651 North Posey Field of Dreams Invita-
       tional
     North Posey High School
     5900 High School Road
     Poseyville, IN 47633
     812-673-4242
     www.northposey.k12.in.us/North_Posey
     _High_School.htm
     email: highschool@northposey.k12.in.
     us

652 North Stafford Invitational Hermitage
       Classic

     839 Garrisonville Road
     Stafford, VA 22554
     540-658-6150
     Fax 540-658-6158
     www.nshs.net

653 Northeast Florida Marching Band Festi-
       val
     Nathan Bedford Forrest Senior High
       School
     5530 Firestone Road
     Jacksonville, FL 32244-1599

654 Northeast Missouri State Marching
       Contest
     Northeast Missouri State University
     Kirksville, MO 63501

655 Northern Arizona University Marching
       Band Festival
     c/o Administrative Assistant
     Northern Arizona University Bands
     Northern Arizona University
     Flagstaff, AZ 86001

656 Northern Illinois University Preview of
       Champions
     School of Music
     DeKalb, IL 60115
     815-753-1551
     Fax 815-753-1759
     www.niu.edu/music

657 Northern Kentucky Marching Band Fes-
       tival
     Campbell County High School
     25 West Lickert Road
     Alexandria, KY 41001
     859-635-4161
     Fax 859-448-4886
     www.campbell.k12.ky.us/cchs

658 Northern Nash Band Classic (USSBA)
     Northern Nash High School
     4230 Green Hills Road
     Rocky Mount, NC 27804

659 Northwest Arkansas Invitational March-
       ing Classic

Siloam Springs High School
1500 West Jefferson
Siloam Springs, AR 72761
479-524-3104
http://sssd.k12.ar.us/band/marching
classic

660 Northwest Guilford Marching Band Fall
Festival
Northwest Guilford High School
5240 Northwest School Road
Greensboro, NC 27409
336-605-3300
Fax 336-605-3310
http://www.nwvikingband.org

661 Northwestern Bandfest (OMEA)
Northwestern High School
5650 Troy Road
Springfield, OH 45502
937-964-1324
Fax 937-964-6006

662 Norwin Festival (PIMBA)
Norwin Senior High School
251 McMahon Drive
North Huntingdon, PA 15642
www.homestead.com/norwinband
aides/NorwinBandAidesIndex.html

663 Oakton Classic
Oakton High School
2900 Sutton Road
Vienna, VA 22180
703-281-7939
www.oaktonbands.com

664 Ohio County Band Festival
Ohio County High School
1400 S. Main Street
Hartford, KY 42347

665 Ohio Music Education Association
(OMEA)
Contest sites: Cambridge Cavalcade
of Bands, Piqua Marching Band Invi-
tational, Philo Challenge, Westland
Open, Rhythm in Blue Invitational,
Lancaster High School Band of Gold
Invitational, Art in Motion, Tipp City
Invitational, Highland Marching Band
Festival, Ottawa Glandorf High School
Parade of Bands, Cloverleaf Caval-
cade of Sound, Talawanda Marching
Braves Invitational, Columbus Grove
"Eyes with Pride," Music in Motion,
Findley High School Band Festival,
Logan Elm Marching Band Classic,
Southwest Invitational, Hilliard
Marching Band Invitational, Band-O-
Rama, Mid-West Ohio Marching Band
Festival, Pickerington Marching Band
Festival, Lexington Festival of Cham-
pions, Grove City High School March-
ing Band Invitational, Northwestern
Bandfest, Pride of Holgate Band Con-
test, Rock Hill Band Contest, Blue
and White Invitational, Licking Valley
Band Fest, Winchester Marching
Band Classic, "Band-O-Rama," Buck-
eye Classic, Bonanza of Bands, Mau-
mee Music in Motion, Trojan Invita-
tional, Athens Marching Invitational
Festival, Miami Trace Marching Band
Invitational, Nordonia Festival of
Bands, Mid Ohio Classic, Shawnee
March-O-Rama, Annual Band Expo,
Claymout Band Round Up, Wester-
ville North Marching Band Classic,
Pride of Belpre Marching Band Invi-
tational, Shawnee Showcase, Cardinal
Marching Band Invitational, Kettering
Classic, Copley High School March-
ing Band Invitational, River View
Marching Band Invitational, Buckeye
Classic Band Invitational, Meadow-
brook Festival of Bands, North Coast
Marching Band Festival, Thomas
Worthington Preview of Champions,
Lockland Band Invitational, Southern
Ohio Marching Band Classic, Tecum-
seh High School Showcase of Bands,
Sounds of the Stadium, Swanton
Bulldog Bowl, BC Classic, Versailles
Marching Band Invitational, Tri-Val-
ley Classic, Newark Marching Band
Invitational, Fort Frye Pageant of
Bands, Brunswick Sound Spectacular,
Green Festival of Bands, New Phila-
delphia Field Competition. Finals:
Kent State University, Dayton Wel-
come Stadium

Northampton Area Senior High School Twirlers (Northampton, PA)

666 Okefenokee Sound of Gold Marching Championship (GMEA; site: Memorial Stadium)
Ware County High School
700 Victory Drive
Waycross, GA 31501
912-287-2351
Fax 912-287-2358
www.ware.k12.ga.us/wchs_band.htm

Old Dominion Dixie Classic *see* Dixie Classic

667 Omaha Marching Invitational
Harry A. Burke Omaha Public High School
12200 Burke Street
Omaha, NE 68154
402-557-3200

668 Onalaska High School (WSMA)
700 Hilltopper Place
Onalaska, WI 54650
www.onalaska.k12.wi.us/building/hs/
index.htm
608-783-4561, x5349

669 Opp High School
502 North Maloy Street
Opp, AL 36467
334-493-4561

670 Ottawa Glandorf High School Parade
of Bands (OMEA)
Ottawa Glandorf High School
630 Glendale Road
Ottawa, OH 45875
419-523-5702, x20
Fax 419-523-6346
email: deskinB@oghs.noacsc.org

671 Owasso Invitational Marching Contest
(OSSAA)
Owasso High School
12901 E. 86th Street North
Owasso, OK 07055
918-272-1856

672 Owen J. Roberts Cavalcade of Bands
(CBA)
Owen J. Roberts High School
901 Ridge Road
Pottstown, PA 19465
610-469-5100
www.ojr.k12.pa.us

673 Oxon Hill High School Marching Band
Competition
Oxon Hill High School
6701 Leyte Drive
Oxon Hill, MD 20745
301-749-4300
http://oxonhillhs.pgcps.org

674 Ozarko Invitational Marching Festival
Southwest Missouri State University
901 South National Avenue
Springfield, MO 65804
417-836-5000
www.smsu.edu

675 Pacific Coast Invitational Marching
Band Championships (site: Sprague
H.S., Salem, OR)
c/o Karl Raschkes
Music/Drama Coordinator
Curriculum Planning and Coordination
2575 Commercial Street S.E.
Salem, OR 97302

676 Pacific Grove Band Festival (NCBA)
Pacific Grove High School
615 Sunset Drive
Pacific Grove, CA 93950
831-372-3310
Fax 831-646-6660
www.pghs.org

677 Pageant of Bands
Manzano High School
12200 Lomas Blvd. NE
Albuquerque, NM 87122
505-292-0090
Fax 505-291-6854

678 Paoli Invitational
Paoli Junior-Senior High School
Pride of Paoli Band Boosters
501 Elm Street
Paoli, IN 47454
812-723-7301 (Fax same)
www.simplyinstrumental.com/contests/
contest_paoli02.shtml

679 Parade of Champions
School of Music
James Madison University
800 S. Main Street
Harrisonburg, VA 22807
540-568-6656
www.jmu.edu/music/mrd/poc.html

680 Park Hills Central Rebel Invitational
Central R-III
200 High Street
Park Hills, MO 63601-2524
573-431-2616
Fax 573-431-2107
www.dese.state.mo.us/directory/094086.
html
email: dstevens@central-ph.k12.mo.us

681 Patriot Invitational Band Competition
     (field show plus parade)
     Denbigh High School
     259 Denbigh Blvd.
     Newport News, VA 23608
     757-886-7700
     www.dhspatariots.com/Invitational/
     patriot_invite.htm

682 Patuxent Invitational Marching Band
     Competition (TOB)
     Patuxent High School
     12485 Rousby Hall Road
     Lusby, MD 20657
     410-535-7806
     Fax 410-535-7875
     http://users.erols.com/star.wolf/News.
     htm

683 Peach State Marching Festival (GMEA)
     Rome City School Band Booster Asso-
     ciation
     Rome High and Middle School Bands
     P.O. Box 6202
     Rome, GA 30161
     email: romebandboosters@romebands.
     org

684 Pender Band Invitational
     Pender High School
     5380 NC Highway 53 West
     Burgaw, NC 28425
     http://www.angelfire.com/band/pender
     band

685 Pennsauken (USSBA)
     Pennsauken High School
     800 Hylton Road
     Pennsauken, NJ 08110

686 Penns Grove Classic Marching Band
     Competition (USSBA)
     Penns Grove High School
     Harding Highway
     Carneys Point, NJ 08069
     856-299-6300
     www.pennsgrove.k12.nj.us/pghs/Page
     _1x.html

687 Perkiomen Valley Tournament of Bands
     (TOB)
     Perkiomen Valley High School
     509 Gravel Pike, Rt. 29 & Trappe Road
     Collegeville, PA 19426
     610-489-1230

688 Philo Challenge (OMEA)
     Philo High School
     200 Broad Street
     Philo, OH 43771
     740-674-5201
     Fax 740-674-5202
     email: cporter@alltel.net

689 Phoenix Festival of Bands
     Dalton L. McMichael High School
     Mayodan, NC 27027

690 Phoenixville Cavalcade of Bands (CBA)
     Phoenixville Area High School
     1200 Gay Street
     Phoenixville, PA 19460
     610-933-6694
     Fax 610-933-6009
     www.pasd.com/phantomband

691 Pickerington Marching Band Festival
     (OMEA)
     Pickerington High School
     300 Opportunity Way
     Pickerington, OH 43147
     614-833-3062

692 Pike Central Invitational
     Pike Central High School
     1810 State Road
     Petersburgh, IN 47567
     812-354-8478

693 Pinson Valley
     Pinson Valley High School
     6895 North 75 Highway
     Pinson, AL 35126
     205-379-5100

694 Piqua Marching Band Invitational
     (OMEA)
     Piqua High School

1 Indian Trail
Piqua, OH 45356
937-773-6314
Fax 937-778-4514
email: sphill@bright.net

695 Plainfield Invitational
Plainfield High School
709 Stafford Road
Plainfield, IN 46168
317-839-7711
Fax 317-838-3671
www.plainfield.k12.in.us/hschool/
    curric/band

696 Plattsmouth Marching Invitational
1916 E. Highway 34
Plattsmouth, NE 68048
402-296-3322

697 Plymouth-Whitemarsh Cavalcade of
    Bands (CBA)
Plymouth-Whitemarsh High School
201 E. Germantown Pike
Plymouth Meeting, PA 19462
610-825-1500
Fax 610-828-5280
http://listen.to/pwband
email: pwband@hotmail.com

698 Power Surge Festival of Bands
North Davidson Senior High School
7227 Old Highway 52
Lexington, NC 27295
http://www.davidson.k12.nc.us/ndhs/
    index.htm

699 Powhatan Fall Classic
Powhatan High School
4135 Old Buckingham Road
Powhatan, VA 23139
804-598-5710
www.powhatanclassics.com

700 Preview of Champions
Ben Davis High School
1200 North Girls School Road
Indianapolis, IN 46214
317-244-7691

Fax 317-243-5506
www.wayne.k12.in.us/bdmusd

701 Preview of Champions
Mt. Pleasant High School
700 Walker Road
Mt. Pleasant, NC 28124
704-436-9321
www.cabarrus.k12.nc.us/mphs/band.
    htm

702 Pride of Belpre Marching Band Invita-
    tional (OMEA)
Belpre High School
612 3rd Street
Belpre, OH 45714
740-423-3000
Fax 740-423-3003

703 Pride of Florida Marching Band Contest
    (FMBT)
Cape Coral High School
2300 Santa Barbara Blvd.
Cape Coral, FL 33991
941-772-9222
PrideofFlorida@yahoo.com

704 Pride of Holgate Band Contest (OMEA)
Holgate High School
103 Frazier Street
Holgate, OH 43527
419-264-2521
Fax 419-264-1965

705 Princeton Invitational
Princeton Community High School
RR 4, Box 49
Princeton, IN 47670
812-385-2591
Fax 812-386-1535
www.princetonbands.homestead.com/
    index.html

706 Prospect Knight of Champions
Prospect High School
801 West Kensington Road
Mt. Prospect, IL 60056

707 Pryor Marching Festival
Pryor High School

1100 SE Ninth Street
Pryor, OK 74361
918-825-2340

708 Pulaski County Marching Band Invitational
Pulaski County High School
511 E. University Drive
Somerset, KY 42503

709 Pursuit of Excellence (site: Southwest State University)
Marshall High School
401 South Saratoga Street
Marshall, MN 56258
507-537-6920
Fax 507-537-6931
www.marshall.k12.mn.us/our_schools.htm

710 Putnam City Marching Festival (site: Putnam City Stadium)
Putnam City Schools
5401 N.W. 40th
Oklahoma City, OK 73122

711 Quest for the Best
Bethel High School
P.O. Box 253, 1 School Street
Bethel, CT 06801
203-794-8620

712 Quincy Senior High Invitational
Quincy High School
3322 Maine Street
Quincy, IL 62301
217-224-3770

713 Reading High School Cavalcade of Bands (CBA)
Reading Senior High School
801 N. 13th Street
Reading, PA 19604
610-371-5751

714 The Rebel Classic (MSBA)
Boone County High School
7056 Burlington Pike
Florence, KY 41042-1681

715 Rebel Classic Invitational Field Show
c/o Helen Sur, Band Director
Champlin Park High School
6025 109th Avenue North
Champlin, MN 55316
763-506-7074
www.marching.com/events/champlin park.html

716 Red Lion Cavalcade of Bands (CBA)
Red Lion High School
696 Delta Road
Red Lion, PA 17356
717-246-1611

717 Renegade Review
Union High School
6636 South Mingo
Tulsa, OK 74133
918-459-5540
www.renegaderegiment.com

718 Reno Preview of Champions (NCBA)
c/o Jerry Willis (775-851-5630)
Galena High School
3600 Butch Cassidy Way
Reno, NV 89511
775-851-5630
Fax 775-851-5607
www.galenahigh.com

719 Review of Champions (NCBA)
Lincoln High School
6844 Alexandria Place
Stockton, CA 95207
209-653-8919

720 Rhythm in Blue Invitational (OMEA)
Amelia High School
1351 Clough Pike
Batavia, OH 45103
513-753-5120, x80
Fax 513-753-2419
email: pease_j@hccanet.org

721 Ridley Festival of Bands (USSBA)
Ridley High School
Morton Avenue
Folsom, PA 19033

619-534-1900
Fax 610-534-5470

722 Ripley Marching Invitational
Ripley High School
Ripley, TN 38063
www.lced.net/rhs

723 River View Marching Band Invitational
(OMEA)
River View High School
26496 SR 60 N
Warsaw, OH 43844
740-824-3521
Fax 740-824-3760

724 Riverside Community College (Western
Band)
4800 Magnolia Avenue
Riverside, CA 92506-1299
909-222-8000
Fax 909-222-8036

725 Rock Hill Band Contest (OMEA)
Rock Hill High School
2171 County Road 26
Ironton, OH 45638
740-533-6048
Fax 740-533-6051

726 Rocky Mountain Band Competition
University Bands
Department of Music
Brigham Young University
C-550 HFAC
P.O. Box 26410
Provo, UT 84602-6410

727 Rosemount Marching Band Festival
Rosemount High School
3335 West 142nd Street
Rosemount, MN 55068
651-423-7501
Fax 651-423-7511
www.isd196.k12.mn.us/schools/rhs

728 Route 66 Marching Band Classic
Rolla Senior High School
900 Bulldog Run

Rolla, MO 65401
573-458-0140
Fax 573-458-0147
http://rolla.k12.mo.us/Rhs/rhs/index.
html
email: mnew@rolla.k12.mo.us

729 Royal Classic
Royal High School
1402 Royal Avenue
Simi Valley, CA 93065
www.royalbands.com

730 Rumble in the Jungle (BOA)
South View High School
4800 Elk Road
Hope Mills, NC 28348
http://www.svband.com

731 Russell Invitational
Russell High School
709 Red Devil Lane
Russell, KY 41169

732 Russellville Contest
Russellville High School
210 E. 7th Street
Russellville, KY 42276

733 Saint Bernard High School (USSBA)
1593 Norwich New London Turnpike
Uncasville, CT 06382

734 St. Louis Gateway Marching Band Festival (site: Edward Jones Dome)
c/o Herb Duncan
314-469-5908

735 Salem Invitational
Salem Community Schools
500 North Harrison Street
Salem, IN 47167

736 San Marcos Field Show
San Marcos High School
4750 Hollister Avenue
Santa Barbara, CA 93110
805-967-4581
Fax 805-967-8358

737 Sandy Creek Invitational Tournament
       of Bands (GMEA)
     Sandy Creek High School
     360 Jenkins Road
     Tyrone, GA 30290
     770-969-2843, x261
     www21.brinkster.com/scitob/directions.
       html

738 Santa Barbara High School
     700 East Anapamu Street
     Santa Barbara, CA 93103
     805-966-9101
     Fax 805-965-6872

739 Santa Cruz High Band Review
     Santa Cruz High School
     415 Walnut Avenue
     Santa Cruz, CA 95060
     831-429-3960

740 Sea of Sounds Band Competition
     Middletown Area High School
     1155 North Union Street
     Middletown, PA 17057
     717-948-3300
     Fax 717-948-3329

741 Sea Side Band Classic
     Swansboro High School
     161 Queens Creek Road
     Swansboro, NC 28584
     http://www.marchingpirates.org

742 Seventy-First High School Marching
       Band Invitational
     Seventy-First High School
     6764 Raeford Road
     Fayetteville, NC 28304
     http://71stband.homestead.com

743 Shawnee High School (CBA)
     600 Tabernacle Road
     Medford, NJ 08055
     609-654-7544
     www.1r.k12.nj.us/site/shawnee/body1.
       html

744 Shawnee March-O-Rama (OMEA)
     Shawnee High School

     1675 East Possum Road
     Springfield, OH 45502
     937-325-9296
     Fax 937-328-5389

745 Shawnee Showcase (OMEA)
     Lima Shawnee High School
     3333 Zurmehly Road
     Lima, OH 45806
     419-998-8016
     Fax 419-998-8026

746 Shelby Golden Classic
     Shelby High School
     230 E. Dixon Blvd.
     Shelby, NC 28152
     http://www.blueridge.net/scs/shs/shs.
       htm

747 Shelby Valley Contest
     Shelby Valley High School
     125 Douglas Park
     Pikeville, KY 41501

748 Sherando Invitational Marching Band
       Competition
     Sherando High School
     185 S. Warrior Drive
     Stephens City, VA 22655
     540-869-3995
     www.sherandoband.org/contact.htm

749 Showcase of Bands
     Shelby County High School
     1701 Frankfort Road
     Shelbyville, KY 40065

750 Showcase of Champions
     Auburndale High School
     1 Bloodhound Trail
     Auburndale, FL 33823-9209
     941-965-6209
     www.auburndaleband.com

751 Showcase of Champions
     Mt. Pleasant High School
     700 Walker Road
     Mt. Pleasant, NC 28124
     704-436-9321

752 Sierra Cup Classic (Western Band)
California State University-Fresno
5241 N. Maple Avenue
Fresno, CA 93740-8027
559-278-4240
www.csufresno.edu/music

753 Silver Regiment Invitational (FMBT)
Lake Howell High School
4200 Dike Road
Winter Park, FL 32792
407-320-9050
Fax 407-320-9025
www.lakehowell.scps.k12.fl.us/non
fuser.html

754 Somerset Musictown Festival (includes
non-competitive parade and field
show)
Somerset High School
Somerset, MA 02722

755 Sounds of Pride Marching Band Field
Show
Blaine High School
12555 University Avenue, NE
Blaine, MN 55434-2199
763-506-6677
www.marching.com/events/blaine.html
email: shawn.kolles@anoka.k12.mn.us

756 Sounds of the Patriots (TOB)
Red Land High School
560 Fishing Creek Road
Lewisberry, PA 17339
717-938-6561
www.wssd.k12.pa.us/RL/RL.home.html

757 Sounds of the Stadium (OMEA)
Harrison High School
9860 West Road
Harrison, OH 45030
937-367-4169
Fax 513-367-7251

758 South Carolina State Fair Marching
Band Festival
c/o Philip C. McIntyre

South Carolina Band Director's Associ-
ation
James F. Byrnes High School
P.O. Box 187, Highway 290
Duncan, SC 29334

759 South Central Kentucky Marching Band
Classic
Glasgow High School
1601 Columbia Avenue
Glasgow, KY 42141

760 South Coast Invitational (Western Band)
Costa Mesa High School
2650 Fairview Road
Costa Mesa, CA 92626
714-424-8700
Fax 714-424-8770

761 South Laurel Band Classic
South Laurel High School
201 S. Laurel Road
London, KY 40744

762 South Rowan Cavalcade of Bands
South Rowan High School
1655 Patterson St.
China Grove, NC 28023
http://www.srhsband.4t.com

763 South St. Paul Field Show
South St. Paul High School
700 Second Street North
South St. Paul, MN 55075
651-457-9408
Fax 651-457-9455
www.sostpark.k12.mn.us

764 South Spencer Invitational
South Spencer High School
South Spencer Band Boosters
2225 South U.S. Highway 231
Rockport, IN 47635
www.simplyinstrumental.com/contests/
contest_sspencer02.shtml

765 South Western High School Cavalcade
of Bands (CBA)
South Western Senior High School

200 Bowman Road
Hanover, PA 17331
717-633-4818

766 Southeast Missouri Band Association
     Marching Festival
     Charleston High School
     606 South Thorn Street
     Charleston, MO 63834
     573-683-3761

767 Southeastern Classic
     Newton Conover High School
     338 West 15th Street
     Newton, NC 28658
     http://www.nchsband.org

768 Southern California School Band & Or-
     chestra Association
     Contest sites: Moreno Valley Field
     Tournament, J. F. Kennedy High
     School Field Tournament, Poway Pre-
     view of Champions, Rowland Field
     Tournament, Rubidoux High School
     Field Show Tournament, Bonita Vista
     Field Tournament, El Camino/West
     High Field Tournament, Etiwanda
     Artistry in Motion, Valencia High
     School Classic (Placentia), Baldwin
     Park High School Invitational Field
     Tournament, Claremont Field Tour-
     nament, Rising Star Invitational Field
     (Scripps Ranch), Simi Valley High
     School Field Tournament, Golden
     State Field Classic (Glen A. Wilson
     High School), Loara Field Tourna-
     ment, Mt. Carmel Tournament of
     Bands, Ramona SW Regional, Chino
     Invitational Field Show, Hart Ram-
     page Field Tournament, Lester Oaks
     Field Tournament, Mira Mesa Invita-
     tional Field Tournament, Sierra Vista
     Annual Field Tournament, Los Altos
     Field Tournament, Capistrano Valley
     Field Tournament, Oxnard Field
     Tournament, Vista Invitational Field
     Tournament, Westminster Annual
     Field Show, Arcadia Festival of Bands,
     Centennial High School (Bakersfield),
     Moorpark Field Tournament, Sa-
     vanna Field Tournament, Temecula

Valley Classic, West Covina Field
Tournament, Antelope Valley Invita-
tional, Royal Classic, Eisenhower
Field Tournament, Palmdale Field
Show, Santa Barbara Field Tourna-
ment

769 Southern Kentucky Marching Band Fes-
     tival
     Bowling Green High School
     1801 Rockingham Avenue
     Bowling Green, KY 42104-3347

770 Southern Ohio Marching Band Classic
     (OMEA)
     Portsmouth West High School
     15332 US Highway 52
     West Portsmouth, OH 45662
     740-858-1103
     Fax 740-858-1110

771 Southern Showcase of Champions
     (FMBT)
     Santa Fe High School
     16331 NW U.S. 441
     Alachua, FL 32615
     386-462-1125
     Fax of 386-462-1711
     www.sbac.edu/~sfhs/geninfo.htm
     email: RaiderRegi@AOL.COM

772 Southern Star Invitational Band Festival
     and Competition (GMEA)
     South Gwinnett Band Association
     South Gwinnett High School
     2228 E. Main Street
     Snellville, GA 30078
     770-736-4302
     www.southern-star.net/home.html

773 Southern States Marching Band Festival
     Camden High School
     1022 Ehrenclou Drive
     Camden, SC 29020
     803-425-8930
     Fax 803-424-2861
     www.kershaw.k12.sc.us/chs/main.htm
     email: webmaster@chs.kershaw.k12.sc.
     us

774 Southland Band Classic
     Enterprise High School
     500 Watts Avenue
     Enterprise, AL 36330

775 Southwest Invitational (OMEA)
     Xenia High School
     303 Kinsey Road
     Xenia, OH 45385
     937-372-6983, x117
     Fax 937-374-4390

776 Spartan Sounds of Success Marching
       Band Festival
     Central Davidson Senior High School
     2747 NC Highway 47
     Lexington, NC 27292
     http://www.geocities.com/cdhsspartan

777 Spirit of the South Marching Festival
     Tift County High School Band
     One Blue Devil Way
     Tifton, GA 31794
     email: wleonard@tiftschools.com

778 Sprayberry Southern Invitational Festi-
       val (GMEA)
     Sprayberry High School
     2525 Sandy Plains Road
     Marietta, GA 30062
     770-509-6111
     Fax 770-509-6114

779 Spruce Creek
     Spruce Creek High School Bands
     801 Taylor Road
     Port Orange, FL 32127
     904-756-7253
     Fax 904-761-5659
     www.creekband.org

780 Stafford High School
     33 Stafford Indian Lane
     Stafford, VA 22405
     540-371-7200
     Fax 540-371-2389
     www.staffordhighschool.com

781 Stallion Classic Band Competition
     South Columbus High School

     40 Stallion Drive
     Tabor City, NC 28463
     http://www.tpinter.net/schs

782 Starfest
     Marshall County High School
     416 High School Road
     Benton, KY 42025-7017

783 State of Illinois Marching Band Invita-
       tional
     School of Music
     Illinois State University
     Campus Box 5660
     Normal, IL 61761
     309-438-7631
     www.arts.ilstu.edu/music
     email: music@ilstu.edu

784 Stephen Foster Classic
     Bardstown High School
     400 N. 5th Street
     Bardstown, KY 40004

785 Sterling High School (USSBA)
     501 South Warwick Road
     Somerdale, NJ 08083
     856-784-1333
     Fax 856-784-1234
     http://sterling.k12.nj.us/music/march.
       html

786 Sullivan Marching Festival
     Sullivan High School
     1073 East Vine
     Sullivan, MO 63080
     573-468-5181
     Fax 573-860-3524
     http://eagles.k12.mo.us/high/hsindex.
       htm

Sun Bowl *see* Wells Fargo Sun Bowl Music
Festival

787 Super Bowl of Sound (GMEA)
     Central-High School
     113 Central Road
     Carrollton, GA 30116
     770-834-3386

Fax 770-832-0103
www.lionpride.org

788   Super Bowl of Sound (FMBT)
Miami Coral Park High School
8865 SW 16 Street
Miami, FL 33165
305-226-6565, x2256
Fax 305-553-4648
www.coralparkband.com
email: jnoble@coralparkband.com

789   Superchief Marching Festival (USSBA)
Piscataway High School
100 Behmer Road
Piscataway, NJ 08854-4173
732-981-0700
Fax 732-981-1985
www.piscataway.net/about/contactinfo.
html

790   Swain County High School Marching
Band Festival
Swain County High School
1415 Fontana Road
Bryson City, NC 28713
http://www.swain.k12.nc.us/high/band.
htm

791   Swanton Bulldog Bowl (OMEA)
Swanton High School
206 Cherry Street
Swanton, OH 43558
419-826-3045
Fax 419-826-1611

792   Talawanda Marching Braves Invitational
(OMEA)
Talawanda High School
101 W. Chestnut Street
Oxford, OH 45056
513-523-4137, x223
Fax 513-523-0504
email: bhiler@po.tcs.k12.oh.us

793   Tar Heel Invitational
University of North Carolina at Chapel
Hill
Music Department

212 Hill Hall
CB #3320
Chapel Hill, NC 27599
919-962-5695
www.unc.edu/depts/music/uncbands

794   Tarpon Springs Outdoor Music Festival
(FMBT)
Tarpon Springs High School
1411 Gulf Road
Tarpon Springs, FL 34689
727-943-4900, x132
http://tshs.pinellas.k12.fl.us
Beank143@aol.com

795   Taylor County Marching Invitational
Taylor County High School
300 Ingram Avenue
Campbellsville, KY 42718-1625

796   Tecumseh High School Showcase of
Bands (OMEA)
Tecumseh High School
9830 W. National Road
New Carlisle, OH 45344
937-845-4500
Fax 937-845-4547

797   Tell City Invitational
Tell City High School
Tell City Band Boosters
P.O. Box 174
Tell City, IN 47586
www.simplyinstrumental.com/contests/
contest_tellcity02.shtml

798   Tennessee Valley Invitational Marching
Competition
Muscle Shoals High School
1900 Avalon Avenue
Muscle Shoals, AL 35661
256-389-2682

799   Texas Tech Marching Festival
Kappa Kappa Psi & Tau Beta Sigma
Texas Tech University
Lubbock, TX 79408
mainly west Texas area high schools

800   Thomas Worthington Preview of Champions (OMEA)
Thomas Worthington High School
330 W. Dublin Granville Road
Worthington, OH 43085
614-883-2263
Fax 614-883-2260

801   Thousand Oaks Field Show
Thousand Oaks High School
2323 N. Moorpark Road
Thousand Oaks, CA 91360

802   Thunder at the Mountain (GMEA)
Kennesaw Mountain High School
1898 Kennesaw Due West Road
Kennesaw, GA 30152

803   Tidewater Festival
Indian River High School
1969 Braves Trail
Chesapeake, VA 23325
757-578-7000
Fax 757-578-7004

804   Tipp City Invitational (OMEA)
Tippecanoe High School
555 N. Hyatt Street
Tipp City, OH 45371
937-669-5912
Fax 937-667-0912
email: sparks@tippcity.k12.oh.us

805   Todd County Central Contest
Todd County Central High School
806 S. Main Street
Elkton, KY 42220

806   Tournament of Bands (TOB)
Liberty High School
5855 Bartholow Road
Eldersburg, MD 21784
www.geocities.com/libertyband

807   Tournament of Bands
Madison Central High School
705 N. 2nd Street
Richmond, KY 40475

808   Tournament of Bands (TOB)
Patuxent High School
12485 Rousby Hall Road
Lusby, MD 20657
410-539-7806
Fax 410-535-7875
www.patuxentband.org

809   Tournament of Bands (TOB)
West Deptford High School
1600 Old Crown Point Road
Westville, NJ 08093
856-848-6110
www.wdeptford.k12.nj.us/High_School/
high.htm

810   Tournament of Bands Association (DE, MD, NC, NJ, NY, PA, MD, OH, WV; championships held at Lackawanna County Stadium, PA)
High school members, Delaware: Brandywine, Caravel Academy, Caesar Rodney, Christiana, Concord, Lake Forest, Laurel, McKean, Salesianum, William Penn; Maryland: Arundel, Broadneck, Chopticon, Colonel Richardson, Elkton, North East, Northern Maryland, Queen Anne County, Rising Sun, Severna Park, South Carroll, Westminster; New Jersey: Absegami, Audubon, Brick, Clearview, Delsea, Deptford, Eastern Regional, Edgewood, Egg Harbor, Florence, Gloucester City, Governor Livingston, Haddon Heights, Hammonton, Holy Cross, Kingsway, Northern Garrett, Penns Grove, Pleasantville, Shawnee, Southern Regional, Sterling, Toms River East, Triton, Washington Township; Ohio: Wadsworth; Pennsylvania: Bellefonte, Bensalem, Bermudian Springs, Berwick, Bloomsburg, Carlisle, Catasauqua, Cedar Crest, Central Bucks West, Cocalico, Cumberland Valley, Delone Catholic, East Pennsboro, Emmaus, Governor Mifflin, Hanover, Hazleton, Henderson, Lebanon, Lebanon Catholic, Lock Haven, Mechanicsburg, Montrose, Northern Lebanon, Northern York, Penncrest, Pocono Mountain, Redland, Shamokin, Sun Valley,

Williamsport, Wyoming Area; Virginia: Kempsville, Louisburg, Princess Anne, Salem; West Virginia: Central Martinsburg, Hedgesville, Jefferson, Keyser, Preston County

811   Tournament of Bands Competition (TOB)
Deptford Township High School
575 Fox Run Road
Deptford, NJ 08096
856-232-2713
Fax 856-374-9145
www.deptford.k12.nj.us

812   Tournament of Champions (NCBA)
Fairfield High School
205 East Atlantic Avenue
Fairfield, CA 94533
707-438-3015
Fax 707-421-3977
www.fsusd.k12.ca.us

813   Tournament of Champions
Western Carolina University
Cullowhee, NC 28723
http://www.prideofthemountains.com

814   Trabuco Hills (Western Band)
Trabuco Hills High School
27501 Mustang Run
Mission Viejo, CA 92691
949-768-1934

815   Treasure Coast Crown Jewel Marching Band Festival (FMBT)
Vero Beach High School
1707 16th Street
Vero Beach, FL 32961-6208
772-562-1621
Fax 772-564-4720
http://crownjewel.vero-beach.fl.us
email: SrigleyK@vetrol.com

816   Trinity Band Classic
Trinity High School
5746 Trinity High School Drive
Trinity, NC 27370
www.geocities.com/trinitybluecrew

817   Tri-State Band Festival (includes parade)
c/o Luverne Area Chamber of Commerce
102 East Main
Luverne, MN 56156-1831
888-283-4061
www.marching.com/events/luverne.html
email: luvernechamber@dtgnet.com
includes Minnesota, Iowa, South Dakota

818   Triton Tournament of Bands (TOB)
Triton High School
250 Schubert Avenue
Runnemede, NJ 08078
856-939-4500
Fax 856-939-4724
www.TritonRHS.org
email: webmaster@tritonhighschool.com

819   Tri-Valley Classic (OMEA)
Tri-Valley High School
46 E. Muskingum Avenue
Dresden, OH 43821
740-745-1141
Fax 740-754-6415

820   Trojan Classic
Olympic High School
4301 Sandy Porter Road
Charlotte, NC 28273
http://www.olympictrojanband.com

821   Trojan Invitational (OMEA)
Troy High School
151 W. Staunton Road
Troy, OH 45373
937-335-5938
Fax 937-332-6738

822   Trojan Tournament of Bands (FMBT)
Lely High School
1 Lely High School Blvd.
Naples, FL 34113
941-417-4517
ReaneyWi@Collier.K12.FL.US

823   United States Scholastic Band Association (USSBA)

University of Delaware Band Day 2002 (Newark, DE)

Connecticut contest sites: Bunnell H.S. (Stratford), St. Bernard H.S. (Uncasville), Waterford H.S., Montville H.S. (Oakdale), Norwich Free Academy H.S. (Norwich), Cheshire H.S. (Cheshire), Robert E. Fitch H.S. (Groton), Rocky Hill H.S., Southington H.S. (Southington); Delaware site: Mt. Pleasant H.S. (Frawley Stadium, Wilmington); Georgia site: South Gwinnett H.S. (Snellville); Maryland site: Howard County Music in Motion (Columbia); Massachusetts sites: Blackstone-Millville H.S. (Blackstone), King Phillip Regional H.S. (Wrentham), Reading Memorial H.S.; New Jersey sites: Audubon H.S., Brick Memorial H.S., Brick Township H.S., Bridgeton H.S., Burlington Township H.S., Carteret H.S., Cherokee H.S. (Marlton), Cinnaminson H.S., Delaware Valley Regional H.S. (Frenchtown), Delsea Regional H.S. (Franklinville), Eastern Regional H.S. (Voorhees), Edison H.S., Egg Harbor H.S., Franklin H.S. (Somerset), Gateway Regional H.S. (Woodbury Heights), Haddonfield H.S., Hasbrouck Heights H.S., Hillsborough H.S., Jackson Memorial H.S., John P. Stevens H.S. (North Edison), Lenape Regional H.S. (Medford), Lindenhurst H.S., Manalapan H.S., Manchester Township H.S. (Lakehurst), Millville H.S., Montclair, North Brunswick H.S., Northern Highlands H.S. (Allendale), North Warren H.S. (Blairstown), Nutley H.S., Penns Grove H.S. (Carneys Point), Pennsville Memorial H.S., Piscataway H.S., Morris Hills H.S., Roselle Park H.S., Franklin H.S., Ridgewood H.S., North Warren H.S., Piscataway H.S., Pompton Lakes H.S., North Rockland H.S., Mount Olive H.S. (Flanders), Morris Knolls H.S., Westfield H.S., Hunterdon Central H.S. (Flemington), Toms River H.S., Verona H.S., Boonton H.S., Pequannock H.S. (Pompton Plains), Perth Amboy H.S., Scotch Plains-Fanwood H.S. (Scotch Plains), Somerville H.S., South Brunswick H.S. (Monmouth

Junction), Sterling H.S. (Somerdale), Vineland H.S., West Deptford H.S. (Westville); New York sites: Copiague H.S., Brentwood H.S., Monsignor Farrell H.S., Division Avenue H.S. (Levittown), East Ramapo H.S. (Spring Valley), Hofstra, Hicksville H.S., Mahopac H.S., Mineola H.S. (Garden City), Sachem H.S., Huntington H.S. North Carolina site: Northern Nash H.S. (Rocky Mount); Pennsylvania sites: Central Bucks-West H.S. (Doylestown), Greencastle-Antrim H.S. (Greencastle), Northampton Area H.S., North Penn H.S. (Lansdale), Northwestern Lehigh H.S., Nazareth Area H.S., Olney H.S. (Philadelphia), Phoenixville H.S., Ridley H.S. (Folsom), Shamokin H.S., Mid-Valley H.S., Souderton H.S., Stroudsburg H.S., Upper Dublin H.S. (Ft. Washington), Upper Moreland H.S. (Willow Grove), West Perry H.S.; Virginia site: Kempsville H.S. Championships sometimes held at J. Birney Crum Stadium, Allentown, PA. State championship round initiated in 2002.

824 University Interscholastic League (TX)
     Contest sites include: Odessa, Nacogdoches, Waco, Alice, Bedford, Mesquite, San Antonio, Alief ISD, Duncanville

825 University of Arizona Band Day
     School of Music and Dance
     Music Bldg., Room 166
     Tucson, AZ 85721
     520-621-1683
     Fax 520-621-1916
     www.arts.arizona.edu/uabands/band day
     email: dotson@u.arizona.edu

826 University of Colorado Band Day Festival (exhibition)
     University Bands
     Campus Box 302
     University of Colorado
     Boulder, CO 80309-0302

827 University of Connecticut Band Day (exhibition)
     University of Connecticut Marching Band
     Dr. David L. Mills, Director
     U-12, Department of Music
     University of Connecticut
     Storrs, CT 06269-1012
     www.ucmb.uconn.edu/bandday.html

828 University of Delaware Band Day (massed band exhibition)
     Department of Music
     AMY E. duPont Music Bldg.
     University of Delaware
     Newark, DE 19716
     302-831-2577
     www.music.udel.edu

829 Upper Darby High School Band-A-Lympics (TOB)
     Upper Darby High School
     601 Lansdowne Avenue
     Drexel Hill, PA 19026
     610-622-7000
     www.angelfire.com/band2/udbop/marching.html

830 Upper Dublin (USSBA)
     Upper Dublin High School
     800 Loch Alsh Avenue
     Fort Washington, PA 19034
     215-643-8900
     Fax 215-643-0229

831 Upper Moreland (USSBA)
     Upper Moreland High School
     300 Terwood Road
     Willow Grove, PA 19090
     215-706-2386

832 Valhalla Marching Band Festival
     Parkview High School
     516 West Meadowmere
     Springfield, MO 65807
     417-895-2396
     www.phsband.com/vmbf/home.html
     email: valhalla@phsband.com

833 Valley View High School (Western Band)
13135 Nason Street
Moreno Valley, CA 92555
909-485-5720

834 Valleyfest Showdown
Valley High School
1140 35th Street
West Des Moines, IA 50266
515-226-2600
www.wdm.k12.ia.us/valley

835 Vanderbilt Marching Invitational
Vanderbilt University
P.O. Box 1637 B
Nashville, TN 37235-1637
615-343-2263
Fax 615-327-1328
www.vanderbilt.edu/vuband/vmiapp/
2002entryform.htm
email: vuband@vanderbilt.edu

836 Versailles Marching Band Invitational
(OMEA)
Versailles High School
459 S. Center Street
Versailles, OH 45380
937-526-4427
Fax 937-526-4356

837 Viking Classic
Union Pines High School
1981 Union Church Road
Cameron, NC 28326
910-947-5511

838 Viking Invitational
North Forsyth High School
5705 Shattalon Drive
Winston-Salem, NC 27105
http://wsfcs.k12.nc.us/nforsyth

839 Vintage Band Review (NCBA)
Vintage High School
1375 Trower Avenue
Napa, CA 94558
707-753-3620
Fax 707-253-3604
www.vhs.nvusd.k12.ca.us

840 Virginia State Marching Band Festival
c/o Virginia Music Educators Association and Virginia Band and Orchestra
Directors Association
West, Central, Northeast, and Southeast high school contest sites

841 Virginia Band and Orchestra Directors
Association (VBODA)
Contests: Oakton Classic (Oakton
High School; www.oaktonbands.com),
Hermitage Classic (Chester Fritz Stadium, Richmond; 804-672-3345, Charlottesville Cavalcade Marching Band
Contest (Charlottesville High School;
804-295-8453, Jefferson Classic (Monticello High School; marchingmus
tangs.cjb.net), George Wythe Band
Festival (George Wythe High School;
gwband.wytheville.com/festival),
Sherando Invitational Marching Band
Competition (Sherando High School;
540-869-3995); James Madison University Parade of Champions (James
Madison University, Harrisonburg;
www.jmu.edu/music/mrd)

842 Warrior Invitational Marching Festival
(GMEA)
Gordon Central High School
335 Warrior Path
Calhoun, GA 30701
706-629-7391
Fax 706-625-5376
www.gcbe.org/gchs/index.htm

843 Waseca Marching Classic
Waseca High School
1717 2nd Street NW
Waseca, MN 56093-2299
507-835-5470
Fax 507-835-1724
www.waseca.k12.mn.us/sch/hs/whs.
htm

844 Washington Marching Festival
Washington High School
600 Blue Jay Drive
Washington, MO 63090
636-239-4717

www.washington.k12.mo.us/schools/
whs/index.html

845 Watsonville High School Invitational
Field Show
Watsonville High School
Watsonville, CA 95076

846 Waukesha South (WSMA)
South High School
401 East Roberta Avenue
Waukesha, WI 53186
262-970-3778
Fax 262-970-3720
www.waukesha.k12.wi.us/wauk/high/
south.asp
email: mhansen@waukesha.k12.wi.us

847 Waukesha West (WSMA)
3301 Saylesville Road
Waukesha, WI 53189
262-970-4005
Fax 262-970-3920
www.waukesha.k12.wi.us/wauk/high/
west.asp
email: dstraus@waukesha.k12.wi.us

848 Waunakee Fall Invitational
Waunakee High School
Waunakee, WI 53597

Wells Fargo Sun Bowl Music Festival *see*
Music Tours Unlimited, Inc.

849 West Carrollton Invitational (Central
States Judges Assn.)
West Carrollton Senior High School
5833 Student Street
West Carrollton, OH 45449
937-435-2211
Fax 937-435-2315

850 West Central Illinois Field Show Com-
petition
c/o West Central Illinois Marching Band
Association
Jacksonville High School
Jacksonville, IL 62650

851 West Chester University Cavalcade of
Bands (CBA)
School of Music
West Chester University
West Chester, PA 19383
610-436-2495
www.wcupa.edu/stu/band

852 West Chester University Invitational
School of Music
West Chester University
West Chester, PA 19383
610-436-2495
www.wcupa.edu/stu/band

853 West Covina High School Field Tournament
West Covina High School
1609 E. Camero Avenue
West Covina, CA 91791

854 West Craven Marching Band Festival
West Craven High School
2600 Streets Ferry Road
Vanceboro, NC 28586
252-523-2600
http://schools.craven.k12.nc.us/WCH/
band.html

855 Western Band Association
Contest sites include: Merced, Mo-
desto, Live Oak, Gilroy, Clovis,
Logan, Thousand Oaks, San Marcos,
Costa Mesa, Valley View, Mission
Viejo, Trabuco Hills, Riverside Com-
munity College
High school members include:
Aliso Niguel, Aloha, Amador Valley,
American Fork, Arlington, Arroyo,
Atascadero, Atwater, Ayala, Beyer,
Buchanan, Buena, Bullard, Burroughs,
Canyon Springs, Capistrano Valley,
Carlsbad, Centennial, Central, Ceres,
Chaparral, Clayton Valley, Clovis,
Clovis West, Corona, Costa Mesa,
Davis, Del Oro, Dos Pueblo, Downey,
El Toro, Etiwanda, Exeter, Fallbrook,
Fountain Valley, Fremont, Gilbert,
Gilroy, Grace Davis, Green Valley,
Hanford, Highland, Homestead,

Hoover, Indio, Johansen, John Burroughs, John F. Kennedy, Laguna Hills, La Habra, Lancaster, Las Vegas, Lemoore Union, Liberty, Live Oak, Logan, Los Banos, Los Gatos, Madera, Mater Dei, McClatchy, Merced, Milpitas, Mission Viejo, Modesto, Monta Vista, Moreau Catholic, Moreno Valley, Mt. Miguel, Mt. Pleasant, Mt. View, Newburry Park, North Salinas, Nogales, Oak Grove, OakMont, Oceanside, Ocean View, Orange Glen, Pacifica, Page, Palmdale, Ramona, Redlands, Ridgeview, Riverband, Rosamond, Saddleback, San Marcos HB, San Marcos SM, Santa Margarita, Saratoga, Selma, Serrano, South Hills, Spring Creek, Taft, Thousand Oaks, Torrance, Trabuco Hills, Tulare Western, Upland, Valencia, Valley Christian, Valley View, West Bakersfield, West Covina, West, Westlake, Westmont, Yerba Buena, Yucaipa

856 Western Illinois University Marching Band Classic
Western Illinois University
Macomb, IL 61455
309-298-1505
www.wiu.edu/marchingband/html/mb classic.html

857 Western Kentucky Invitational March for the Gold
Heath High School
4330 Metropolis Lake Road
West Paducah, KY 42086-9791

Western Scholastic Marching Band Conference *see* Western Band Association

858 Western States High School Band Competition
University of Utah
Salt Lake City, UT 84112

859 Westerville North Marching Band Classic (OMEA)
Westerville North High School
950 County Line Road

Westerville, OH 43082
614-797-6248
Fax 614-895-6079

860 Westland Open (OMEA)
Westland High School
146 Galloway Road
Galloway, OH 43119
614-851-7076
Fax 614-870-5531
email: rwmcnutt@msn.com

861 Westminster Field Show (SCSBOA)
Westminster High School
14325 Goldenwest Street
Westminster, CA 92683-4905
714-893-1381

862 Westside Band Review (NCBA)
Orestimba High School
707 Hardin Road
Newman, CA 95360
209-862-2629
Fax 209-862-0259

863 Wetumka Marching Competition
Wetumka High School
P.O. Box 8
410 East Benson Street
Wetumka, OK 74883-0008
405-452-3291

864 White Oak High School Marching Band Festival
White Oak High School
1001 Piney Green Road
Jacksonville, NC 28546
http://www.geocities.com/wohsband

865 Wilson Sound Panorama (TOB)
Wilson High School
Wilson High School
West Lawn, PA 19609
610-670-0185

866 Winchester Marching Band Classic (OMEA)
Canal Winchester High School
300 Washington Street
Canal Winchester, OH 43110

614-920-2656
Fax 614-833-2163

867 Wisconsin Lutheran High School
(WSMA)
330 North Glenview Avenue
Milwaukee, WI 53213-3379
414-453-4567
Fax 414-453-3001
www.wlhs.k12.wi.us/contact.htm

868 WSMA (Wisconsin School Music Association) State Championships
Department of Music
Greenhill Center of the Arts
University of Wisconsin-Whitewater
Whitewater, WI 53190
800-621-8744
Fax 262-472-2808
http://academics.uww.edu/music/contact%20us/Index.html
email: music@uww.edu

869 Wolf River Marching Classic
Cordova High School

1800 Berryhill Road
Cordova, TN 38016
901-759-4540
Fax 901-759-4545
www.cadetsofcordova.org

870 Wyoming State High School Marching
Band Championship
Events Center
Casper, WY 82601

871 Youngsville Middle & Senior High
School (Lakeshore Marching Band
Association/Pennsylvania Federation
of Contest Judges)
College Street
Youngsville, PA 16371
814-563-7573

872 Zia Marching Band Fiesta
Department of Music
University of New Mexico
Albuquerque, NM 87131-1411
Fax 505-277-5568

Associations and Contest Sponsors

873 All American Association of Contest
Judges
1627 Lay Blvd.
Kalamazoo, MI 49001

874 All Japan Marching Band & Baton
Twirling Association
408 10-8 Nishi-Gotanda Zcho-Me
ShnaGawa-Ku
Tokyo, Japan JP141
+81-33-493-6357

875 American Drum Line Association
J. Greg Perry, President
1034 Westbrook Street
Corona, CA 92880
909-270-0670
www.amdrumassn.org

876 Association of Texas Small School
Bands

15310 Amesbury Lane
Sugar Land, TX 77478
281-494-2151
www.atssb.org
email: execsec@atssb.org

877 Bands of America (BOA)
526 Pratt Avenue North
Schaumburg, IL 60193
800-848-BAND
Fax 847-891-1812
www.bands.org
email: boainfo@bands.org

878 British Youth Band Association
www.byba.org.uk

Cadets Marching Band Cooperative *see*
United States Scholastic Band Association

879 Canadian Band Association
Jim Forde, President
17 Coronet Avenue
Halifax, NS, B3N 1L4
Canada
902-427-7501
Fax 902-427-7498
www3.sk.sympatico.ca/skband/cba.html
email: jimforde@psphalifax.ns.ca

880 Cavalcade of Bands Association
c/o Bill Powers, President
3745 Jonas Drive
Landisville, PA 17538
717-898-0276
Fax 717-898-5518
http://cavalcadeofbands.com
email: bill_powers@hempfield.k12.pa.
us

881 Central States Judges Association
c/o Dick Turner, Executive Director
4458 Aspen Drive
Hamilton, OH 45011
513-509-1010
email: csjal@aol.com

882 Colorado Bandmasters Association
c/o Mike Snell, Executive Secretary
8271 South Krameria Way
Englewood, CO 80112
www.coloradobandmasters.org

883 Danish National Association of Music
Corps
Landsgardeforeningen af 1992
Oresundsveg 148
DK-2300 Copenhagen S
Denmark
Phone: +45 70 23 80 80
Fax +45 70 23 80 90
www.lgf.dk/eng/default.asp
e-mail: landskontor@lgf.dk

884 Eastern Marching Band Associates
(EMBA)
www.maaemba.org

885 Five Star Brass Productions, Inc.
www.fivestarbrass.com

886 Florida Bandmasters Association
www.flmusiced.org/fba
email: fbawebsite@cs.com

887 Florida Marching Band Tournament
(FMBT)
P.O. Box 1972
Apopka, FL 32704 or 33991?
407-889-7024
Fax 407-889-4772
www.floridabandtournament.com

888 Georgia Music Educators Association
(GMEA)
www.gmea.org

889 Hong Kong Marching Band Association
P.O. Box 87071
To Kwa Wan Post Office
Kowloon, Hong Kong
852-9129-5229
Fax 852-2774-2932
email: hongkongmarchingbandassocia
tion@hotmail.com

890 Indiana State School Music Association,
Inc.
P.O. Box 50620
Indianapolis, IN 46250-0620
317-585-4600
www.issma.net/index2.html

891 Iowa Bandmasters Association, Inc.
c/o Roxianne Classen, President
3615 Kingman Blvd.
Des Moines, IA 50311
515-226-2636
www.bandmasters.org

892 Iowa High School State Marching Band
Contests
Iowa High School Music Association
1605 S. Story Street
P.O. Box 10
Boone, IA 50036
515-432-2013
Fax 515-432-2961
www.ihsma.org
email: alan@ihsma.org

893 Judges Association of Mid America (JAMA) (Missouri, Kansas, Oklahoma, Nebraska, Midwest)
c/o Brad Simon
4104 Trail Road
Lawrence, KS 66049
785-843-6587
www.jamahome.org
email: Simon@jamahome.org

894 Kansas Bandmasters Association
c/o Frank Tracz, President
Kansas State University
226 McCain
Manhattan, KS 66506
785-532-5740
www.kansas.net/%7Ecmrcam/Kba.htm

Kentucky Marching Band Board of Control *see* Kentucky Music Educators Association

895 Kentucky Marching Band Evaluators Association
www.kmea.org/FESTIVAL/KMBEA. htm

896 Kentucky Music Educators Association (KMEA)
c/o Jim Fern, Executive Secretary
P.O. Box 65
Calvert City, KY 42029
270-395-4821
Fax 270-395-7156
affiliated with Music Educators National Conference; individual contests plus East and West Regionals and Kentucky High School Marching Band Championships

897 Lakeshore Marching Band Association (sites: Bradford, Youngsville)
www.Lmba.us

898 Marching Band Association of Southern California
200 Main Street, Suite 104-401
Huntington Beach, CA 92648

899 Metro American Adjudicators (judges Eastern Marching Band Associates)
www.maaemba.org

900 Michigan Competing Band Association (MCBA)
www.michcompband.org

901 Mid-America Competing Band Directors Association (MACBDA)
c/o Ken Paris
5009 Thorson Road
Sun Prairie, WI 53590
608-834-7825
www.macbda.org
email: kenneth.paris@att.net

902 Mid-American Performing Arts Association (MAPAA; Arkansas, Oklahoma, Texas)
www.geocities.com/broadway/orcestra/ 6615

Mid-Atlantic Judges Association *see* Cavalcade of Bands Association

903 Mid-States Band Association (MSBA)
Greg Mills, President
Kings High School
5500 Columbia Road
Kings Mill, OH 45034
513-398-8050, x11042
www.midstatesba.org

904 Mississippi High School Activities Association, Inc.
P.O. Box 244
Clinton, MS 39060
601-924-6400
Fax 601-924-1725
www.misshsaa.com
email: mhsas@netdoor.com

905 Missouri Bandmasters Association
c/o Kurt Bauche, President
573-701-1310, x129
www.missouribandmasters.org
email: admin@missouribandmasters. org

906 Musical Arts Conference (MAC)
c/o Carman T. Dragone, Publicity Director
2125 Fairfield Avenue

Bridgeport, CT 06605
203-384-1241
www.musicalartsconference.com
email: webmaster@musicalartsconfe
rence.com

907 National Judges Association (founded
1960; judges Tournament of Band Association)
c/o Dominic Fulginiti, Director
703 Robert Street
Mechanicsburg, PA 17055
717-697-2570
Fax 717-737-1483
www.tob.org

908 Nebraska Music Educators Association
William A. Roehrs, President
7232 Carmen Drive
Lincoln, NE 68516-5631
402-423-6784
Fax 402-423-6798
http://whs_band.tripod.com/infor-
mat.htm
email: wroehrs@lps.org

909 New England Scholastic Band Association
c/o Anthony S. Di Carlo, Fall Activities
Director
246 West Street
South Weymouth, MA 02188
781-331-9500
Fax 781-331-6636
www.nesba.org

910 New York Field Band Conference
c/o Chris Centner, President
Phoenix High School
552 Main Street
Phoenix, NY 13135
315-695-1606
Fax 315-695-1618
www.nysfbc.org
email: ccentner@phoenix.k12.ny.us

911 Northern California Band Association
(NCBA)
c/o Kris Harper

Cupertino High School
10100 Finch Avenue
Cupertino, CA 95014
www.ncbaonline.org

912 Northwest Marching Band Circuit
(NWMBC)
c/o Todd Zimbelman, President
Associate Director of Bands
School of Music
1225 University of Oregon
Eugene, OR 97403
541-346-5670
Fax 541-346-6188
www.marchingband.org

913 Ohio Music Educators Association
(Affiliated with Music Educators National Conference, 1902 Association
Drive, Reston, VA 22091)
c/o Steven Stroup, President-Elect
116 Karns Drive
Dover, OH 44622
330-364-7134
www.omea-ohio.org
email: stroup@bright.net
or: c/o John Purdy, OMEA Marching
Band Affairs Chair
937-335-5938
www.omea-ohio.org
email: purdy-j@troy.12.oh.us

914 Oklahoma Secondary School Activities
Association (OSSAA)
P.O. Box 14590
Oklahoma City, OK 73113-0590
405-840-1116
Fax 405-840-9559
conducts West, East, Northwest,
Southwest, Northeast and Southeast
Regionals

Pennsylvania Federation of Contest Judges
see Pennsylvania Interscholastic Marching
Band Association

915 Pennsylvania Interscholastic Marching
Band Association (PIMBA)
c/o Tom Snyder, PIMBA President

West Allegheny High School
205 West Allegheny Road
Imperial, PA 15126
724-695-8690
www.pimba.org
email: president@pimba.info
    School competition sites: Elizabeth-
    Forward, Kiski, Gateway, McGuffey,
    McKeesport, Mars, Norwin, South-
    moreland, West Allegheny, Woodland
    Hills

916 South Carolina Band Director's Associ-
    ation
c/o Philip C. McIntyre
Marching Committee Chair
James F. Byrnes High School
P.O. Box 187, Highway 290
Duncan, SC 29334

917 South Dakota Bandmasters
www.sdbandmasters.org

918 Southern California School Band and
    Orchestra Association (SCSBOA)
11770 Warner Avenue, Suite 110
Fountain Valley, CA 92708
714-979-2263
www.scsboa.org
email: scsboa@pacbell.net

919 Summer Bands International
c/o Dave Schaafsma
222 West 19th Street
Upland, CA 91784
909-981-1454
email: director@soundmachine.org

920 Texas Music Educators Association
PO Box 49469
Austin, TX 78765

921 Tournament of Bands Association
c/o William Wildemore, National Judges
    Association Business Manager
134 Germantown Avenue
Plymouth Meeting, PA 19462
610-825-1825
Fax 610-828-3401
www.tob.org

922 United States Scholastic Band Associa-
    tion (USSBA)
c/o Youth Education in the Arts (formed
    with The Cadets, Carolina Crown
    and Crossmen Drum & Bugle Corps)
P.O. Box 506
Bergenfield, NJ 07621
201-384-8822
www.yea.org

923 University Interscholastic League (UIL)
c/o Richard Floyd, State Director of
    Music
P.O. Box 8028
Austin, TX 78722
512-471-5883

924 Virginia Band and Orchestra Directors
    Association (VBODA)
c/o Bill Berg, Marching Festival Chair-
    man
Chancellor Middle School
6320 Harrison Road
Fredericksburg, VA 22407
540-786-8099
Fax 540-785-9392
www.vboda.org

925 West Tennessee School Band and Or-
    chestra Association
www.wtsboa.com

926 Western Band Association (formerly
    Western Scholastic Marching Band
    Conference)
Kathy Whitcomb, Administrator
1710 San Luis Road
Walnut Creek, CA 94596
925-938-8917
www.westernband.org

927 Wisconsin School Music Association
    (WSMA)
4797 Hayes Road
Madison, WI 53704
800-589-9762
Fax 608-249-5532
www.wsmamusic.com/activities/march
    _band.html

928   World Association of Marching Show
Bands
Chinook RPO Box 30353
Calgary, Alberta T2H 2W1

Canada
www.wamsb.org
Note: Addresses may change as new
presidents and chief judges are elected.

Selected Bibliography

Articles

929   Ake, H. Worth. "Consistency—A Much
Used Word with Many Meanings for
Judges, Instructors and Competi-
tors." *Drum Corps News*, June 16, 1982,
p. 8.

930   Bauerlein, Chuck. "Keeping Up with a
Marching Band." *Daily Local News*
[West Chester, PA], November 9,
2001, p. A3.

931   Bough, T. "Corps-Style Percussion Tips
for High School Marching Bands." *Instrumentalist* (October 2001): 52–55.

932   Brown, Elene C. "Music in Motion: 1992
Band Cavalcade Showcased." *Daily
Local News* [West Chester, PA], Octo-
ber 15, 1992, p. F2.

933   Casavant, Albert R. "The Adjudication
Process." *Instrumentalist* (August 1979):
23–24.

934   Clements, Phillip. "Marching with a
Method." *Instrumentalist* (June 1999):
40, 42, 44.

935   _____. "Saving Time During Marching Rehearsals." *Instrumentalist* (August 1998): 50, 52, 54.

936   _____. "Start with a Show Theme
Then Add Music and Drill." *Instrumentalist* (August 2000): 48, 50, 52.

937   "Corps Style Marches On with One
Show Per Year: An Overview of Current Trends in Marching Bands." *Instrumentalist* (November 2000): 12–19.

938   Dunnigan, P. "The Best Marching Bands
Never Skip the Warm-Up." *Instrumentalist* (October 2001): 46–49.

939   Foster, Robert E. "Some Suggestions
from a Marching Band Adjudicator."
School Musician, Director & Teacher
(August/September 1979): 10, 61–62.

940   "Fun Is Instrumental to These Compe-
titors." [Tournament of Band cham-
pionships] *Philadelphia Inquirer*, November 16, 1998, pp. A1, A10.

941   Greenstone, Paul. "Philosophy of
School Marching Bands." *School Musician, Director & Teacher* (October
1983): 10.

942   Guegold, William. "Substance, Not
Style." *Instrumentalist* (January 1992):
80.

943   Hindsley, Mark H. "Adjudication in Per-
spective." *School Musician, Director &
Teacher* (March 1980): 20–21.

944   Hong, Sherman. "Adjudicating the
Marching Percussion Section." *Instrumentalist* (October 1981): 86–89.

945   Kastens, L. Kevin. "Adding Variety to
Create More Interesting Shows." *Instrumentalist* (June 2001): 44–46, 48,
56.

946   _____. "From Paper to Field Drills:
Clear Instructions Improve Marching
Band Rehearsals." *Instrumentalist*
(July 1999): 34, 36, 38, 40.

947 Kenney, Edward L. "Bands Face Field of Tough Competition." *Sunday News Journal* [Wilmington, DE], October 28, 1984, pp. G1, G4.

948 Lambrecht, Richard, and Barbara Prentice. "A Checklist for Marching Bands." *Instrumentalist* (September 1990): 44, 49, 50, 52, 54.

949 Lautzenheiser, Tim. "Adjudication: Who is the Real Judge?" *Instrumentalist* (September 1982): 114, 116.

950 _____. "Marching Band Competitions: Friend or Foe?" *Instrumentalist* (August 1981): 64.

951 Lovel, Walter. "The Contest Controversy." *Instrumentalist* (October 1983): 116.

952 "Marching Band Madness." *Sunset* (October 1981): 100–101.

953 Miller, Robert F. "How to Pick a Marching Band Contest." *Instrumentalist* (July 1984): 20, 22.

954 Moeny, Eugene E. "The Unification of Adjudication for Marching Bands and Contests." *School Musician, Director and Teacher* (October 1966): 70–71, 77.

955 Moyer, Ray. "Perfection?" *Instrumentalist* (January 1983): 86–87.

956 Neidig, Kenneth. "Realism, Efficiency, and Contest Excellence." *Instrumentalist* (September 1983): 31.

957 Rawlings, Randall. "Ten Weeks to Go." *Instrumentalist* (July 1980): 25.

958 Rockefeller, David R. "Rifles, Pom-Poms, Flags, and Music?" *Music Educators Journal* (December 1982): 31–32.

959 Rogers, George L. "What Do Students and Parents Really Think?" *Instrumentalist* (September 1983): 22–24.

960 Ruby, Neil. "Hosting a Marching Competition." *Instrumentalist* (February 2001): 60, 62, 64.

961 Saucedo, Richard, and Michael Pote. "A Coordinated Approach to Music and Drill Designs." Interview by Catherine Sell Lenzini. *Instrumentalist* (August 2000): 13–17.

962 Sherry, Heather Rakauskas. "Colorguard Designs for Maximum Effect." *Instrumentalist* (August 2000): 26–27, 29–30.

963 Sochinsky, James R., and Vernon Burnsed. "The Band Interest Survey." *Instrumentalist* (September 1983): 29–30.

964 Soltwedel, Judy. "The Director's View." *Instrumentalist* (September 1983): 24, 26.

965 Stansberry, John C. "Soft Corps (An Alternative to Hard Corps)." *Instrumentalist* (October 1979): 21–22.

966 "Student Musicians at Athletic Events: Half-Time Education?" *Music Educators Journal* (December 1978): 24–31.

967 Telesco, Joseph. "Marching Styles—The Words That Cause Debate." *Instrumentalist* (September 1984): 120.

968 Van Vorst, Charles E. "Corps Style Bands: The Best of Both Worlds." *Instrumentalist* (April 1983): 6–7.

Books and Monographs

969 Bennett, George T. *Field Routines for Marching Band Contests and Public*

Exhibitions. Marching Maneuver Series, Vol. VI. Chicago, IL: Gamble Hinged Music Company, 1938.

970 _____. *Grooming the Marching Band for High School Contests.* Marching Maneuver Series, Vol. III. Chicago, IL: Gamble Hinged Music Company, 1937.

971 _____. *Required and Special Maneuvers for High School Marching Band Contests.* Marching Maneuver Series, Vol. IV. Chicago, IL: Gamble Hinged Music Company, 1937.

972 Bilik, Jerry H. *Gridiron Showmanship.* Ann Arbor, MI: Jerry Bilik Music, 1974.

973 Dunnigan, Patrick. *Marching Band Techniques.* Northfield, IL: Instrumentalist Company, 1998.

974 Ryder, Dan. *Techniques of Marching Band Show Designs.* Austin, TX: Dan Ryder Field Drills, 2000.

975 Smith, Gary E. *The System: A Marching Band Guide.* 2000. [self-published]

976 Snoeck, Kenneth. *Contemporary Drill Design.* Oskaloosa, IA: C. L. Barnhouse, 1981.

977 Spohn, Charles L., and Richard W. Heine. *The Marching Band: Comparative Techniques in Movement and Music.* Boston: Allyn and Bacon, 1969.

Part 3
Drum Corps

Drum and Bugle Corps, often abbreviated to Drum Corps, is, like marching band, a fairly well kept secret, but each summer many stadiums nationwide reverberate to the strains of brass and percussion as children, teens, adults, and grandfolks compete under the aegis of such organizations as Drum Corps International (DCI) and Drum Corps Associates (DCA). It's a grueling season for members and the support staff that must transport and feed mini-armies. For instance, the 4th of July, 2002, found the Bluecoats parading in Bristol, Rhode Island, in the morning before busing south to Philadelphia for an early evening parade. Next day they rehearsed 35 miles west of Philadelphia at a middle school. The following day they performed in competition in Hershey—another 75 miles to the northwest.

There are still some all-male DCI members (Madison Scouts, Cavaliers) corps. Internationally, there is a growing corps movement in Europe, especially Britain, and in Japan.

Besides brass and percussion, a drum corps is composed of silk (flag) and rifle squads. In light of the fact that most high school marching band members play woodwinds, there have been movements to introduce non-brass instruments into the corps.

DCI is composed of "junior" corps. Members' ages range from 14 to 22. Maximum corps number for Division I is 135. There are also Division II (61–128 members) and Division III (up to 60 members) corps that also have championships. Some corps have been formed with the recognition that many high school and college musicians have summer jobs and therefore concentrate their performances on weekends in a specific region, e.g., the Jersey Surf travels the northeast. The top 25 corps comprise the voting membership of DCI. Many corps draw on several states for their members and headquarters change. The Sky Ryders used to hale from Kansas. Now it's Texas. The Crossmen have moved around southeastern Pennsylvania, northern Delaware, and New Jersey.

Drum Corps Associates was organized in 1965. There are no age restrictions on membership. A DCA corps numbers 128. As of 2002 there were 18 DCA member corps.

Competition schedules are found in DCI Today and Drum Corps World, www.dcacorps. org and www.dci.org.

Associations

978 DCI Atlantic (administered by Drum
Corps International)
246 West Street
South Weymouth, MA 01288
617-331-9500
Fax 617-331-6636

979 DCI Division II and III Office
4601 Holt Avenue
Milwaukee, WI 53219
414-327-2847
Fax 414-543-8289
www.dcm-online.org

980 DCI Pacific
372 Florin Road, #303

Sacramento, CA 95831
916-429-9545

981 Drum Corps Associates
P.O. Box 374
Monmouth Beach, NJ 07750
732-222-3835
www.dcacorps.org

982 Drum Corps France
32/6 rue Leon Blum
59100 Roubaix
France
03-20-75-43-93
Fax 03-20-45-17-83
membres.lycos.fr/drumcorps

983   Drum Corps Germany
      Hans-Peter Rosswag
      Hohe Strasse 35
      63069 Offenbach
      Germany
      +49 (0 177-4476026
      http://web3.athen076.server4free.de
      www.drumcorps-germany.de.vu

984   Drum Corps International (DCI)
      470 South Irmen Drive
      Addison, IL 60101
      630-628-7888
      Fax 630-628-7971
      www.dci.org
      email: dci@dci.org

985   Drum Corps Japan
      c/o Mr. Akira Konno
      3-15-11-205 Aoto
      Katsushika-ku, Tokyo 125-0062
      Japan
      Phone & Fax 03-3838-3315

986   Drum Corps Midwest
      c/o Roman Blenski, Executive Director
      4601 W. Holt Avenue
      Milwaukee, WI 53219
      414-327-2847
      www.dcm-online.org

987   Drum Corps United Kingdom
      c/o Jill Boyington, Secretary
      Croft House, Garden Street
      Sheffield S1 4BJ
      England
      (+44   0114 249 1922
      Fax (+44   0114 249 1933
      www.dcuk.org.uk

988   Eastern Massachusetts Association
      c/o Harry Sampson, Executive Director
      8 Highland Avenue
      Stoneham, MA 02180-1870
      781-438-3631

989   Federation des Associations Musicales
         du Quebec (F.A.M.Q.)

c/o Suzie Proulx, Executive Director
4545 Avenue Pierre-De Coubertin
C.P. 1000—Succursale M,
Quebec H1V 3R2
Canada
514-252-3025
Fax 514-252-4303
www3.sympatico.ca/ath/famq.html

990   Field Band Foundation
      c/o Retha Cilliers
      P.O. Box 5353
      Durban 4000
      South Africa
      27-31-572-4672
      Fax 27-31-306-2166
      www.fieldband.org.za

991   Friends of Drum Corps Quebec
      c/o Andre Theriault, President
      Les Amis du Drum Corps
      Quebecois (ADCQ), Canada
      www3.sympatico.ca/ath/index.html

992   Garden State Circuit
      c/o Tom Maiello, President
      91 West 28th Street
      Bayonne, NJ 07002
      201-788-1935
      www.gardenstatecircuit.homestead.
         com

993   Ontario Drum Corps Association
      c/o Bill Faulds
      1176 Christina Street N.
      Sarnia, Ontario N7V 3C3
      Canada
      877-634-6322
      Fax 519-336-8307
      www.odca.org
      email: odca@golden.net

994   Sponsors of Musical Enrichment, Inc.
         (S.O.M.E.)
      P.O. Box 9010
      Stockton, CA 95208

Corps Addresses

DCI Division I

995 Blue Devils
4065 Nelson Avenue
Concord, CA 94520
925-689-2918
Fax 925-689-0384
www.bluedevils.org

996 Blue Knights
1137 South Jason Street
Denver, CO 80223
303-777-1937
www.bknights.org

997 Bluecoats
P.O. Box 2733
North Canton, OH 44720
330-699-1572
Fax 330-899-0350
www.bluecoats.com

998 Boston Crusaders
Notre Dame Education Center
50 W. Broadway, 4th Floor
South Boston, MA 02127
617-268-4600
Fax 617-268-4688
www.crusaders.com

999 Cadets
P.O. Box 506
Bergenfield, NJ 07621-0506
201-384-8822
Fax 201-384-6882/8882
www.yea.org

1000 Carolina Crown
227-A Main St.
Ft. Mill, SC 29715
803-547-2270
www.carolinacrown.org
email: crown@carolinacrown.org

1001 Cavaliers
P.O. Box 501
Rosemont, IL 60018-0501

847-685-8412
www.cavaliers.org

1002 Colts
P.O. Box 515
1101 Central Avenue
Dubuque, IA 52004-0515
563-582-4872
Fax 563-582-7317
www.colts.org

1003 Crossmen
P.O. Box 506
Bergenfield, NJ 07621-0506
201-384-8822
Fax 201-384-6982
www.yea.org

1004 Glassmen
P.O. Box 352080
Toledo, OH 43635-2080
419-452-6553
Fax 419-452-6600
www.glassmen.org

1005 Kiwanis Kavaliers
25010 Highway Market RPO
Kitchener, Ontario N2A 3A2
Canada
519-894-0222
www.kavaliers.com

1006 Madison Scouts
P.O. Box 948
Madison, WI 53701
608-241-3171
Fax 608-249-6975
www.madison-scouts.org

1007 Magic of Orlando
P.O. Box 690426
Orlando, FL 32869
407-679-1575
www.magicorlando.org

1008 Phantom Regiment
202 W. State Street, Suite 514

Aftermath Indoor Drumline (Quakertown, PA)

Rockford, IL 61101
815-965-6777
www.regiment.org

Milwaukee, WI 53219
414-327-2847
www.pioneer-corps.org

1009 Pioneers
4601 West Holt Avenue

1010 Santa Clara Vanguard
1795 Space Park Drive

Santa Clara, CA 95054
408-727-5534
Fax 408-727-8730
www.scvanguard.org

1011 Seattle Cascades
P.O. Box 55100
Seattle, WA 98155
206-367-6695
www.seattlecascaces.com

1012 Southwind
P.O. Box 948
Madison, WI 53701
608-241-3171
Fax 608-249-6975
www.southwind.org

1013 Spirit from JSU (Jacksonville State
University)
P.O. Box 1295
Jacksonville, AL 36265
256-782-5562
www.spiritdrumcorps.org
www.marchingsoutherners.org

Spirit of Atlanta *see* Spirit from JSU

1014 Troopers
P.O. Box 375
Casper, WY 82602-0375
307-472-2141
Fax 307-235-6236
www.troopersdrumcorps.org

DCI Division II and III

1015 Americanos
1615 Drum Corps Drive
Menasha, WI 54952
920-722-5543
www.canos.org

1016 Blue Stars
P.O. Box 2523
LaCrosse, WI 54602
608-782-3219
www.bluestars.org

1017 Capital Regiment
1444 Demorest Road
Columbus, OH 43228
614-539-0366
Fax 614-539-0376
www.capitalregiment.org

1018 East Coast Jazz
P.O. Box 53
Malden, MA 02148
781-388-9411
www.eastcoastjazz.org

1019 General Butler Vagabonds (chose not
to participate in 2001)
Library, PA

1020 Jersey Surf
131 S. White Horse Pike
Berlin, NJ 08009
856-753-3786
Fax 856-767-1535
www.JerseySurf.org

1021 Les Senateurs
1446 rue Lepine
Joliette, Quebec J6E 4B5
514-753-5686

1022 Mandarins
P.O. Box 22297
Sacramento, CA 95822
916-395-8310
Fax 916-395-6104
www.mandarins.org

1023 Marion Glory Cadets
434 West Church Street
Marion, OH 43302
740-382-3013
Fax 740-375-8073
www.marioncadets.org

1024 Patriots
2145 Buffalo Road
Rochester, NY 14624-1507
716-247-9670
www.patriotsdrumcorps.com

Upper Darby High School Indoor Drumline (Drexel Hill, PA)

1025 Raiders
P.O. Box 133
Hillsdale, NJ 07646
201-573-8392
www.raidersdbc.org

1026 Spartans
73 East Hollis Street
Nashua, NH 03060-6303
603-889-2760
Fax 603-889-4710
www.spartansdbc.org

1027 Teal Sound
830 Cavalla Road
Atlantic Beach, FL 32233
904-997-6566
www.tealsound.org

1028 Vanguard Cadets
1795 Space Park Drive
Santa Clara, CA 95054
408-727-559
www.scvanguard.org

1029 Yamato
8955 Poppy Lane
Riverside, CA 92503
909-352-9573
www.yamatodrumcorps.org

International Division

1030 Taipei Yuehfu
P.O. Box 22-270
Taipei, Taiwan
Republic of Korea
886-2-2322-5027
www.yuehfu.org
U.S.A. liaison: 1 620 8th Avenue, #17,
Greeley, CO 80631; 970-356-1748

Other Junior Corps

1031 Allegiance Elite
3650 19th Street NE, #15
Calgary, Alberta T2E 6V2
Canada

403-250-2263
email: director@allegianceelite.org

1032 Alliance
P.O. Box 20227
El Cajon, CA 92021
619-442-9148
www.sandiegoalliance.org

1033 Bandettes
103 River Road
Sault Ste. Marie, Ontario P6A 6C3
Canada
705-759-3192
Fax 705-759-3192
email: royf.wilson@sympatico.ca

1034 Blue Devils "B"
4065 Nelson Avenue
Concord, CA 94520
925-689-2918
www.bluedevils.org

1035 Blue Devils "C"
4065 Nelson Avenue
Concord, CA 94520
925-689-2918
www.bluedevils.org

1036 Blue Saints
102 Jacob Street
Sudbury, Ontario P3Y 1E5
Canada
705-692-5464
email: ripplechip22@aol.com

1037 Cadets of New York City
359 Herkimer Street
Bronx, NY 11216
718-363-0266
www.cadets_nyc.tripod.com

1038 Capital Sound
P.O. Box 948
Madison, WI 53701
608-241-3171
www.capital-sound.org

1039 Citations
P.O. Box 379

Burlington, MA 01803
617-272-7111
www.citations.org

1040 Colt Cadets
P.O. Box 515
Dubuque, IA 52001-0515
563-582-4872
www.colts.org

1041 Decorah Kilties
509 Goose Island Drive
Decorah, IA 52101
319-382-4363

1042 Delta Brigade
14101 Pleasant Hill Road
Alexander, AR 72002
501-407-8024
www.deltabrigade.com

1043 Dutch Boy
192 Grey Fox Drive
Kitchener, Ontario N2E 3R1
Canada
519-744-3291
www.dutchboydrumcorps.com

1044 Edmonton Strutters
Box 20055
Beverly Postal 57
Edmonton, Alberta T5J 3K6
Canada
403-473-3548

1045 Emerald Knights
P.O. Box 1142
Cedar Rapids, IA 52406
www.emeraldknights.org

1046 Esperanza
P.O. Box 502591
San Diego, CA 92150-2591
858-391-1311
www. EsperanzaCorps.org

1047 Glory Cadets
434 West Church Street
Marion, OH 43302

740-382-3013
www.marioncadets.org

1048 H.Y.P.E.
344 Magnolia Drive
Hamilton, Ontario L9C 6N7
905-318-7376

1049 Impulse
2039 Goldeneye Place
Costa Mesa, CA 92626
714-239-4408
ww.impulseyoutharts.org

1050 Jersey Surf
131 South White Horse Pike
Berlin, NJ 08009
856-753-DRUM
Fax 856-767-1535
www.jerseysurf.org

1051 Joliet Kingsmen
307 Hobbs Road
Joliet, IL 60435
815-834-1500

1052 Jubal
Box 8189
3301 CD Dordrecht
The Netherlands
011-31-78-6184850
www.jubal.org

1053 Kingsmen
201 North Hickory
Joliet, IL 60455
815-834-1500

1054 Kips Bay Crusaders
1930 Randall Avenue
Bronx, NY 10473
718-893-8600

1055 Knight Storm
586 Montgomery Street
Chicopee, MA 01020
413-534-4970
www.knightstorm.org

1056 Lake Erie Regiment
113 W. 10th Street
Erie, PA 16501
814-456-5300
www.leregiment.org

1057 Legend of Texas
3107 Interstate 27
Lubbock, TX 79404
888-484-5463
Fax 806-741-1374
www.angelfire.com/tx2/legendof
    texas/contact.html

1058 Lehigh Valley Knights
P.O. Box 786
Allentown, PA 18105
610-799-8186
www.LehighValleyKnights.org

1059 Les Sentinelles
102 Michel-DuGué
Varennes, Quebec J3X 1H5
Canada
514-425-2050

1060 Les Stentors
CP 24001 Belvedere
Sherbrooke, Quebec J1H 6J4
Canada
819-563-3013
www.interlinx.qc.ca/~stentors

1061 McCollough Royal Knights
3450 Delfry Lane
Woodbridge, VA 22192
703-515-1475

1062 Oregon Crusaders
32838 Old Bunker Hill Road
St. Helens, OR 97051
503-397-4876
www.oregoncrusaders.org

1063 Pacific Crest
21231 Fountain Springs
Diamond Bar, CA 91765
714-744-7057
Fax 909-468-2802
www.pacific-crest.org

The Phantom Regiment Drum Corps (Rockford/Loves Park, IL)

1064 Patriots Praise
P.O. Box 292242
Phelan, CA 92329-2242
760-868-5846

1065 Phoenix
738 Pine Drive
Brick, NJ 08523
732-928-9699
richski@cybercomm.net

1066 Pride of Soka
1-236 Tangi-cho
Hachioji, Tokyo 192
Japan
(0427) 50-6234

1067 Pride of the Lions
2272 Pasqua Street
Regina, Saskatchewan S4T 4M4
306-791-6221

1068 Quebec Alliance
1446 rue Lépine
Joliette, Quebec J6E 4B5
Canada

1069 Quest
P.O. Box 23610
Brooklyn, NY 11202
718-515-4723
www.questdbcorps.org

1070 Racine Scouts
2030 Taylor Avenue
Racine, WI 53403
414-554-4949

1071 Raiders
P.O. Box 76
Lodi, NJ 07644-0076
201-573-8302
www.raidersdbc.org

1072   Revolution
       9155 Tree Village
       San Antonio, TX 78250
       210-682-9052
       www.revolution-corps.org

1073   San Diego Alliance
       P.O. Box 20227
       El Cajon, CA 92021
       619-442-9148
       www.sandiegoalliance.org

1074   Scenic City
       P.O. Box 11072
       Chattanooga, TN 37401
       423-877-3164
       www.buglecorps.com

1075   Silver Knights
       94 Erin Lane
       Ludlow, MA 01056
       413-547-8998

1076   Spirit of America
       P.O. Box 2831
       Orleans, MA 02653
       508-255-3999
       www.gdaf.org

1077   Spirit of Newark
       120 Roseville Avenue
       N___ __k, NJ 07107
       ___-___-1172
       ___w.spiritofnewark.org

1078   Strångnås
       c/o Lars Ostlund
       Oxhagsv 31 D
       645 51 Strångnås
       Sweden
       046-0152/193 05

1079   Tampa Bay Thunder
       P.O. Box 271621
       Tampa, FL 33688
       813-969-0904
       www.tampabaythunder.org

1080   Targets
       276 Spikenard Circle

       Springfield, MA 01129
       413-783-2405
       www.targetsdbc.org

1081   Teal Sound
       830 Cavalla Road
       Atlantic Beach, FL 32233
       904-249-6462
       www.tealsound.org

1082   Vanguard Cadets
       1795 Space Park Drive
       Santa Clara, CA 95054
       408-727-5534, x20
       Fax 408-727-8730
       www.scvanguard.org

1083   West Coast Sound
       www.westcoastsound.org

1084   Yokohama Scouts
       8955 Poppy Lane
       Riverside, CA 92503
       909-352-9573
       www.hamakko.or.jp/~y_scouts

Senior Corps (Drum Corps Associates)

1085   Allegheny Night Storm
       P.O. Box 6484
       Allegheny Station
       Pittsburgh, PA 15212
       412-231-1349
       www.a-nightstorm.org

1086   Bayou City Blues
       17707 Windy Point Drive
       Spring, TX 77379
       281-320-9192
       www.geocities.com/Broadway/Stage/
       1798

1087   Blue Grass Brass
       7209 Chestnut Tree Lane
       Louisville, KY 40291

1088   Brigadiers
       1860 West Fayette Street
       Syracuse, NY 13204

315-468-5710
www.brigadiers.com

1089 Buccaneers
P.O. Box 13032
Reading, PA 19612-3032
610-275-1654
www.readingbuccaneers.org

1090 Bushwackers
5 Lower Rocks Lane
Norwalk, CT 06851
201-339-6348
www.bushwackers.org

1091 Caballeros
P.O. Box 170
Hawthorne, NJ 07507
973-523-5371
www.cabs.org

1092 Chieftains
P.O. Box 786
Allentown, PA 18108
610-799-8186
email: Ivchiefs@aol.com

1093 Chops, Inc.
P.O. Box 14774
Minneapolis, MN 55414
800-486-9207
www.chopsinc.com

1094 Corps Vets
1860-D Briarcliff Circle, NE
Atlanta, GA 30329
404-886-0269
www.corpsvets.org

1095 The Crusaders
P.O. Box 1524
Rochester, NY 14615
716-634-7891
www.rochcrusaders.org

1096 Empire Statesmen
341 Ridge Road East
Rochester, NY 14621
716-266-2232
www.statesmen.org

1097 Generations
P.O. Box 503
Seekonk, MA 02771
ourworld.cs.com/_ht_a/generations
   879/id17.htm

1098 Govenaires
P.O. Box 235
St. Peter, MN 56082
507-345-5857

1099 Heat Wave of Orlando
3300 Harrison Avenue
Orlando, FL 328304
407-857-9702
www.heatwavecorps.org

1100 Hurricanes
P.O. Box 471
Derby, CT 06418
203-269-3771
www.ct-hurricanes.org

1101 Kilties
P.O. Box 085235
Racine, WI 53408-5235
262-634-2100
www.kilties.org

1102 Kingston Grenadiers
P.O. Box 1342
Kingston, Ontario K7L 5C6
Canada
613-378-6420

1103 The Los Angeles Conquistadors
12477 Crystal Ranch Road
Moorark, CA 93021
805-657-0471
www.conquistadors.org

1104 Mighty St. Joe's
7132 Thwing Road
LeRoy, NY 14482
716-768-8687
www.mightystjoes.com

1105 Minnesota Brass, Inc.
P.O. Box 7341

Jersey Surf Drum Corps (Camden County, NJ)

St. Paul, MN 55107
www.mnbrassinc.org
email: mnbrass@writeme.com

1106 Northernaires
P.O. Box 201
Menominee, MI 49858
user.cybrzn.com/-nadc

1107 Northwest Venture Sr.
432 Rose Court
Mt. Vernon, WA 98273
360-428-8149
www.nwventure.org

1108 Renegades, Sr.
P.O. Box 50091
San Francisco, CA 94159-0051
www.renegades.org

1109 River City Regiment Sr.
2237 Sandcastle Way
Sacramento, CA 95833

916-564-0861
email: Info@rivercityregiment.org

1110 San Francisco Renegades
4937 Spur Way
Antioch, CA 94509
925-706-8198

1111 Skyliners
P.O. Box 343
Linden, NJ 07036
908-925-3523
www.skyliners.org

1112 SoCal Dream, Sr.
P.O. Box 5369
Buena Park, CA 90622
714-239-4408
www.SoCalDream.org

1113 Sunrisers
44 Brittany Lane
Nagatuck, CT 06770

203-720-2858
www.sunrisers

Harrisburg, PA 17106
888-970-0217
www.westshoremen.org

1114 Westshoremen
P.O. Box 60594

Drum Corps International
Championship Winners

1115 2003 Blue Devils (site: Orlando, FL)
Cavaliers
Cadets
Phantom Regiment
Santa Clara Vanguard
Boston Crusaders
Bluecoats
Madison Scouts
Crossmen
Carolina Crown
Magic of Orlando
Spirit from JSU

1116 2002 Cavaliers (site: Madison, WI)
Blue Devils
Cadets
Santa Clara Vanguard
Boston Crusaders
Phantom Regiment
Bluecoats
Glassmen
Crossmen
Spirit
Magic of Orlando
Seattle Cascades

1117 2001 Cavaliers (Buffalo, NY)

1118 2000 Cadets (College Park, MD)
Cavaliers (tie)

1119 1999 Blue Devils (Madison, WI)
Santa Clara Vanguard (tie)

1120 1998 The Cadets (Orlando, FL)

1121 1997 Blue Devils (Orlando, FL)

1122 1996 Blue Devils (Orlando, FL)
Phantom Regiment (tie)

1123 1995 Cavaliers (Buffalo, NY)

1124 1994 Blue Devils (Boston, MA)

1125 1993 Cadets of Bergen County (Jackson, MS)

1126 1992 Cavaliers (Madison, WI)

1127 1991 Star of Indiana (Dallas, TX)

1128 1990 Cadets of Bergen County (Buffalo, NY)

1129 1989 Santa Clara Vanguard (Kansas City, MO)

1130 1988 Madison Scouts (Kansas City, MO)

1131 1987 Garfield Cadets (Madison, WI)

1132 1986 Blue Devils (Madison, WI)

1133 1985 Garfield Cadets (Madison, WI)

1134 1984 Garfield Cadets (Atlanta, GA)

1135 1983 Garfield Cadets (Miami, FL)

1136 1982 Blue Devils (Montreal, Canada)

1137 1981 Santa Clara Vanguard (Montreal, Canada)

Tri-High Creek Indoor Guard (Runnemede, NJ)

1138 1980 Blue Devils (Birmingham, AL)

1139 1979 Blue Devils (Birmingham, AL)

1140 1978 Santa Clara Vanguard (Denver, CO)

1141 1977 Blue Devils (Denver, CO)

1142 1976 Blue Devils (Philadelphia, PA)

1143 1975 Madison Scouts (Philadelphia, PA)

Selected Bibliography

Articles

1147 "Beating the Drums for the Corps."
Sports Illustrated (August 10, 1987): 18.

1148 Boehm, Mike. "It's Brass and Percus-
sion with a *Blast!* Theater: The No-
Story Spectacle Is Not Your Average
Drum and Bugle Corps. It Has Its
West Coast Premiere at OCPAC
This Week in Costa Mesa." *Los An-
geles Times* (Orange County Edi-
tion), December 25, 2001, p. F-2.

1149 Cahill, Michael J. "A Capsule History
of the Drum and Bugle Corps." *The
Instrumentalist* (June 1982): 6–9.

1150 Dyroff, Denny. "*Shockwave* Expands
Musical Boundaries." *Daily Local
News Weekender* [West Chester, PA],
November 15, 2002, pp. 3, 12.

1151 Faram, Mark. "Music for the Years."
The American Legion, V. 147, No. 6
(1999): 26. [re Empire Statesmen and
drum corps competition]

1152 Hartsough, Jeff, and Logozzo, Derrick.
"Sixty Years of Drum Corps." *Percussive Notes*, V. 36, No. 1 (1998): 18.

1153 Irwin, Leo. "Music in Motion." *55
Hours Plus* [*News Journal*, Wilmington, DE], November 15, 2002, pp.
18–20. [re *Blast II: Shockwave*]

1154 _____. "Show Strikes a Familiar Chord
for UD Marching Band Assistant."
55 Hours Plus [*News Journal*, Wilmington, DE], November 15, 2002, p.
18. [re *Blast II: Shockwave*]

1155 Kachin, Denise Breslin. "Everything
but 76 Trombones." *Philadelphia Inquirer*, June 6, 1991, pp. 4CC–5CC
plus cover photo.

1156 Karis, Al. "A Little History: Notable
Anniversaries in the Drum Corps
Activity." *Drum Corps World* (April
1982): 10.

1157 Koizumi, Katsuyuki. "Corps Questions." *The Instrumentalist* (October
1982): 8. "The Author Replies" by
Michael Cahill.

1158 McCarthy, Pat, and Paul McCarthy.
"The Art of Drum Corps Percus-
sion—Some Comments About the
Past, Present and Future Trends."
Drum Corps News (January 27, 1982):
8–9.

1159 McGrath, William A. "The Contribu-
tion of Senior Drum and Bugle Corps
to Marching Percussion." *Percussionist* (Spring/Summer 1980): 149–176.

1160 McTaggart, Mark. "Can Drum Corps
Help Your Drum Playing?" *Modern
Drummer*, V. 24, No. 8 (2000): 136.

1161 "Management & Instructors of Top
Twenty-Five Corps." *Drum Corps
News* (June 2, 1982): 8–9.

1162 "Marching Band vs. Drum Corps: One
Marching Member's Opinion." *Percussive Notes* (July 1983): 56–57.

1163 Mason, Brian. "Auditioning for a Drum
Corps." *Percussive Notes*, V. 37, No. 5
(1999): 37.

1164 Merle, Renae. "What's a Billionaire to Do When He Gets Tired of the Stent Biz? Why, Put a Musical on Broadway, of Course; But *Blast!* Is a Bust with the Critics." *Wall Street Journal*, April 19, 2001, pp. A1, A4.

1165 Murray, Allan. "Field Bands and Drum Corps—South African Style." *Percussive Notes*, V. 36, No. 3 (1998): 33.

1166 "The 1983 Drum Corps Hit Parade, Management, Instructors, Historical Notes." *Drum Corps News*, July 8, 1983, pp. 8–9, 13–15.

1167 Orgill, Roxane. "No Strings: Summer with the Drum and Bugle Corps." *Wall Street Journal*, September 18, 1990, pp. A18, A28.

1168 Roznoy, Richard T. "The Drum Corps International Championships." *Instrumentalist* (June 1978): 24–27.

1169 Spalding, Dan C. "The Evolution of Drum Corps Drumming." *Percussionist* (Spring/Summer 1980): 116–131.

1170 "Sports Medicine Practiced in Regiment's Musical Sport." *DCI Today* (November-December 1992): 8–9.

1171 Taylor, Barbara. "Ambassadors Celebrate 10 Seasons: Practice, Parades and Competitions Are a 'Way of Life' for the Members." *Newmarket-Aurora Era* [Canada], April 4, 1984.

1172 Vickers, Steve. "Drum Corps Moves Into the '80s." *Instrumentalist* (June 1980): 18–19.

1173 _____. "The Drum Corps World in 1982." *Instrumentalist* (June 1982): 10–11.

1174 _____. "1984 Report: Drum Corps World." *Instrumentalist* (June 1984): 9–11.

1175 Weiss, Lauren Vogel. "Percussion Today: Drum Corps Meets Drumset: DCI Drumset Champion Daniel Villanueva." *Modern Drummer*, V. 24, No. 4 (2000): 122.

1176 Wulf, Steve. "Beating the Drums for the Corps." *Sports Illustrated* (August 10, 1987): 18.

Books

1177 Bennett, George T. *New and Novel Formations for Marching Bands and Drum Corps.* Marching Maneuver Series, Vol. VII. Chicago, IL: Gamble Hinged Music Company, 1938.

1178 Blake, Richard I. *The Music of the Hawthorne Caballeros.* Lynn, MA: Fleetwood Records, 1961.

1179 *Competitive Drum Corps, There and Then ... to Here and Now.* Des Plaines, IL: Olympic Printing, 1981.

1180 Drum Corps International. *The 1992 Summer Music Games.* Lombard, IL, 1992. [souvenir championships program features 20-year history of DCI]

1181 Drum Corps World. *A History of Drum & Bugle Corps.* Madison, WI, 2002.

1182 Johnson, Scott, and Blue Devil Percussion Staff. *The Line: The Blue Devil Book of Drumming.* Addison, IL: Drum Corps International.

1183 Petty, Mark A. *Corps Style Percussion Techniques.* Troy, MI, 1976.

1184 Popp, Jodeen E. *Competitive Drum Corps.* Des Plaines, IL: Olympic Printing, 1979.

Website

1185 www.drumcorpsplanet.com

Part 4
Fund-Raising

The ways to raise money for a trip, instruments, or uniforms are limited only by one's imagination. Candy always sells but does not provide a high profit margin. Raffles can net plenty, but even turkey or ham raffles are illegal in some states. Records and cassettes made from concerts or field shows are novel but can be expensive. Ditto band performance videos. Cheap jewelry is virtually a one-time-only method. Other traditional ways to raise money are sausage and cheese, hoagies or other types of sandwiches (preferably made on a school's in-service day so that lunchtime deliveries can be made to local businesses), pizza kits, spaghetti dinners, flowers, dance-a-thons, ceramic Christmas ornaments, candles, fruit, car washes, bingo, auctions, plant sales, and selling refreshments at concerts, games, and competitions. Less traditional so far are running a haunted house at Halloween (be aware of liability) and arranging with a mall to wrap shopper's gifts.

One method for raising funds that can net one hundred percent profit for the student or music fund is a band calendar. Use one photo per month, featuring action shots plus different band sections (woodwinds, brass, percussion, drum major, majorettes, flags, rifles). Printing costs can be defrayed through local businesses that supply business cards for reproduction around each photo and pay, say, $25 per ad. Six ads per month equals $150, twelve months times $150 equals $1,800, and voila, the printing cost is negligible. Sell the calendar cheap, and sell a lot. Remember to take the photos early—during band camp or early in the autumn season—so the calendars can be printed and sold before Christmas.

To obtain a truck or trailer to transport equipment, canvas local businesses. In exchange for the vehicle, the business gets free publicity via logos on the side. This might also work for small tractors hauling percussion equipment and the drum major podium to the sidelines.

Fund-Raising Organizations and Products

Note: Phone book Yellow Pages include a fund-raising category.

1186 Action Events, Inc. (bouncers, moon-walk, slides)
888746-7072
www.fun1.com/kidszone.htm

1187 All American Fundraising
P.O. Box 220
Waterloo, NE 68069
800-228-9028
www.allamericanfr.com
email: comments@allamericanfr.com

1188 America's Fundraising Network (candles, candy, keyrings, lollipops)
P.O. Box 52167
Knoxville, TN 37950
www.americasfundraising.com

1189 America's Premier Fundraisers
P.O. Box 65A
Cumberland Center, ME 04021-0665
800-976-1787
Fax 207-878-4188
www.PremierFundraisers.com
email: mail@premierfundraisers.com

1190 ArtAuctionFundraiser.com
761 Coates Avenue
Holbrook, NY 11741
888-676-7700
Fax 631-471-6741
www.artauctionfundraiser.com

1191 Bazaar World
396 Avenel Street
Avenel, NJ 07001-1117
732-634-8240
http://fundraising.webshq.com/show.
php3?Which=689860

1192 B-Craft Fund Raising Products
5801 65th Avenue, North
Minneapolis, MN 55429
763-537-3000
http://fundraising.webshq.com/sow.
php3?Which=689869

1193 Boston's Best Fundraising
43 Norfolk Avenue
South Easton, MA 02375
877-937-2633
Fax 508-230-0298
www.coffeeandmorefundraising.com
email: sales@coffeeandmorefundrais
ing.com

1194 Buckeye Donkey Ball Company
P.O. Box 345
Marengo, OH 43334-0345
www.donkeyball.com
419-253-4600
email: info@donkeyball.com

1195 C.C.I. Fundraising
18813 Willamette Drive
West Linn, OR 97068-1711
503-697-7495
Fax 503-697-5913
www.cdcoupon.com
email: info@cdcoupon.com

1196 CEI
917 SW Oak Street #306
Portland, OR 97205-2829
503-226-0717
http://fundraising.webshq.com/show.
php3?Which=689877

1197 Century Resources Inc.
3730 Lockbourne Road
Columbus, OH 43207
800-444-7977
Fax 614-492-2462
www.centuryresources.com
email: dpalmo@centres.com

1198 Cherrydale Farms
www.cherrydale.com

1199 Collegiate Specialty Company
44 River Street
Troy, NY 12180-4448
518-272-8911
http://fundraising.webshq.com/show.
php3?Which=689863

1200 Cornucopia Snack Foods Company
4671 Highway Avenue
Jacksonville, FL 32254
800-385-0093
Fax 904-384-7796
www.funfoodusa.com/fundraisers.htm
email: funfood@bellsouth.net

1201 Creative Garden Concepts, Inc.
240 Main
Grandview, MO 64030
888-BIOMATS
www.biomat.com
email: sales@biomat.com

1202 Crest Fruit Company
100 North Tower Road
Alamo, TX 78516
956-787-9971
Fax 956-787-1428
www.gotexan.org/cgi-bin/tame_mem
ber.idc?tame_iud=1509
email: crestmrkt@aol.com

1203 Cromers P-Nuts
1235 Assembly Street.
P.O. Box 163
Columbia, SC 29202
800-322-7688
Fax 803-779-0731
www.cromers.com

1204 Dutch Mill Bulbs Inc.
25 Trinidad Avenue
P.O. Box 407
Hershey, PA 17033
800-533-8824
www.dutchmillbulbs.com

1205 eFundraising.com
1320 Rt. 9
Champlain, NY 12919

800-561-8388
www.efundraising.com
email: service@efundraisingcorp.com
Canada: 33 Prince Street
Montreal, Quebec H3C 2M7

1206 Entertainment Publications
5009 Pacific Highway East, #5-0
Tacoma, WA 98424-2657
253-922-1822
http://fundraising.webshq.com/show.
php3?Which=689866

1207 Fancy's Catering
4666-C South Mingo Road
Tulsa, OK 74146
918-622-6836
Fax 918-622-0359
http://9186226836.area-wide.com

1208 Florida Indian River Groves
P.O. Box 2764
Vero Beach, FL 32961
800-468-3168
Fax 772-492-0898
www.floridaindianrivergroves.com
email: admin@floridaindianrivergroves.
com

1209 Fly Technology (TotalPort internet ac-
cess software]
www.flytechnology.com [access code:
bandkids]

1210 Four Point Products (custom im-
printed loose-leaf products)
106 Gamma Drive
Pittsburgh, PA 15238-2949
800-456-6603
Fax 412-967-9898
www.fourpoint.com

1211 Friendship House (musical gifts, awards)
29313 Clemens Road, #2-G
P.O. Box 450978
Cleveland, OH 44145-0623
800-791-9876
Fax 440-871-0858

www.friendshiphouse.com
email: info@friendshiphouse.com

1212 Fun Services (bouncers, slides, moon-
walks, dunk tank)
1065 South 76th Avenue
Bridgeview, IL 60455
800-511-4FUN
Fax 708-233-6983
www.funservicesil.com

1213 Fund Raisers Ltd.
601 E. 44th Street #6
Boise, ID 83714-4833
208-377-9011
http://fundraising.webshq.com/show.
php3?Which=689871

1214 Fund Raising at its Best
c/o St. Louis PECO Flake Candy Company
877-263-9661
www.the-candyman.com

1215 Fundever (software)
3100 FiveForks Trickum, Suite 401
Lilburn, GA 30047
www.fundever.com

1216 Fundraising Beads Programs
888-511-2323
www.fundraisingbeads.com

1217 FundRaising.com (candy, cheesecake,
cookie dough)
800-443-5353
www.fundraising.com

1218 FundraisingDirect.com
c/o MusicFundraising.com
4 Mill Park Ct., Dept. MS
Newark, DE 19713
800-238-7916
Fax 302-366-8995
www.musicfundraising.com
email: info@musicfundraising.com

1219 Fundraising.WebsHQ.com.com
1001-A East Harmony Road, #512

South Brunswick High School Visual Ensemble (Monmouth Junction, NJ)

Fort Collins, CO 80525
970-225-6989
Fax 240-352-0684
http://fundraising.webshq.com/contactus.php3
email: info@Fundraising.WebsHQ.com
Companies associated with this site: Bazaar World (NJ), CEI (OR), Collegiate Specialty Company (NY), Entertainment Publications (WA), Fancy's Catering (OK), Fund Raisers Ltd. (ID), Golden Donuts (GA), Kids Korner Gift Shop (CA), Knight's Popcorn Company (WI), McGuire Industries (FL), Open Option Inc. (NY), Partners Coffee Company (GA), Sunshine Selections Inc. (NY), Team Sale Company (TN), Tri-State Sales Inc. (NH), Troll Book Fairs Corporation (TN)

1220 Gertrude Hawk Chocolates (chocolate, peanut butter)
9 Keystone Park
Dunmore, PA 18512
800-342-7556
www.gertrudehawk.com
email: customerservice@gertrude
hawk.com

1221 Gold Medal Products Company
10700 Medallion Drive
Cincinnati, OH 45241-4807
800-543-0862
Fax 800-542-1496
www.gmpopcorn.com
email: info@gmpopcorn.com

1222 Golden Donuts
625 45th Street
Columbus, GA 31904
706-660-8783
http://fundraising.webshq.com/show.
php3?Which=689873

1223 Golden Gem Growers, Inc.
P.O. Drawer 9
Guard Main Gate
Umatilla, FL 32784

352-669-2101
Fax 352-669-1993

1224 Hale Indian River Grove
P.O. Box 700217
Wabasso, FL 32970
800-327-4768
www.halegroves.com/vrr

1225 Henco, Inc.
205 Henco Drive
Selmer, TN 38375
901-645-3255

1226 Hershey's Food Corporation
800-803-6932
www.hersheysfundraising.com

1227 Impressions in Stone (commemorative bricks, plaques)
13 South Milwaukee Avenue
Vernon Hills, IL 60061
888-883-0310
Fax 847-883-0305
www.impressionsinstone.com
email: info@impressionsinstone.com

1228 Indian River Fruit Sales
P.O. Box 2764
Vero Beach, FL 32969

1229 Jackson Fundraising
800-994-7882
www.candyfundraising.com
email: info@candyfundraising.com

1230 Joe Corbi's Wholesale Pizza Inc.
1430 Desoto Road
Baltimore, MD 21230
800-322-1689
Fax 410-525-0531
www.joecorbi.com

1231 Kathryn Beich (candy)
800-431-1248
www.kathrynbeich.com

1232 Kids Korner Gift Shop
7741 Alabama Avenue #10

Canoga Park, CA 91304-4946
http://fundraising.webshq.com/show.
   php3?Which=689875

1233   Kids Korner Gift Shoppes
       2705 185th Avenue East
       Sumner, WA 98390
       800-KIDS-NOW
       Fax 253-891-4112
       www.kidskornerusa.com
       email: kidskornerusa@worldnet.att.
       net

1234   Langdon Barber Groves
       P.O. Box 13540
       Fort Pierce, FL 34979
       800-766-7633
       Fax 800-878-3613
       www.lbg.org
       email: info@lbg.org

1235   McGuire Industries
       772 Washburn Road #B
       Melbourne, FL 32934
       http://fundraising.webshq.com/show.
          php3?Which=689874

1236   Mickman Bros. Nurseries
       14630 Highway 65
       Anoka, MN 55304
       763-434-4047
       Fax 763-434-4611

1237   Music Rewards Fundraising
       2103 Stratford Court, Suite 1NE
       Highlands Ranch, CO 80126
       800-770-0458
       www.raisemoremoney.com/contact/
          index.htm

MusicFundraising.com *see* FundraisingDi-
rect.com

1238   Music-T's
       1031 Eastgate
       Midlothian, TX 76065
       800-587-4287
       www.music-ts.com

1239   Musitoods (apparel)
       512 River Trace Cove
       Marion, AR 72364
       888-687-9327
       Fax 870-739-3333
       www.musitoods.com
       email: bandtshirts@musitoods.com

Nestle-Beich Candies *see* Kathryn Beich

1240   Old Time Coffee Company
       7960 Soquel Drive, Suite B-360
       Aptos, CA 95003-3972
       800-498-7070
       Fax 408-920-0495
       www.oldtimecoffee.net/fundraising.
          html
       email: info@oldtimecoffee.net

1241   Open Option Inc.
       590 Plutarch Road
       Highland, NY 12528-2912
       845-255-7439
       http://fundraising.webshq.com/show.
          php3?Which=689870

1242   Pacific West Marketing
       20 Ana Capri
       Laguna Nigel, CA 92677
       949-363-9129
       Fax 949-363-8429
       www.pacificwestmarketing.com
       email: Ed@Pacificwestmarketing.com

1243   PackJam.com
       866-722-5526
       www.packjam.com

1244   Parker Indian River Groves
       P.O. Box 1208
       Vero Beach, FL 32961-1208
       888-544-3871
       Fax 865-591-8882
       www.citrusfruit.com/fund.htm
       email: info@citrusfruit.com

1245   Partners Coffee Company
       4225 Westfield Drive S.W.
       Atlanta, GA 30336-2651

Penns Grove High School Red Devil Marching Band (Penns Grove, NJ)

404-344-5282
http://fundraising.webshq.com/show.
    php3?Which=689861

1246 Pennsylvania Dutch Funnel Cake
    Company
P.O. Box 35
Sewell, NJ 08080
856-629-9936
Fax 856-629-9937
www.funnelcake.net
email: funnelman@funnelcake.net

1247 Personal Touch Fundraising, Inc.
P.O. Box 355
Kershaw, SC 29067
866-475-9244
Fax 803-475-4201
http://members.tripod.com/ptfund
    raising/id6_m.htm
email: bet@camden.net
1248 Profit Potentials

800-597-0416
www.profitpotentials.com

1249 Quality Citrus Packs (California)
800-684-6000
www.qualitycitruspacks.com

1250 Quality Direct
c/o Patty Merritt
P.O. Box 7004
Springfield, IL 62791

1251 Rada Mfg. Co.
P.O. Box 838
905 Industrial Street
Waverly, IA 50677
800-311-9691
Fax 800-311-9623
www.radamfg.com
email: customerservice@radamfg.com

1252 Revere Fundraising
P.O. Box 751

Montgomery, AL 36101
800-876-9967
Fax 334-273-4688
email: reverefundraising@mindspring.
com

1253 Riversweet Citrus
11350 66th Street North, Suite 102
Largo, FL 33773-5524
800-741-0004
Fax 727-545-5367
www.riversweet.com

1254 Ross Galleries, Inc. (art auctions, ad
books, raffles)
761-D Coates Avenue
Holbrook, NY 11741
631-471-6700
email: robert@rossgalleries.com

1255 Sherwood Forest Farms
1900 North Northlake Way, Suite 135
Seattle, WA 98103
800-767-7778
Fax 206-545-7888
www.sherwoodforestfarms.com
email: sherwood@sherwoodforest
farms.com

1256 Sport Supply Group
1901 Diplomat Drive
Farmers Branch, TX 75234
800-774-6972
www.officialfundraising.com
email: dparks@sportsupplygroup.com

1257 Sportdecals
P.O. Box 358
Crystal Lake, IL 60039
800-435-6110
Fax 800-557-3322
www.sportdecals.com
email: sports@sdind.com

1258 Sunshine Selections Inc.
555 Stowe Avenue
Baldwin, NY 11510
516-378-7295
http://fundraising.webshq.com/show.
php3?Which=689868

1259 Sunsweet Fruit, Inc.
P.O. Box 2120
Vero Beach, FL 32960
561-569-1234
Fax 561-562-0302

1260 Supreme Citrus, Inc.
P.O. Box 828
Mission, TX 78572

1261 Team Sale Company
903 Northern Avenue
Signal Mountain, TN 37377-2848
423-886-6721
http://fundraising.webshq.com/show.
php3?Which=689876

1262 Thomas Fund Raising (candles,
cheesecake, cookies, fudge, steaks)
2119 Kermit Highway
Odessa, TX 79761
800-583-7858
Fax 915-333-2619
www.thomasfundraising.com

1263 Tomoro Fundraising
25 Van Dyke Avenue
New Brunswick, NJ 08901
800-777-1189, x21
Fax 732-296-8919
www.tomorro.com
email: cynthia@tomorro.com

1264 Tom-Wat (cheese, Christmas ornaments, dolls, nuts, wrapping paper)
185 Plains Road
Milford, CT 06460
800-243-9250, x625
www.tomwat.com
email: sales@tomwat.com

1265 Tootsie Roll Industries, Inc.
Chicago, IL 60629
www.tootsie.com

1266 TPC (Thomas Proestler Company)
Cash & Carry (cakes and pies, Fan-
nie May candy, pizza)
309-787-4041, x176

Archbishop Ryan High School Marching Band (Philadelphia, PA)

www.tpcinfo.com/cashcarry/fundrais
ing.html

1267 Tri-State Sales Inc.
494 Elm Street
Manchester, NH 03109
603-668-0505
http://fundraising.webshq.com/show.
php3?Which=689865

1268 Troll Book Fairs Corporation
604 Airpark Center Drive
Nashville, TN 37217-2923
615-367-9145
http://fundraising.webshq.com/show.
php3?Which=689872

1269 World's Finest Chocolate, Inc.
4801 South Lawndale
Chicago, IL 60632-3062
800-932-3863
www.wfchocolate.com

Association

1270 Association of Fund Raising Distributors and Suppliers
5775 Peachtree-Dunwoody Road,
Bldg. G, Suite 500
Atlanta, GA 30342
404-252-3663
www.afrds.org

Selected Bibliography

Articles

1271 Booker, Roderick. "Free Trips for Students with Stunning Sub Sales." Instrumentalist (June 2000): 38, 40, 42.

1272 Cornock, Ruth. "Fund-Raising Tips for
Bands on the Move." Instrumental-
ist (October 1983): 58, 60–62.

1273 Darnall, Josiah. "Fund-Raising Ideas
Ripe for the Picking." Instrumentalist (April 1987): 27–28, 30.

1274 "Fundraising: Community-Friendly
Fundraising." School Band and Orchestra (June 2002): 44–47.

1275 Laich, Ralph. "You Don't Stumble
Over Mountains." School Musician,
Director & Teacher (December
1982): 6–9.

1276 Neiman, Marcus L. "Fund-raising
Without Fruit." Instrumentalist (July
1996): 36, 38, 40.

1277 Nortrup, Megan, and Warren Haston.
"Three Fundraising Programs That
Generate Big Profits." Instrumen-
talist (June 2001): 28, 30, 32.

1278 Rohner, James M. "Fundraising for
Fun and Very Large Profits." Instrumentalist (December 1994): 12–17.

1279 Tubbs, Ann Marie. "What a Way to
Make a Buck." Instrumentalist (January 1982): 82.

Books

1280 Arledge, Rick, and David Friedman.
Dynamic Fund Raising Projects.
Chicago: Precept Press, 1998.

1281 Brownrigg, W. Grant. *Effective Corpo-
rate Fundraising.* New York, NY:
American Council for the Arts,
1982.

1282 Edles, L. Peter. *Fundraising: Hands-on
Tactics for Nonprofit Groups.* New
York: McGraw-Hill., 1992.

1283 Flanagan, Joan. *Successful Fundraising:
A Complete Handbook for Volunteers*

and Professionals. New York: McGraw-Hill, 1999.

1284 Keegan, P. Burke. *Fundraising for Non-Profits.* New York: HarperCollins, 1994.

1285 Schaff, Terry, and Doug Schaff. *The Fundraising Planner: A Working Model for Raising the Dollars You Need.* San Francisco: Jossey-Bass, 1999.

Part 5
Indoor Guard

"They're very strong," said one mother about her teenage daughter's indoor guard squad. Strength, stamina, agility, fluidity: These are the elements participants in the "sport of the arts" must possess. And speed. The modern competitive indoor color guard is more often than not a rapidly moving collection of agile, enthusiastic, even aggressive performers versed in dance and equipment handling skill. Some independent guards have no off-season but practice in elementary school gymnasiums throughout the summer. And although the season doesn't begin until January, tryouts normally are held in the fall.

Indoor guard, also known as winter guard, occasionally indoor cavalcade, is a gymnasium competition that takes place in winter and spring and involves junior and senior high school, college, and independent units. For some, indoor guard is an opportunity for the band front (flags, sabers, rifles) to maintain and hone skills during the off-season. For others, indoor is an exciting and challenging activity in its own right. Sometimes twirling squads are part of "indoor."

Indoor guard shows generally begin with sophisticated percussion unit competitions. There are also percussion-only contests. Whether concert (standing) or moving, percussion competition has gained in popularity, and units often incorporate sets and even members of the school's color guard for background color and general effect.

Color guards perform intricate—and frequently dangerous—routines to pre-recorded music: rock, opera, movie, Broadway. All musical genres are grist for the mill, from tributes to film director Stanley Kubrick to a recreation of Alice in Wonderland *to the knights of Arthurian legend.*

Dance training is evident in the balletic and jazz moves of many units. De rigueur for more and more units are portable floors: vinyl tarps spread atop the gym's playing area. This is not mandated by the schools to protect the hardwood or parquet (except perhaps when Bishop Kearney High School intentionally spilled paint and crashed through stunt windows). Rather, the portable floor—the Henderson High School crew calls theirs "The Beast"—gives traction and provides a decorated background complementing the show's theme. Colorful vertical backdrops frame the performers who use flags, rifles, and sabers but also props deemed appropriate to the show: beds on wheels, chimneys spouting dry ice smoke, plywood saloons and locomotives, full-scale gazebos, theater marquees, and paddlewheel steamships, painted or foil-covered Celotex or Tyvek insulation panels, mirrors, tables with checkerboard covers recreating an Italian restaurant, a thirty-foot multi-media violin. Cheap props include rakes, children's hockey sticks, bar stools, folding chairs, and plastic milk boxes nailed to wood to create light platforms.

Associations

1286 All American Judges Association
      P.O. Box 5324
      Hickory, NC 28603
      www.employees.org/~mrogers/CAA/
          judge.html

1287 American Drum Line Association
      (Southern California and the Southwest)
      909-270-0670
      www.amdrumassn.org

1288 Atlantic Indoor Association
      c/o Bob Nicholson,
          President
      P.O. Box 2791
      Springfield, VA 22152
      202-986-7758
      www.atlanticindoor.org
      email: bob@atlanticindoor.org

Auxiliary Dance Alliance *see* TADA

Apex Indoor Guard (Wilmington, DE)

1289 California Color Guard Circuit
c/o Dee Ariza
649 Enos Court
Santa Clara, CA 95051
408-244-4949
Fax 408-244-1670
www.geocities.com/cal_cg_circuit
email: deeguard@ix.netcom.com

1290 Canadian Winter Guard Association
P.O. Box 52288
311-16th Avenue NE
Calgary, Alberta T2E 8K9
Canada
403-710-5890
www.winterguard.ca/contact.htm
email: cwa@calgarywinterguard.com

Carolina All American Judges Association *see*
All American Judges Association

1291 Carolina Indoor Performance Association
c/o Larry McCarter, CIPA Director
864-268-9208
www.cipaonline.org
email: bmccarter@cipaonline.org

1292 Carolina Winter Ensemble Association
www.cwea.us
email: cwea@triad.rr.com

1293 Cavalcade Indoor Association (CIA)
c/o Hugh Williamson
Daniel Boone High School
501 Chestnut Street
Birdsboro, PA 19508
610-582-6100, x141
Fax 610-582-5400
www.cavalcadeofbands.com
email: williams@dboone.k12.pa.us

1294 Cecq
c/o Ginette Ringuette
762 Boulevard
Samson Laval, Quebec H7X 1K1
Canada

1295 Color Guard Netherlands (CGN)
www.colorguard.org/en/main.html
email: info@colorguard.org

Continental Divide Color Guard Circuit *see*
Rocky Mountain Color Guard Association

1296 Eastern Massachusetts Association
c/o Harry Sampson
8 Highland Avenue
Stoneham, MA 02180-1870
781-438-3631

1297 Florida Federation of Cologuards Circuit
P.O. Box 888
Lake City, FL 32056-0888
www.ffcc.org

1298 The Guard Network (website)
c/o Encore Business Network
409 Cameron Circle, Suite 1815
Chattanooga, TN 37402
423-267-8610
www.guardnetwork.com
email: Encore_biz_net@guardnetwork.
com

1299 Gulfcoast Color Guard and Percussion
Circuit
c/o Wilbur Campbell, Executive Director
850-866-6693 (cell)
www.gcgc.org
email: wilbur@gcgc.org or wcampbell
@panacom.com
Western Circuit
c/o Charlie Hernandez
504-472-0251
email: charlie@gcgc.org

1300 Heartland Indoor Drill Association
(HCGA; Iowa, Nebraska, South Dakota)
email: kmoreh00@connectseward.org

1301 Indiana High School Color Guard Association (IHSCGA)
c/o Lee Gibson, Vice President

South Plainfield High School Silver Dreams Indoor Guard (South Plainfield, NJ)

207½ Crane Drive
Crawfordsville, IN 47933
812-448-2661
www.ihscga.org
email: med@clay.k12.in.us

1302 Judges Association of Mid-America
(JAMA)
4104 Trail Road
Lawrence, KS 66049
785-843-6587
www.jamahome.org
email: Simon@jamahome.org

1303 Keystone Indoor Drill Association (PA
and MD; includes drumline and majorette)
c/o Doug Gardner, President
717-338-9652
www.kida.org
email: dgardner@graphcom.com

1304 Massachusetts Judges Association
c/o Patricia Labillios
14 Semont Road
Dorchester, MA 02125
http://massjudges.homestead.com

1305 Metro American Adjudicators (M.A.A.)
c/o Paul Bongiovi
Winter Guard Coordinator
2416 Summit Terrace
Linden, NJ 07036-4930
www.maaemba.org/winterguard.htm
e-mail: maawinterguard@aol.com

1306 Metropolitan American Associates/
EMBA Color Guard
c/o Matthew Cornelisse
336 Standish Avenue
Hackensack, NJ 07601

1307 Michigan Color Guard Circuit (MCGC)
c/o Kari Lynn Clark, MCGC Secretary
2623 Hartline
Rochester Hills, MI 48309
www.mcgc.net
email: secretary@mcgc.net

1308 Mid-America Performing Arts Association (MAPAA; Arkansas, Okla-
homa, Texas)
Oklahoma City, OK
www.geocities.com/broadway/orche
stra/6615/index.html

1309 Mid-Atlantic Indoor Network (M.A.I.N.)
c/o Ginny Kraft
www.geocities.com/main_guards/
home.html

1310 Mid-Continent Color Guard Association (MCCGA; Arkansas, Illinois,
Iowa, Kansas, Missouri)
c/o Ann Duncan
8170 Halsey
Lenexa, KS 66215
www.mccga.org
e-mail: mccga@mccga.org

1311 Mid-East Performance Association
(MEPA)
c/o Josh Johnson, MEPA Coordinator
118 Westpark Road
Dayton, OH 45459
937-434-1121
Fax 937-434-0356
email: mepacgc@fjminc.com

1312 Midwest Color Guard Circuit
c/o Howie Mogil, President
621 North Clinton Street
River Forest, IL 60305
630-455-4473
Fax 630-455-2158
www.midwestcolorguard.com
email: mogil@viskase.com

1313 Mid-York Color Guard Circuit
c/o Dan Jones, President
www.homestead.com/midyork/midy
ork.html
email: jam6700@superior.net

1314 National Judges Association (related
to Tournament Indoor Association)
c/o Dom Fulginiti

703 Roberts Street
Mechanicsburg, PA 17055

1315 New England Scholastic Band Association
c/o Richard Rigolini, Winter Activities Director
257 Main Street
Everett, MA 02149
617-381-0505
www.nesba.org

1316 North East Colorguard Circuit (Western NY, Southern OH, Northern PA)
c/o Allen Buell, Vice President
585-271-3361, x222
http://necgc.tripod.com

1317 North Star Circuit of Colorguards (MN, WI, IA)
c/o Brian Johnson, President
North Star Circuit
P.O. Box 14735
Minneapolis, MN 55414
www.northstarcircuit.org/index.html
email: information@northstarcircuit.org

1318 North Texas Color Guard Association
c/o Melinda Wemhoff, President
10185 Slick Rock Terrace
Frisco, TX 75034
www.ntca-wgi.org
email: mwemhoff@ntca-wgi.org

1319 Northern California Band Association Winter Circuit
c/o Kris Harper
Cupertino High School
10100 Finch Avenue
Cupertino, CA 95014
www.ncbaonline.org

1320 Northwest Pageantry Association
c/o Tiffany Osterling, President
www.nwpageantry.org
email: tkostling@yahoo.com

Ohio Color Guard Circuit *see* Mid-East Performance Association

1321 Oklahoma Color Guard Circuit
c/o Larry Shockley
4005 Stonebridge Circle
Yukon, Oklahoma 73099-3215

1322 Ontario Drum Corps Association (ODCA)
c/o Bill Faulds
1176 Christina Street North
Sarnia, Ontario N7V 3C3
877-634-6322
Fax 519-336-8307
www.odca.org
email: odca@golden.net

1323 Pennsylvania Federation of Contest Judges
c/o Pennsylvania Interscholastic Marching Band Association
Tom Snyder, PIMBA President
West Allegheny High School
205 West Allegheny Road
Imperial, PA 15126
www.pimba.org

1324 Pep & Pageantry Arts Association of Central California
www.ppaacc.com

1325 Rocky Mountain Color Guard Association
c/o Kendra Sparks
303-470-4940

1326 San Joaquin Color Guard Association
c/o Bruce Morow/Clovis School District
1450 Herndon Avenue
Clovis, CA 93611-0567

1327 South Florida Winter Guard Association
c/o Kathy Porter, President
954-463-6359 (Circuit Administrator)
www.sfwga.org/contact_page.html

Upper Darby High School Indoor Guard (Drexel Hill, PA)

1328   Southeastern Color Guard Circuit
       c/o Brian Giddens, Circuit President
       4867 Ashford Dunwoody Road
       Dunwoody, GA 30338
       770-512-8681
       http://scgconline.org

1329   Southern California Color Guard As-
       sociation
       c/o Noreen Roberts
       16401 Golden Gate
       Huntingdon Beach, CA 92649
       or: Lee Carlson
       31-120 Avenida El Mundo
       Cathedral City, CA 92234

1330   TADA (The Auxiliary Dance Alliance)
       P.O. Box 336732
       Greeley, CO 80634
       http://tadaonline.com
       email: info@tadaonline.com

1331   Texas Color Guard Circuit
       P.O. Box 304
       Dickinson, TX 77539-0304
       281-554-7479
       Fax 281-557-2469
       www.texascolorguardcircuit.org

1332   Texas Educational Color Guard Asso-
       ciation (T.E.C.A.)
       c/o Ed Gonzales, T.E.C.A. Secretary
       2551 Loop 337 North
       New Braunfels, TX 78130
       830-625-3800
       Fax 830-625-9453

1333   Three Rivers Winter Ensemble Asso-
       ciation (TRWEA)
       c/o Marcie Mains
       1960 Eden Park Blvd.
       McKeesport, PA 15132
       412-664-3650
       www.homestead.com/TRWEA/con
       tact~main.html

1334   Tournament Indoor Association (TIA)
       (includes percussion, twirling)
       c/o Donna Stout
       1216 W. Woodlawn
       Whitehall, PA 18052
       610-439-3760
       www.tob.org

1335   Tri-State Circuit for the Pageantry Arts
       (Indiana, Kentucky, Ohio; includes
       percussion)
       c/o Tom Acheson, President
       517 E. Main Street
       Alexandria, KY 41001
       859-635-7006
       www.nacnet.org/tristate

1336   Winter Guard Association of South-
       ern California
       c/o Amy Mack, Circuit Administrator
       651 Third Avenue, Suite C
       Chula Vista, CA 91910
       619-476-9225
       Fax 619-422-3740
       www.wgasc.org

1337   Winter Guard International
       7755 Paragon Road, Suite 104
       Dayton, OH 45459-4044
       937-434-7100
       Fax 937-434-6825
       www.wgi.org
       email: office@wgi.org

1338   Winter Guard International Europe
       www.wgieurope.org

1339   Winterguard Arizona
       c/o Alice Hays, President
       www.geocities.com/wgarizona
       email: Richnal@extremezone.com

1340   Winterguard United Kingdom (WGUK)
       (organized by Drum Corps United
       Kingdom)
       www.wguk.org.uk
       email: sec@wguk.org.uk

Percussion Associations

Note: percussion is often covered by the color guard circuit associations.

1341 California Percussion Circuit
Riverside, CA
1342 Central Iowa Percussion
Ankeny, IA

1343 Indiana Percussion
Indianapolis, IN

1344 MCA Winter Activities Circuit
Brooklyn, MI

1345 Minnesota Percussion Association
Waite Park, MN

1346 Musical Arts Conference
Stamford, CT

1347 Percussion Arts Society
Houston, TX

1348 Rocky Mountain Percussion Association
c/o Mike Nevin, President
www.rmpa.org/staff.asp
email: symmen@home.com or rmpa@oneimage.com

1349 Southern California Percussion Alliance
c/o Pete Ellison, President
http://sc-pa.org/contacts.html
email: pellison@sc-pa.org

Band Front and Color Guard Equipment

1350 The Band Hall
P.O. Box 100855
Nashville, TN 37224-0855
615-252-0855
Fax 615-252-2269
www.thebandhall.com

1351 Band Mans Company
3328 Towerwood Drive
Dallas, TX 75234
800-527-2214
www.bandmans.com
email: sales@bandmans.com

1352 Bernie Roe & Associates (includes batons, buttons, flags, percussion, rifles, t-shirts)
P.O. Box 4525
Ithaca, NY 14852
607-257-2834
Fax 607-257-6158
www.lightlink.com/roe

1353 Designs by King (floors, rifles, sabres)
29 Corte Palazzo

Lake Elsinore, CA 92532
909-245-1080
www.designsbyking.com
email: Sales@designsbyking.com

1354 Electra Tarp, Inc. (floor covers)
2900 Perry Drive S.W.
Canton, OH 44706
800-274-1003
Fax 330-477-7702
www.electratarp.com
email: etarp2900@aol.com

1355 Encore Flags
c/o The Guard Network/Encore Business Network
409 Cameron Circle, Suite 1815
Chattanooga, TN 37402
423-267-8610
www.guardnetwork.com/encore_flags
email: encore_flags@guardnetwork.com

1356 The Guard Gear Company
510 Saddlebrook Drive #134

Chichester High School Indoor Guard (Boothwyn, PA)

San Jose, CA 95136
408-236-2093
Fax 707-248-2141
email: ThinkKarma.aol.com

1357 George Miller & Sons
209 E. Church Street
Blackwood, NJ 08012
609-227-1495
Fax 609-227-6924

1358 Peacock's Marching World (includes
maces, batons)
1251 North Tustin Avenue
Anaheim, CA 92807-1603
714-630-7077
Fax 714-630-7241
www.marchingworld.com
email: peacocksmw@aol.com

1359 The Sabre Line
www.sabreline.net

1360 SEFCO Plumes
Division, Kerr's Music World
911 Bigley Avenue
Charleston, WV 25302

1361 Under the Sun Productions (choreography plus flags, fabrics, neck coolers, color guard jackets, fundraising)
882 South Matlack Street, Suite 202
West Chester, PA 19382
800-264-1121
Fax 610-431-6511
http://members.aol.com/utsp2/index.
html
e-mail: undersunpr@aol.com

1362 WinterGarb
1089 Third Avenue, SW #300A
Carmel, IN 46032
800-796-8731
http://wintergarb.com/header.htm
email: estephenieinc@aol.com

Selected Bibliography

Articles

1363 Biondi, Christopher, and Tom Kennedy. "Pizza, Hoagies Rushed to
Stranded Students." *Daily Local News*
[West Chester, PA], March 14, 1993,
pp. A1, A4.

1364 Burns, Caroline. "Field of View Likes
Competing." *Daily Local News* [West
Chester, PA], April 12, 1993, p. A5.
includes two photos.

1365 Dyroff, Denny. "A Spectacle of Music
and Color." *Daily Local News Weekender* [West Chester, PA], July 19,
2002, pp. 3, 7. review of *Blast!*

1366 Fuller, John. "The Flag Corps." *School
Musician, Director & Teacher* (June/
July 1979): 36–39, 46.

1367 Holston, Kim. "They Call It Indoor
Guard." *Twirl* (June/July/August
1980): 16.

1368 Kachin, Denise Breslin. "Amid All That
White, a Parade of Color." *Philadelphia Inquirer*, March 21, 1993, p. CC6.

1369 Kennedy, Tom. "WCU Color Guard
Team Shines in International Show."
Daily Local News [West Chester, PA],
March 23, 1992, pp. A1, B1. Includes
three photos (Tsunami Blue, Phoe-
nix, Field of View)

1370 Masoner, Betty L. "The Guard—With
Color." *School Musician, Director &
Teacher* (May 1981): 18–20.

1371 Meagher, Marlene. "Effective Flags—
A Basic Approach." *Instrumentalist*
(March 1985): 38–40.

1372 Merle, Renae. "What's a Billionaire to Do When He Gets Tired of the Stent Biz?" *Wall Street Journal*, April 19, 2001, p. 1, Ar. [about *Blast!* on Broadway]

1373 Pfeifle, Morell. "The Color Guard." *School Musician, Director & Teacher* (May 1978): 55, 59.

1374 "Points on Painting Your Floor." *Focus* (December, 1999): 12.

1375 Sagen, Dwayne P. "Flags That Visualize Music." *Instrumentalist* (October 1977): 49–54.

Periodicals

1376 *DanceSpirit* (10 issues/yr.)
P.O. Box 2041
Marion, OH 43306-2141
212-265-8890
dancespirit.com
covers WGI championships

1377 *Focus* (3 times/yr.)
Winter Guard International
7755 Paragon Road, Suite 104
Dayton, OH 45459-4044
www.wgi.org

Books

1378 Alfred Publishing Company. *Championship Auxiliary Units.* Sherman Oaks, CA, 1979.

1379 Holston, Kim. *Spin!* Lincoln, NE: Writer's Club Press/iUniverse.com, 2002. [teenage novel with indoor guard backdrop]

1380 Winter Guard International. *2003 WGI Color Guard Adjudication Manual and Rulebook.* Wheat Ridge, CO.

1381 _____. *2003 WGI Percussion Adjudication Manual and Rulebook.* Wheat Ridge, CO.

Videos

1382 Marcocci, Todd. *World of Dance Video.* Ft. Wayne, IN: Marching Show Concepts.

1383 _____. *World of Flags Video.* Ft. Wayne, IN: Marching Show Concepts.

1384 _____. *World of Rifle Video.* Ft. Wayne, IN: Marching Show Concepts.

1385 _____. *World of Sabre Video.* Ft. Wayne, IN: Marching Show Concepts.

1386 Winter Guard International. *Advanced Body and Equipment.* Wheat Ridge, CO.

1387 _____. *The Band Front-Visual Musician.* Wheat Ridge, CO.

1388 _____. *Creating Effect.* Wheat Ridge, CO.

1389 _____. *Equipment—The Next Step.* Wheat Ridge, CO.

1390 _____. *A Guide to Expressive Efforts and Equipment Principles.* Wheat Ridge, CO.

1391 _____. *Instructor's Guide to Flag Technique.* Wheat Ridge, CO.

1392 _____. *Instructor's Guide to Movement Fundamentals.* Wheat Ridge, CO.

1393 _____. *Instructor's Guide to Rifle Technique.* Wheat Ridge, CO.

1394 _____. *Instructor's Guide to Sabre Technique.* Wheat Ridge, CO.

1395 _____. *Instructor's Guide to Staging and Design.* Wheat Ridge, CO.

1396 _____. *Intermediate Body and Equipment*. Wheat Ridge, CO.

1397 _____. *An Introduction to Percussion Ensembles*. Wheat Ridge, CO.

1398 _____. *An Introduction to Winter Guard*. Wheat Ridge, CO.

1399 _____. *The Language of Visual Design*. Wheat Ridge, CO.

Part 6
Military Bands

Directory

1400 Admiral Farragut Academy
501 Park Street North
St. Petersburg, FL 33710
727-384-5500
Fax 727-347-5160
www.farragut.org
email: admissions@farragut.org

1401 Air National Guard (ANG) Band of the
Great Lakes
Attn: Operations Manager
Ohio Air National Guard
2660 South Eber Road
Swanton, OH 43558-9645
419-8684149
www.ohband.ang.af.mil

1402 ANG Band of the Mid-Atlantic
553rd Air Force Band
81 Constellation Court
Middletown, PA 17057-5086
www.paharr.ang.af.mil/553Home.htm

1403 ANG Band of the Northeast
50 Maple Street
Milford, MA 01757
888-301-3103, x7871
Fax 508-233-7882
www.567band.org/contact.asp

1404 ANG Band of the Northwest (560th
Air Force Base)
Fairchild Air Force Base
Spokane, WA 99011
800-344-7034

1405 ANG Band of the Smoky Mountains
(572nd Air Force Band)
McGhee Tyson ANG Base
Knoxville, TN 37701
865-985-3209
www.572tangband.org
email: lengland@wnclink.com

1406 ANG Band of the Southwest (562nd
Air Force Band)
107 Mulcahy Drive

Port Hueneme, CA 93041-4013
805-986-7880
www.calguard.ca.gov/562afband/en
sembles.htm

1407 Armed Forces School of Music
Naval Amphibious Base (Little Creek)
Norfolk, VA 23521-5240
www.eustis.army.mil/som

1408 Army and Navy Academy
P.O. Box 3000
Carlsbad, CA 84647
760-729-2385, x400
www.studyusa.com/boarding/fact
shts/armynavy.htm

1409 Band of the U.S. Air Force Reserve
550 Allentown Road
Robins AFB, GA 31098-2252
478-327-0555
www.afrc.af.mil/ha/band/default.htm

1410 Benedictine Military School
6502 Seawright Drive
Savannah, GA 31406

1411 Camden Military Academy
5201 Highway 1, North
Camden, SC 29020
800-948-6291
www.camdenmilitary.com
email: admissions@camdenmilitary.
com

1412 Carson Long Military Institute (has
drum and bugle corps)
P.O. Box 98-DD
New Bloomfield, PA 17068
717-582-2121
Fax 717-582-8763
www.carsonlong.org
email: carson6@pa.net

1413 The Citadel
171 Moultrie Street
Charleston, SC 29409

Washington Township High School Minuteman Marching Band (Sewell, NJ)

843-953-5000
www.citadel.edu
email: webmaster@citadel.edu

1414 Culver Military Academy
Culver Educational Foundation
1300 Academy Road
Culver, IN 46511-1291
574-842-7000
www.culver.org

1415 Department of the Army Staff Bands
Office
PERSCOM (TAPC-PDZ-B)
Alexandria, VA 22331-0474
703-325-4472

1416 Fishburne Military School
225 South Wayne Avenue
Waynesboro, VA 22980-0277
800-946-7773
www.fishburne.org/band.htm

1417 Florida Air Academy
1950 South Academy Drive
Melbourne, FL 32901
321-723-3211
www.flair.com
email: admissions@flair.com

1418 Fork Union Military Academy
P.O. Box 3212
Fork Union, VA 23055
434-842-3212
Fax 434-842-4300
www.fuma.org
email: akers@fuma.org

1419 Georgia Military College
201 East Greene Street
Milledgeville, GA 31061
800-342-0413
www.gmc.cc.ga.us

1420 Hargrave Military Academy
200 Military Drive
Chatham, VA 24531
434-432-3129
Fax 434-432-3129
www.hargrave.edu

1421 Howe Military School
P.O. Box 240
Howe, IN 46746
www.howemilitary.com

1422 Kemper Military School
701 Third Street
Boonville, MO 65233
800-530-5600
Fax 660-882-3332
www.kemper.org
email: enroll@kemper.org

1423 Lyman Ward Military Academy
P.O. Drawer 550
Camp Hill, AL 36850
256-896-4127
www.lwma.org
email: info@lwma.org

1424 Marine Corps Logistics Base Marine
Band Ceremonial Band
814 Radford Blvd.
Albany, GA 31704-1128
800-952-3352
www.ala.usmc.mil/base
email: mbmatcomcustsvs@matcom.
usmc.mil

1425 Marine Military Academy
320-P Iwo Jima Blvd.
Harlingen, TX 78550
956-423-6006, x251
Fax 956-423-4251
www.mma-tx.org
email: admissions@mma-tx.org

1426 Marion Military Institute
1101 Washington Street
Marion, AL 36756
800-MMI-1842
www.marion-institute.org

1427 Marmion Academy
1000 Butterfield Road
Aurora, IL 60504
630-897-6936
Fax 630-897-7086
www.marmion.org/academy/music.
html#marching

1428 Massanutten Military Academy (band
& drum corps)
614 South Main Street
Woodstock, VA 22664
877-466-6222
www.militaryschool.com / military
school
email: webmaster@militaryschool.com

1429 Midshipman Drum and Bugle Corps
U.S. Naval Academy
Annapolis, MD 21402
www.usna.edu / USNADB / History.htm
email: drumbug@nadn.navy.mil

1430 Missouri Military Academy
204 Grand Avenue
Mexico, MO 65265
888-564-6662
http: / / mma-cadet.org

1431 Navy Band Mid-South
5720 Integrity Drive
Millington, TN 38054-5015
901-874-5784
Fax 901-874-5020
www.bupers.navy.mil / navyband / main.
htm

1432 Navy Band Northwest
Director
1103A Hunley Road
Silverdale, WA 98315-1103
360-315-3447
Fax 360-315-3457
www.band-seattle.navy.mil
email: webmaster@NavyBandNorth
west

1433 New Mexico Military Institute
101 West College Blvd.
Roswell, NM 88201-5173
800-421-5376
www.nmmi.cc.nm.us

1434 New York Military Academy
78 Academy Avenue
Cornwell-On-Hudson, NY 12520
888-275-6962

Fax 845-534-7699
www.nyma.org
email: admissions@nyma.ouboces.org

1435 North Georgia College & State University
The Military College of Georgia
Dahlonega, GA 30579
706-864-1400
www.ngc.peachnet.edu / Military / ind
ex.htm

1436 Northwestern Military Academy Drum
and Bugle Corps
Lake Shore Drive
Lake Geneva, WI 53147

1437 Norwich University (regimental band
& drill team)
158 Harmon Drive
Northfield, VT 05663
800-468-6679
www.norwich.edu / default.htm
email: webmaster@norwich.edu

1438 Oak Ridge Military Academy
P.O. Box 498
Oak Ridge, NC 27310
336-643-4131, x148
Fax 336-643-1797
www.oakridgemilitary.com
email: ormilitary@aol.com

1439 132nd Army Band
2400 Wright Street
Madison, WI 52704-2572
608-242-3490
Fax 608-242-3494
www.bands.army.mil / guard / guard.as
p?UNITNAME=132AB

1440 Randolph-Macon Academy (Air Force
Jr. ROTC program)
200 Academy Drive
Front Royal, VA 22630
800-272-1172
www.rma.edu
email: admissions@rma.edu

William Penn High School Indoor Guard (New Castle, DE)

1441 Riverside Military Academy (Jr. ROTC program)
2001 Riverside Drive
Gainesville, GA 30501
800-GO-CADET
www.cadet.com

1442 St. John's College/HS (regimental band)
2607 Military Road
Washington, D.C. 20015
202-363-2316
Fax 202-686-5162
http://stjohns-chs.org/jrotc/jrotc.htm

1443   St. John's Military Academy
       1101 North Genesee Street
       Delafield, WI 53018
       800-SJ-CADET
       www.sjnma.org/default.asp
       email: admissions@sjnma.org

1444   St. John's Military School (drill and
       rifle teams)
       P.O. Box 827
       Salina, KS 67402-0827
       785-823-7231
       Fax 785-823-7236
       www.sjms.org
       email: scott@sjms.org

1445   SUNY Maritime College
       6 Pennyfield Avenue
       Throggs Neck, NY 10465
       800-642-1874
       www.sunymaritime.edu/core.makka

1446   Texas A & M University
       College Station, TX 77843
       800-TAMU-AGS
       www.aggiecorps.org/index.htm

1447   Texas Military Institute
       20955 West Tejas Trail
       San Antonio, TX 78257-1604
       210-698-7171
       www.tmi-sa.org

1448   312th U.S. Army Reserve Band
       2100 Iowa Street
       Lawrence, KS 66046-2541
       785-843-2189, x108
       Fax 785-331-1400
       www.midville.com/312

1449   U.S. Air Force Academy Drum and
       Bugle Corps ("The Flight of Sound")
       USAF Academy
       Colorado Springs, CO 80840
       719-333-2055
       email: Bill.Smith@USAFA.AF.mil

1450   U.S. Air Force Band ("America's Band")
       210 McChord Street
       Bolling Air Force Base

       Washington, DC 20332-0202
       202-767-4310
       Fax 202-767-0686
       www.bolling.af.mil/band
       email: bandpublicaffairs@bolling.af.mi

1451   U.S. Air Force Band of Flight
       3920 Lear Street
       Wright Patterson AFB, OH
       937-257-6526
       http://bandofflight.wpafb.af.mil/inde
       x.htm
       email:
       AFBF.webmaster@wpafb.af.mil

1452   U.S. Air Force Band of Liberty
       25 Chennault Street
       Hanscom AFB, MA 01731-1718
       781-377-7035
       www.hanscom.af.mil/ESC-BA

1453   U.S. Air Force Band of Mid-America
       900 Chapman Drive
       Scott AFB, IL 62225-5115
       618-229-8188
       Fax 618-229-0284
       www.bandofmid-america.com

1454   U.S. Air Force Band of the Pacific
       (PACAF)
       9477 Pease Avenue
       Elmendorf AFB, AK 99501-2380
       907-552-3081
       Fax 907-552-8179
       www.elmendorf.af.mil/units/band/
       index.htm
       email: katherine.nordeen@elmendorf.
       af.mil

1455   U.S. Air Force Band of the Pacific-
       Asia/BA
       Attn: Director of Operations
       Bldg. 4361 Unit 5075
       Yokota AB, Japan APO AP 96328
       (81)311-755-3218
       Fax (81)042-530-8049
       www.yokota.af.mil/orgs/tenant_unit
       s/band-of-the-pacific/Contact_Us.
       php

1456 U.S. Air Force Band of the Pacific-
Hawaii
340 Kuntz Avenue, Bldg. 1710
Hickam AFB, HI 96853
808-448-0281
Fax 808-448-4322

1457 U.S. Air Force Band of the Rockies
520 Otis Street
Peterson AFB, CO 80914-1620
719-556-9916
Fax 719-556-9963
www.bandoftherockies.com

1458 U.S. Air Force Band of the West
1680 Barnes Avenue
Lackland AFB, TX 78236-5500
210-671-3934
Fax 210-671-4186
www.lackland.af.mil/bow/

1459 U.S. Air Force Heartland of America
Band
109 Washington Square, Suite 111
Offutt AFB, NE 68113-2126
402-294-6046
Fax 402-294-4638
www.offutt.af.mil/Assoc_Units/Band
email: offutt.web.master@offutt.af.mil

1460 U.S. Air Forces in Europe Band
Sembach AFB, Germany
www.usafe.af.mil/direct/band
email: usafebandmail@semback.af.
mil

1461 U.S. Army Band ("Pershing's Own")
Public Affairs Office
204 Lee Avenue
Fort Myer, VA 22211-1199
800-223-3735, x6-0485 (Army Band Liaison)
www.army.mil/armyband

1462 U.S. Coast Guard Band
U.S. Coast Guard Academy
15 Mohegan Avenue
New London, CT 06320
860-701-6810

Fax 860-444-8475
www.cga.edu/band/default.html

1463 U.S. Continental Army Field Band
10 Bernard Road, Quinto Hall
Fort Monroe, VA 23651-1002
757-788-3620
www.tradoc.army.mil/band

1464 U.S. Marine Band ("The President's
Own")
Marine Barracks
8th & I Streets, S.E.
Washington, DC 20390-5000
202-433-5809 (Public Affairs Office)
www.marineband.usmc.mil/con_ind
ex.html

1465 U.S. Marine Drum & Bugle Corps ("The
Commandant's Own")
Marine Corps Recruiting Command Re
Attn: Musician Procurement Supervi-
sor
3280 Russell Road
Quantico, VA 22134-5103
202-433-2927
www.drumcorps.mbw.usmc.mil

1466 U.S. Merchant Marine Academy
Director of Music
300 Steamboat Road
Kings Point, NY 11024-1169
800-732-6267
www.usmma.edu/band/default.htm

1467 U.S. Military Academy Band
OIC Cadet Band
U.S. Military Academy
West Point, NY 10996
845-938-2617
www.usma.army.mil/band

1468 U.S. Naval Academy Band
U.S. Naval Academy
101 Buchanan Road
Annapolis, MD 21402-5080
410-293-1253
www.usna.edu/USNABand
email: pfabe@gwmail.usna.edu

1469 U.S. Naval Academy Drum and Bugle
Corps
Alumni Hall, 675 Decatur Road
U.S. Naval Academy
Annapolis, MD 21402-5086
email: weir@nadn.navy.mil

1470 The U.S. Navy Band
617 Warrington Avenue, S.E.
Washington Navy Yard, DC 20374-
5054
202-433-6090
Fax 202-433-4108
www.navyband.navy.mil
email: Public.Affairs@navyband.navy.
mil

1471 Valley Forge Military Academy & College

1001 Eagle Road
Wayne, PA 19087-3695
800-234-8362
Fax 610-688-1545
www.vfmac.edu
email: admissions@vfmac.edu

1472 Virginia Military Institute
Lexington, VA 24450
www.vmi.edu

1473 Wentworth Military Academy & Junior College
1880 Washington Avenue
Lexington, MO 64067
800-962-7682
Fax 660-259-2677
www.wma1880.org

Drill Teams

1474 Sports Network International (pro-
duces all-service drill contests, including National [Military] High
School Drill Team Championships)
775 Fentress Blvd.

Daytona Beach, FL 32114
386-274-1919
http://www.thenationals.net
email: drill@thenationals.net

Associations

1475 Alliance of North American Pipe Band
Associations
www.anapba.org

1476 Association of Military Colleges and
Schools of the United States
c/o Dr. Lewis Sorley
9429 Garden Court
Potomac, MD 20854-3964
301-765-0695
Fax 301-983-0583
www.amcsus.org

1477 Company of Fifers and Drummers
P.O. Box 277

Ivoryton, CT 06442-0277
860-767-2237
Fax 860-767-9765
http://companyoffifeanddrum.org
email: CompanyHQ@companyoffife
anddrum.org

1478 Corps of Drums Society
62 Gally Hill Road
Church Crookham
Hants. GU12 ORU
United Kingdom
www.soft.net.uk/corpsofdrums

1479 United States Drum-Majors Association (USDMA)

318½ Hyde Park, Suite "H"
Houston, TX 77006-3044
713-529-5989
http://usdma.freeyellow.com

816-756-3390
Fax 816-968-1149
www.vfw.org
email: info@vfw.org

1480 VFW (Veterans of Foreign Wars) National Headquarters
406 West 34th Street
Kansas City, MO 64111

1481 Western United States Pipe Band Association
www.wuspba.org
email: wuspbalist@wuspba.org

Museum

1482 The Museum of Fife & Drum
P.O. Box 277
Ivorytown, CT 06442
860-767-2237

http://copanyoffifeanddrum.org/museum.html
email: companyhq@companyoffifeand drum.org

Military Music Websites

1483 Ceremonial Music Online
www2.acc.af.mil/music/ceremonial

1484 March Music Online
www2.acc.af.mil/music/march

1485 Patriotic Music Online
www2.acc.af.mil/music/patriotic

1486 Songs of the U.S. Air Force
www.af.mil/accband/sounds/afsong.html

1487 Sounds of the Rockies (USAF Band of the Rockies)
www.bandoftherockies.com/media.htm

1488 Sounds of the USAF Reserve
www.afrc.af.mil/hq/band/recordings/default.htm

Selected Bibliography

Articles

1489 Allen, Mary. "They Know the Drill, 500 Students Strong: Competition Draws Junior ROTC Members from Four States." *News Journal* [Wilmington, DE], February 2, 2003, p. 81.

1490 Battisti, Frank. "The Marine Band Turns 200." *Instrumentalist* (December 1998): 90–91.

1491 Blair, Dennis K. "Music in the Military." *Instrumentalist* (November 1986): 54, 56.

1492 Cochran, Alfred W. "Military Bands—An Aid to Music Education." *Instrumentalist* (August 1984): 10.

1493 Garges, Alicia. "The Army Field Band." *Instrumentalist* (September 1998): 99.

1494 Maiello, Anthony J. "The Battle Over Military Bands." *Instrumentalist* (October 1992): 112.

1495 "Merchant Marine Cadets Hear Beat of a Different Drummer." *Journal of Commerce*, November 14, 1991, p. 10A.

1496 Modi, Sorab. "The United States Marine Band." *Ovation* (June 1989): 16–18, 80.

1497 Outerbridge, Laura. "Strike Up the Bands: Military Music Tradition Marches On." *Washington Times Weekend*, May 28, 1992, pp. M4, M5.

1498 Richards, William W. "Percussion in the Military." *Percussive Notes* (October 1984): 31–32.

1499 Schloesser, Dawn. "Military Bands: America's Music-Makers." *School Band and Orchestra* (May 2002): 40–42.

1500 "The U.S. Military Academy Band, West Point." *Instrumentalist* (December 1981): 26-27.

1501 Young, Amanda. "Music in the Military." *Music Educators Journal* (December 1981): 31–35, 54–56.

Books and Dissertations

1502 Adkins, H.E. *Treatise on the Military Band*. Rockville Centre, NY: Belwin, 1945.

1503 Carpenter, Kenneth William. *A History of the United States Marine Band*. [Ph.D. dissertation] Iowa City: University of Iowa, 1970. Excerpted in *ABA Journal of Band Research* (Spring 1971): 23–28.

1504 Cifaldi, Susan. *For Re-enactors Only: Revolutionary War Fife Tunes in the Company Music Books*. Ivoryton, CT: Company of Fifers & Drummers. ebook.

1505 Glasgow, William. *Exhibition Drills*. Harrisburg, PA: Military Service Publishing Company, 1958.

1506 Railsback, Thomas C., and John P. Langellier. *The Drums Would Roll: A Pictorial History of U.S. Army Bands on the American Frontier, 1866–1900*. New York: Sterling Publishing Company, 1988.

1507 United States Department of the Army. *The Marching Band*. Washington, D.C., 1957.

Film

1508 *Cadet Kelly*. Walt Disney Television. 2002.

Periodicals

1509 *The Mace*.
United States Drum-Majors Association
318½ Hyde Park, Suite "H"
Houston, TX 77006-3044

Part 7
Musicians, Instruments and Uniforms

Associations

Academy of Wind and Percussion Arts *see* National Band Association

1510 Alberta Band Association
#209, 14218 Stony Plain Road
Edmonton, AB T5N 3R3
Canada
877-687-4239
Fax 780-488-4132
www.musicalberta.com/aba.html
email: aba@musicalberta.com

1511 American Music Conference (to promote importance of music)
5790 Armada Drive
Carlsbad, CA 92008-4372
760-431-9124
Fax 760-438-7327
www.amc-music.com

1512 American Musical Instrument Society
8551 Research Way, Suite 180
Middleton, WI 53562
www.amis.org
608-836-9000

1513 British Columbia Band Association
c/o 21583 Glenwood Avenue
Maple Ridge, BC V2X 3P9
Canada
www.vcn.bc.ca/bcba

1514 Canadian Band Association Ontario
www.canadianbandassociation.ca/index.htm

1515 College of Piping
16-24 Otago Street
Glasgow G12 8JH
Scotland
United Kingdom
+44 (0) 141 334 3587
Fax +44 (0) 141 587 6068
www.college-of-piping.co.uk./html/contact.html
email: college@college-of-piping.com

1516 Federation des Harmonies du Quebec
c/o Pierre Mailhot Bur
400, Chemin Haskell Hill Rés
Sherbrooke, QC J1M 2A3
Canada
819-822-5455
www3.sk.sympatico.ca/skband/quebec.html

1517 International Clarinet Association
P.O. Box 5039
Wheaton, IL 60189
630-665-3602
Fax 630-665-3848
www.clarinet.org
email: membership@clarinet.org

1518 International Horn Society
8180 Thunder Street
Juneau, AK 99801
907-789-5477
Fax 907-790-4066
www.hornsociety.org
email: hvogel@gci.net

1519 International Trombone Association
College of Music
University of North Texas
P.O. Box 305338
Denton, TX 76203
817-565-2791
Fax 817-382-3435
www.ita-web.org

1520 International Trumpet Guild
Western Michigan University
School of Music
Kalamazoo, MI 49008
616-387-4700
www.trumpetguild.org
email: president@trumpetguild.org

1521 International Tuba-Euphonium Association
c/o Skip Gray
University of Kentucky
School of Music

Lexington, KY 40506-0022
www.iteaonline.org
email: president@iteaonline.org

1522 Manitoba Band Association
http://home.merlin.mb.ca/~mbband/
index.html

1523 MENC: The National Association for
Music Education
1806 Robert Fulton Drive
Reston, VA 20191
800-336-3768
Fax 703-860-1531
www.menc.org

1524 The Mr. Holland's Opus Foundation
Board of Directors & Advisory Council
15125 Ventura Blvd., Suite 204
Sherman Oaks, CA 91403
818-784-6787
Fax 818-784-6788
www.mhopus.org
email: info@mhopus.org

Music Educators National Conference *see*
MENC: The National Association for Music
Education

1525 Music Teachers National Association
441 Vine Street, Ste. 505
Cincinnati, OH 45202-2811
513-421-1420
Fax 513-421-2503
www.mtna.org
email: mtnanet@mtna.org

1526 National Association of Band Instrument Manufacturers
262 West 38th Street, Room 1506
New York, NY 10010-6906
212-302-0801
Fax 212-302-0783
email: assnhdqs@aol.com

1527 National Association of College Wind
and Percussion Instructors
Executive Secretary

Division of Fine Arts
Truman State University
Kirksville, MO 63501
http://nacwpi.org

1528 National Association of Music Merchants
5140 Avenida Encinas
Carlsbad, CA 92008-4391
www.namm.com

1529 National Association of Professional
Band Instrument Repair Technicians, Inc.
P.O. Box 51
Normal, IL 61761-0051
309-452-4257
Fax 309-452-4825
www.napbirt.org
email: napbirt@napbirt.org

1530 National Association of School Music
Dealers
13140 Colt Road, Ste. 320, LB 120
Dallas, TX 75244-5019
972-233-9107, x204
Fax 972-490-4219
www.nasmd.com

1531 National Association of Uniform Manufacturers and Distributors (sponsors
Best Dressed Bands Awards Program)
1156 Avenue of the Americas
New York, NY 10036
212-869-0670
Fax 212-575-2847
www.naumd.com
email: nyoffice@naumd.com

1532 National Band Association
P.O. Box 121292
Nashville, TN 37212
www.nationalbandassoc.org

1533 National Flute Association
c/o Phyllis T. Pemberton, Executive
Director
26951 Ruether Avenue, Ste. H
Santa Clara, CA 91351
661-299-4632

Fax 661-299-6681
www.nfaonline.org
email: nfacentral@compuserve.com

1534   New Brunswick Band Association
c/o Jennifer Hope, President
4-5 Miller Park Drive
Rothesay, NB E2E 2E5
Canada
506-849-7345
Fax 506-832-6054
www3.sk.sympatico.co/skband/new
brunswick.html
email: jhope@nbnet.nb.ca

1535   North American Saxophone Alliance
NASA Membership Director
School of Music
University of Iowa
Iowa City, IA 52242
www.saxalliance.org
email: kenneth-tse@uiowa.edu

1536   Nova Scotia Band Association
c/o Jim Forde, President

17 Coronet Avenue
Halifax, NS B3N 1L4
Canada
902-427-7501
Fax 902-427-7498
www3.sk.sympatico.ca/skband/nova
scotia.html
email: jimforde@psphalifax.ns.ca

1537   Percussive Arts Society
701 NW Ferris Avenue
Lawton, OK 73507-5442
580-353-1455
Fax 580-353-1456
www.pas.org
email: percarts@pas.org

1538   Saskatchewan Band Association
www.saskband.org/main/contacts.
html
email: sask.band@sk.sympatico.ca

Tubists Universal Brotherhood Association
see International Tuba-Euphonium Association

Music Fraternities and Sororities

1539   Kappa Kappa Psi National Honorary
Band Fraternity
P.O. Box 849
Stillwater, OK 74074
800-543-6505
Fax 405-372-2363
www.kkytbs.org
email: kkytbs@kkytbs.org

Modern Music Masters see Tri-M Music
Honor Society

1540   Tau Beta Sigma National Honorary
Band Sorority
P.O. Box 849
Stillwater, OK 74074
800-543-6505
Fax 405-372-2363

www.kkytbs.org
email: kkytbs@kkytbs.org

1541   Tri-M Music Honor Society
c/o Music Educators National Conference (MENC)
1806 Robert Fulton Drive
Reston, VA 20191
800-336-3768
Fax 703-860-1531
www.menc.org
or: DeWayne Roberson
Wisconsin State Tri-M Chair
Watertown Senior High School
825 Endeavor Drive
Watertown, WI 53098
920-262-7500, x3413
email: robersond@watertown.k12.
wi.us

Instrument Manufacturers and Distributors

The Yellow Pages of the telephone book will include local stores. Buy-sell newspapers and the internet are helpful for those seeking used instruments.

1542 Aberdeen Bagpipe Supply
P.O. Box 841918
Houston, TX 77284-1918
281-859-8546
Fax 281-463-2169
wwws.aberdeenbagpipe.com
email: aberdeen@wt.net

1543 Accent Music
5615 Concord Pike
Wilmington, DE 19803
877-3ACCENT
www.accentmusic.com
email: info@accentmusic.com
and: 5810-A Kirkwood Highway
Newark, DE 19808

Adams Musical Instruments *see* Pearl

1544 Adams Percussion
247 Red Clay Road #102
Laurel, MD 20724
301-362-0867
email: adamspercussion@netzero.net

1545 Allied Music Corporation
P.O. Box 288
Elkhorn, WI 53121

1546 Altus Flutes America, Inc.
600 South Lake Avenue, Suite 406
Pasadena, CA 91106
800-806-7965
Fax 626-844-9305
www.altusflutes.com
email: info@altusflutes.com

1547 American Way Marketing
4561 Pine Creek Road
Elkhart, IN 46515
219-295-6633

1548 Antigua Winds Inc.
5438 Stoneshire Drive
San Antonio, TX 78218

1549 Ardsley Musical Instrument Company
165 Broadway
Hastings-on-Hudson, NY 10706

1550 Armstrong Woodwinds
P.O. Box 787
Elkhart, IN 46515

1551 Artley Woodwinds
1000 Industrial Parkway
Elkhart, IN 46516

1552 Avedis Zildjian Co.
22 Longwater Drive
Norwell, MA 02061

Bach *see* Selmer Company

1553 The Band Company
231 North Main Street
Kernersville, NC 27284
336-993-7436
Fax 336-993-7846
email: thebandcompany@aol.com

1554 Band Instrument Service Company
1232 Harvestowne Industrial Drive
St. Charles, MO 63304
636-441-7707
Fax 636-922-0474
email: info@bandinstrumentservice.
com

1555 Bandstand, Inc.
9222 Broadway
Brookfield, IL 60513

1556 Barrington Music Products, Inc.
22159 N. Pepper Road
P.O. Box 550
Barrington, IL 60010
847-382-3210
Fax 847-382-3250
email: lasax@lasax.com

Governor Livingston High School Highlander Marching Band (Berkeley Heights, NJ)

1557 BayWoodwind Products
P.O. Box 3935
Westlake Village, CA 91361

1558 Benge Professional Brass (includes
trumpets)
c/o United Musical Instruments U.S.A.,
Inc.
P.O. Box 727
Elkhart, IN 46515

1559 Black Swamp Percussion LLC
13493 New Holland Street, Suite E
Holland, MI 49424
616-738-3190
Fax 616-738-3105
www.cin.es/mallets/usa.htm
email: info@blackswamp.com

1560 Boosey & Hawkes Musical Instruments,
Inc.
10949 Pendelton Street
Sun Valley, CA 91352-1522

800-426-7068
Fax 818-252-6351
www.boosey.com
email: marketing.usa@boosey.com

1561 Brannen Brothers—Flutemakers, Inc.
58 Dragon Court
Woburn, MA 01801

1562 Brook Mays Music Group
8701 John Carpenter Freeway, Suite
230
Dallas, TX 75247
800-637-8966
www.brookmays.com
email: CustomerService@brookmays.
com

Buffet Crampon woodwinds *see* Boosey &
Hawkes Musical Instruments, Inc.

1563 Calato/Regal Tip
4501 Hyde Park Blvd.
Niagara Falls, NY 14305

1564 Calicchio Brass Musical Instruments
6409 Willoughby Avenue
Hollywood, CA 90038

1565 Cannonball Musical Instruments
461 West Parkland Drive
Sandy, UT 84070
801-563-3081
Fax 801-563-3263
www.cannonballmusic.com
email: sheryl@cannonballmusic.com

1566 Cascio Interstate Music
P.O. Box 510865
13819 W. National Avenue
New Berlin, WI 53151
262-789-7600
www.casciointerstate.com

1567 Cincinnati Fluteworks
621 Clemmer Ave., #13
Clifton Heights
Cincinnati, OH 45219

1568 Civil and Military Arts, Ltd.
Amersham, England
    makes gear by hand and paints
    equipment and instruments, e.g.,
    drums

1569 Columbus Percussion
5052 North High Street
Columbus, OH 43214
800-775-7372
Fax 614-885-4761
www.thedrumclub.com
email: mail@columbuspercussion.com

1570 Conn Band Instruments
P.O. Box 727
Elkhart, IN 46515
    includes tuba conversion tube
    marching accessory kit

1571 Cushing Bagpipe Company
3866 Shovel Hollow Road (County Rt.
    28)
Andover, NY 14806
607-478-8188
www.lightlink.com/mcushing

1572 Custom Music Company
1930 Hilton
Ferndale, MI 48220
800-521-6380
Fax 248-546-8296
www.custommusiccorp.com
email: cmctuba@aol.com

1573 Dale's Drum Shop
4440 Fritchey Street
Harrisburg, PA 17109
877-704-5682
www.dales-drums.com

1574 Dean Yang Flutes
P.O. Box 14038
Detroit, MI 48214
800-71-PIPER
Fax 248-645-5446
www.dean-yang.com
email: yang@dean-yang.com

1575 DEG Music Products, Inc.
P.O. Box 968
N3475 Springfield Road
Lake Geneva, WI 53147
800-558-9416
Fax 262-248-7953
www.degmusic.com
email: sales@degmusic.com

1576 Dillon Music Web Store
325 Fulton Street
Woodbridge, NJ 07095
732-634-3399
Fax 732-634-4932
www.dillonmusic.com

1577 Drelinger Flute Mouthpiece Company
P.O. Box 146
N. White Plains, NY 10603

The Drum Club.com see Columbus Percussion

1578 Drum Heaven
P.O. Box 1831
Jamaica Plain, MA 02129

1579 Drum Workshops
101 Bernoulli Circle
Oxnard, CA 93030

1580 DrumNetwork.com
15 Orchard Park Road Unit 17
Madison, CT 06443
800-295-0803
Fax 603-754-3967
email: marcel@drumz.com

1581 Drums Ltd. (A. Bill Crowden's)
222 S. Jefferson
Chicago, IL 60661

1582 Drums Unlimited Inc.
4928 St. Elmo Avenue
Bethesda, MD 20814

Dynasty Eagle Marching Percussion *see* DEG
Music Products, Inc.

1583 E.M. Winston Band Instruments Company
38-44 West 21st Street
New York, NY 10010
212-463-7197
Fax 212-229-0642
www.emwinston.com
email: sales@emwinston.com

1584 East Texas Music
5170 Twin City Highway
Groves, TX 77619
800-371-2586
Fax 409-962-8884
email: eastxmus@swbell.net

1585 Edmund Nielsen Woodwinds, Inc.
61 East Park Boulevard
Villa Park, IL 60181

1586 Edmund's Double Reeds
12513 Parker Lane
Clinton, MO 64735

1587 Edward Almeida Flutes
17 Arrowhead Drive
Tiverton, RI 02878

1588 Edwards Instrument Company
530 South Highway H
Elkhorn, WI 53121

1589 e-flutes.com
877-565-2811
www.e-flutes.com

1590 Emerson Musical Instruments, Inc.
P.O. Box 310
Elkhart, IN 46515-0310
219-522-1675
www.emersonflutes.com

1591 Evans (drumheads)
c/o J. D'Addario
P.O. Box 290
Farmingdale, NY 11735
www.evansdrumheads.com

1592 F.A. Reynolds Company
P.O. Box 2669
Westfield, NJ 07091
888-554-5354
Fax 908-789-3025
www.feolds.com

1593 F.E. Olds & Son, Inc.
P.O. Box 2669
Westfield, NJ 07091
888-554-5354
Fax 908-789-3025
www.feolds.com

1594 Fall Creek Marimbas
1445 Upper Hill Road
P.O. Box 118
Middlesex, NY 14507
716-554-4011
Fax 716-554-4017
www.marimbas.com
email: pangaia@earthlink.com

1595 The Flute Exchange
1418 Deertrail Road
Boulder, CO 80302

1596 Flute Specialists, Inc.
120 W. 11 Mile Road, Suite 12

Royal Oak, MI 48067
888-590-5722
Fax 248-548-9407
www.flutespecialists.com
email: info@flutespecialists.com

1597 Flute World
29920 Orchard Lake Road
Farmington Hills, MI 48334

1598 Fox Products Corporation
P.O. Box 347
South Whitley, IN 46787
219-723-4888
Fax 219-723-6188

Frank's Drum Shop, Inc. *see* Drums Ltd.

1599 G. Leblanc Corporation
P.O. Box 1415
7001 Leblanc Blvd.
Kenosha, WI 53141-1415
262-658-1644
Fax 262-658-2824
www.gleblanc.com
email: gleblanc@gleblanc.com

1600 G. Pruefer Manufacturing Company,
Inc.
1669 Hartford Avenue
Johnston, RI 02919

1601 Gemeinhardt Company, Inc.
P.O. Box 788
57882 State Road 19 South
Elkhart, IN 46515

1602 Geneva International Corporation
29 East Hintz Road
Wheeling, IL 60090
847-520-9970
Fax 847-520-9593

1603 Getzen Company, Inc.
530 S. County Road
P.O. Box 440
Elkhorn, WI 53121
262-723-4221
Fax 262-723-4245

www.getzen.com
email: egetzen@elknet.net

1604 Giardinelli Band Instruments Company
7845 Maltage Drive
Liverpool, NY 13090
800-288-2334
www.giardinelli.com

1605 Gibson Guitar (also distributes Slingerland drums)
309 Plus Park Blvd.
Nashville, TN 37217
800-444-2766
www.gibson.com

1606 Hammig Piccolos/Westwind Musical
Products
1214 Fifth Street
Coralville, IA 52241

1607 Hardy's Musical Instrument Company,
Inc.
30462 C.R. 12 West
Elkhart, IN 46514

1608 Hayes House of Music
2011 W. 6th Street
Topeka, KS 66606

1609 Hermes Musical Instruments
2020 North Aurora Drive #5
Nogales, AZ 85621

1610 Hughes & McLeod Ltd.
Alwood Lodge
5 Blackcauseway Road
Strangford
County Down BT30 7LX
Northern Ireland
+44 02844 881 880
Fax +44 02844 881 880
www.bagpipers.co.uk/contact.htm
email: info@bagpipers.co.uk

1611 Idaho Percussion
1618 W. Jefferson
Boise, ID 83702

Pennsauken High School Indoor Guard (Pennsauken, NJ)

888-609-9494
Fax 208-395-0314
email: salesdesk@idahopercussion.com

1612 In Tune (percussion, bagpipes, brass, woodwind)
P.O. Box 7264
50 Mayor Avenue
St. John's NF A1E 3Y4
Canada
800-563-4114
Fax 709-726-7047
www.intune.ca
email: intune@nfld.com

1613 International Strings (distributed by F.E. Olds and Son, Inc.)
P.O. Box 2669
Westfield, NJ 07091
888-554-5354
Fax 908-789-3025

Interstate Music *see* Cascio Interstate Music

1614 J.D'Addario & Company (drumheads, strings, Vandoren reeds)
595 Smith Street
P.O. Box 290
Farmingdale, NY 11735
631-439-3300
Fax 631-439-3333
www.planet-waves.com or www.dad dario.com
email: mail@planet-waves.com

1615 John Lunn Flutes
23 Fletcher Road
Newport, NH 03773

1616 Jupiter Band Instruments
P.O. Box 90249
Austin, TX 78709-0249
512-288-7400
Fax 512-288-6445
www.jupitermusic.com
email: bi@jupitermusic.com

1617 Kaman Music Corporation (drums, mallets, racks)

P.O. Box 507
Bloomfield, CT 06002
860-509-8888
Fax 860-509-8891

1618 Kanstul Musical Instruments
231 East Palais Road
Anaheim, CA 92805
888-526-7885
Fax 714-563-1661
www.kanstul.net
email: sales@kanstul.net

1619 Kastuck Percussion Studio, Inc.
P.O. Box 4313
Winchester, VA 22604
540-667-5188
www.kanstuck.com

1620 King Musical Instruments
P.O. Box 787
Elkhart, IN 46515

1621 Kintail (bagpipes)
113 Barrack Street
Glasgow G4 0UE
Scotland
United Kingdom
+44 (0) 141 553 0902
Fax +44 (0) 141 553 0903
www.kintail.co.uk

1622 Knilling String Instruments
1400 Ferguson Avenue
St. Louis, MO 63133

Kp3, L.L.C. Malletech Instruments *see* Marimba Productions, Inc.

1623 Landell Flutes
529 Williams Hill Road
Richmond, VT 05477

1624 Latin Percussion, Inc.
160 Belmont Avenue
Garfield, NJ 07026

1625 Linton Woodwinds
1013 Alma Street
Elkhart, IN 46514

1626 Little Piper (new and used flutes)
P.O. Box 14038
Detroit, MI 48214
248-540-7970
Fax 248-645-5446
www.little-piper.com

1627 Lonestar Percussion
10611 Control Place
Dallas, TX 75238
214-340-0835
www.lonestarpercussion.com

1628 Ludwig Industries
Box 310
Elkhart, IN 46515
219-522-1675
Fax 219-522-0334
www.ludwig-drum.com

1629 Lyons Music Products
P.O. Box 1003
Elkhart, IN 46515-1003
800-292-4955
Fax 219-251-3545

1630 M. Khalid Pipe Company (bagpipes
and other instruments)
Raja Bazar
Sialkot-51310
Pakistan
+92 432-580048
Fax +92 432-586759
www.khalidpipe.com
email: info@khalidpipe.com

1631 MacLeon Highland Supplies (bagpipes)
136 Bridgegate
Glasgow G1 5HZ
Scotland
United Kingdom
+44 (0) 141 553 1513
Fax +44 (0) 141 552 0795
www.scotbagpipes.com
email: macleod@scotbagpipes.com

1632 MajesticDrumline.com
8 Floral Lane
East Stroudsburg, PA 18301

570-476-5761
www.majesticdrumline.com
email: president@majesticdrumline.
com

1633 Malmark, Inc. (handbells)
P.O. Box 1200
Plumsteadville, PA 18949
800-426-3235
Fax 215-766-0762
www.malmark.com
email: malmark@voicenet.com

1634 Marimba One
www.marimba1.com

1635 Marimba.org
www.marimba.org

1636 Marimba Productions, Inc.
P.O. Box 467
Asbury Park, NJ 07712
732-774-0011
Fax 732-774-0033

1637 Martin Guitar Company
510 Sycamore Street
Nazareth, PA 18064
610-759-2837
www.mguitar.com

1638 Maryland Drum Company
47 Loveton Circle, Suites L-M
Sparks, MD 21152
410-472-3306
Fax 410-472-1784
www.marylanddrum.com

1639 Mateki Flutes U.S.A. & Canada
621 Clemmer Avenue #13
Cincinnati, OH 45219

1640 Medley Music
1041 Lancaster Avenue
Bryn Mawr, PA 19010
610-527-3090

1641 Meisel Stringed Instruments
32 Commerce Street

Concord High School Golden Raider Marching Band (Wilmington, DE)

P.O. Box 90
Springfield, NJ 07081-0090
973-379-5000
Fax 973-379-5020
www.meiselmusic.com
email: meiselmusic.com

1642 Menchey Music Service, Inc.
888-MENCHEY
www.MencheyMusic.com

1643 Miyazawa Flutes, Ltd./Hammig Piccolos
1214 Fifth Street
Coralville, IA 52241

1644 Muncy Winds Music Company
P.O. Box 1274
Boone, NC 28607
800-333-6415
Fax 828-963-8990
www.muncywinds.com
email: info@muncywinds.com

1645 Muramatsu America (flutes)
P.O. Box 344
Bloomfield Hills, MI 48303
248-540-6424
Fax 248-645-5446
www.muramatsu-america.com
email: flute@muramatsu-america.com

1646 Music Go Round (used instruments)
4153 Lawrenceville Highway, Suite 8
Lilburn, GA 30047
770-931-9190
Fax 770-931-7560
email: mgrlilburnga@home.com

1647 Musical Innovations of the Mid-West
P.O. Box 3624
Bloomington, IL 61702-3624
309-827-3297
email: jmcedo@yahoo.com

1648 Musicalmerchandise.com
6400 A Woodward Avenue
Downers Grove, IL 60516

800-895-3267
Fax 630-968-8530
www.musicalmerchandise.com
email: support@musicalmerchandise.
     com

1649 musicgear4sale.com
13852 Wyandotte Street
Van Nuys, CA 91405
818-994-7697 (Fax same)
email: info@musicgear4sale.com

1650 Musician's Friend, Inc.
P.O. Box 4370
Medford, OR 97501
800-391-8762
Fax: 541-776-1370
www.musiciansfriend.com

1651 Musicrafts International, Inc.
4111 Todd Lane
Austin, TX 78744
     sells Jupiter wind instruments and
     percussion

Musser (vibes) *see* Selmer Company

1652 Nagahara Flutes
131 Stedman Street #7
Chelmsford, MA 01824

Naill Bagpipes (David Naill & Co.) *see* Robert Wallace

1653 National Educational Music Company,
     Ltd.
1181 Route 22
Box 1130
Mountainside, NJ 07092
800-526-4593
Fax 908-789-3025
www.nemc.com
email: info@nemc.com

1654 National Music, Inc.
826 Massachusetts Avenue
Arlington, MA 02174

1655 National Music Supply of Florida
P.O. Box 1421
St. Petersburg, FL 33733

1656 Orpheus Music
13814 Lookout Road
San Antonio, TX 78233

1657 Paiste America, Inc. (cymbals, gongs,
     chimes)
460 Atlas St.
Brea, CA 92621

1658 Parker Music Company
2047 Wade Hampton Blvd.
Greenville, SC 29615
800-922-8824
http://members.tripod.com/parker
     music2047/parkermusic2047.html

1659 Patterson Cable Snares
4003 Willow Green
San Antonio, TX 78217

1660 Pearl Corporation
549 Metroplex Drive
P.O. Box 111240
Nashville, TN 37211
615-833-4477
www.pearldrums.com

1661 Pearl Flutes
13814 Lookout Road
San Antonio, TX 78233

1662 Pegasus Stringed Instrument Company
530 East Lexington Avenue, Suite 125
Elkhart, IN 46516-3503

1663 The Percussion Center & Music Spectrum
1701 North Harrison Street
Fort Wayne, IN 46802

1664 The Percussion Source
1212 5th Street
Coralville, IA 52241

1665 Philip Muncy Woodwinds
      RR 4, Box 174B
      Banner Elk, NC 28604

1666 Premier Percussion USA, Inc.
      915 N. Lenola Road
      Moorestown, NJ 08057
      856-231-8825

1667 PRO-MARK
      10707 Craighead Drive
      Houston, TX 77025-5899
      800-233-5250
      Fax 713-669-8000
      www.promark-stix.com
      email: info@promark-stix.com

1668 Rayburn Musical Instrument Com-
      pany, Inc.
      263 Huntington Avenue
      Boston, MA 02115

1669 REMO, Inc. (drums)
      28101 Industry Drive
      Valencia, CA 91354
      805-294-5600
      www.remo.com
      email: customerservice@remo.com

1670 Robert Wallace (bagpipes)
      P.O. Box 341
      Glasgow G33 6DZ
      Scotland
      United Kingdom
      +44 (0) 141 779 1750
      Fax +44 (0) 141 779 9763
      www.sol.co.uk/w/whistlebinkies/pip
        es.corres.htm
      email: robwallpipes@aol.com

Rogers Drum Company *see* Brook Mays
  Music Group

1671 Ross Mallet Instruments, Inc.
      P.O. Box 90249
      Austin, TX 78709
      512-288-7400
      Fax 512-288-6445
      email: info@rossmallet.com

1672 Ruthies Music House
      599 North Louisiana Avenue #8
      Asheville, NC 28806
      www.ruthiesmusic.com

1673 Sabian Ltd. (cymbals, gongs)
      219 Main Street
      Meductic, New Brunswick E6H 2L5
      Canada
      506-272-2019
      Fax 506-272-2040
      www.sabian.com

1674 Saga Musical Instruments (includes
      Celtic instruments)
      350 Harbor Way South
      San Francisco, CA 94080
      650-588-5558

1675 Sagerman Flutes
      P.O. Box 790
      Waldeboro, ME 04572
      207-529-5420

1676 Saied Music Company
      3259 S. Yale Avenue
      Tulsa, OK 74135
      918-742-5541
      Fax 918-744-9573
      email: hhollingsworth@saiedmusic.
        com

1677 Sam Ash Music
      2100 Route 38
      Cherry Hill, NJ 08002 (+ other loca-
        tions)
      609-667-6696
      or: 278 Duffy Avenue
      Hicksville, NY 11802
      516-932-6400
      Fax 516-931-3881
      email: satsnyder@aol.com

1678 Sankyo Flutes U.S.A./Global
      18521 Railroad St.
      City of Industry, CA 91748

1679 Saxophone Shop, Ltd.
      2834 Central St.
      Evanston, IL 60201

1680 Schilke Music, Inc. (instruments and
mouthpieces)
4520 James Place
Melrose Park, IL 60160
312-922-0570

1681 Schulmerich Bells
P.O. Box 903
Carillon Hill
Sellersville, PA 18960-0903
800-77-BELLS
Fax 215-257-1910
www.schulmerichbells.com
email: HomeOffice@schulmerichbells.
com

1682 The Selmer Company (distributes Bach
brass instruments)
P.O. Box 310
Elkhart, IN 46515-0310
219-522-1675
Fax 219-522-0334
www.selmer.com

1683 Seth Gallagher Workshop (Irish bag
pipes)
10 Garden Street
Cold Spring, NY 10516
845-265-5508
www.uilleann.com/pipes.html
email: seth@uilleann.com

1684 Shar Music Company
26 Cumberland Street
Toronto, Ontario M4W 1J5
Canada
416-960-8494
Fax 416-960-1478
email: shar@globalserve.net

1685 Shar Products Company (stringed instruments)
P.O. Box 1411
Ann Arbor, MI 48106
800-248-7427
Fax 800-997-8723
www.sharmusic.com
email: fineinst@sharmusic.com

1686 Slingerland Drum Company (part of
Gibson Guitar)
138 12th Avenue N.
Nashville, TN 37203
800-4-GIBSON
Fax 615-255-4078
www.gibson.com/products/slinger
land/contact.html
e-mail: relations@gibson.com

1687 Stingray (percussion)
1228 B 53rd Street
Mangonia Park, FL 33407

1688 Straubinger Flutes, Inc.
5920 S. East Street
Indianapolis, IN 46227

1689 Sun Percussion
11921 Audrey Avenue
Torrance, CA 90505
888-563-4033
Fax 310-378-3356

1690 Suzuki Corporation
P.O. Box 261030
San Diego, CA 92196
858-566-9710
Fax 858-560-1069
www.suzukimusic.com

1691 Sweetheart Flute Company
32 S. Maple Street
Enfield, CT 06082

1692 TAMA (percussion)
c/o Tama Drum Catalog
Department WBST
1725 Winchester Road
Bensalem, PA 19020
www.tama.com
email: contact@tama.com

1693 Taylor's Music
116 W. Gay Street
West Chester, PA 19380
610-696-1812
www.taylorsmusic.com

Windber Area High School "A" Guard (Windber, PA)

1694 Tradewinds (flutes)
2733 Shelter Island Drive, #303
San Diego, CA 92101

1695 TreeWorks Chimes
443 Chestnut Street
Nashville, TN 37203

1696 The Tuba Exchange
1825 Chapel Hill Road
Durham, NC 27707
800-869-8822
Fax 919-493-8822
www.tubaexchange.com
email: info@tubaexchange.com

1697 United Musical Instruments U.S.A.,
Inc. (distributes Armstrong flutes,
Conn and Benge trumpets, King
trombones and trumpets)
1000 Industrial Parkway
P.O. Box 727
Elkhart, IN 46515

219-295-0079
Fax 219-295-8613
www.unitedmusical.com
email: email@unitedmusical.com

1698 Verne Q. Powell Flutes, Inc.
One Clock Tower Place, Suite 300
Maynard, MA 01754
978-461-6111
Fax 978-461-6155
www.powellflutes.com
email: cg@powellflutes.com

1699 Vic Firth (drumsticks, mallets)
65 Commerce Way
Dedham, MA 02026
www.vicfirth.com

Vintage One (trumpets, flugelhorns) *see*
United Musical Instruments U.S.A., Inc.

1700 Vintage Drum Center
2243 Ivory Drive

Libertyville, IA 52567-8533
800-729-3111
Fax 641-693-3101
www.vintagedrum.com/contact.htm
email: vintagedrum@lisco.com

Western Music Specialty Company *see* Roper Music

1701 Westwind Musical Products
1214 5th Street
Coralville, IA 52241

1702 Wichita Band Instrument Company, Inc.
2525 E. Douglas
Wichita, KS 67211

William Lewis & Son *see* Selmer Company

1703 Wm. S. Haynes Company, Inc.
12 Piedmont Street
Boston, MA 02116

1704 The Wind Shop
3367 Ellen Avenue
Hebron, KY 41048-9637
606-689-5066 (Fax same)

1705 Woodwind & Brasswind
4004 Technology Drive
South Bend, IN 46628
800-348-5003
Fax 574-251-3501
www.woodwindbrasswind.com
email: catalogs@wwandbw.com

1706 Yamaha Corporation of America
Band & Orchestral Division
3445 East Paris Ave. S.E.
P.O. Box 899
Grand Rapids, MI 49518-0899
616-940-4900
Fax 616-949-7721
www.yamaha.com/band

1707 Yamaha Music Corporation (keyboards, synthesizers)
6600 Orangthorpe Avenue
Buena Park, CA 90620

1708 Zzounds.com (guitar and percussion Internet e-tailer)
www.zzounds.com

Instrument Accessories

1709 AAIIRR Power/AcoustiCoils (bore insert for brass and wind)
1234 S. Quince Way
Denver, CO 80231
303-751-0673 (+fax)
www.dmamusic.org/acousticoils
email: aai-irr@uswest.net

AccuBore Clarinet Tuning Barrels *see* DEG Music Products, Inc.

1710 Aerospace Lubricants, Inc. (includes Alisyn Valve, Slide and Key Oil)
1600 Georgesville Road
Columbus, OH 43228
614-878-3600
Fax 614-878-1600

1711 A-K Medical Software (Brace Guard orthodontic embouchure aid)
P.O. Box 50329
Columbia, SC 29250

1712 Altieri Instrument Bags
3003 Arapahoe Street, Sutie 221
Denver, CO 80205
303-291-0658
Fax 303-744-1434
www.altieribags.com
email: donna@altieribags.com

1713 Archives (music writing paper)
210 Route 109
P.O. Box J
E. Farmingdale, NY 11735

1714 Arundo Reed & Cane
Rt. 3, Box 298
Hillsboro, OR 97124

1715 Aztec Shield (banner shields)
927 Sanford Avenue
Wilmington, CA 90744
310-835-1700
Fax 310-835-1223
email: holograph@lansnet.com

1716 Beatsticks.com
P.O. Box 260702
Pembroke Pines, FL 33026
email: info@beatsticks.com

1717 Braceguard Distributor
105 Canyon Road
West Monroe, LA 71291
877-349-2725
Fax 318-397-1686
email: rlacas@bayou.com

1718 Burnham Enterprises
P.O. Box 177
Clinton, MS 39060
800-729-0535
Fax 601-924-5782
email: burnhamenterprises@earthlink.
net

1719 Chartier Reeds
P.O. Box 13344
Albuquerque, NM 87192
800-729-7333
Fax 505-888-1064
chartierreeds.com
email: chartier@chartierreeds.com

1720 Chili con Cases (cases for touring equipment)
9831 S. 78th Avenue
Hickory Hills, IL 60457
708-430-4150
Fax 708-599-0028
email: chiliconcases@earthlink.net

1721 Emerald Reed Company
P.O. Box 1422
Port Townsend, WA 98368-0032

1722 Gamble Music Company
1313 W. Randolph Street, Dept. 0997
Chicago, IL 60607
800-621-4290
Fax 312-421-7979
www.gamblemusic.com
email: custserv@gamblemusic.com

1723 Goldline Percussion Products (mallet
stands)
P.O. Box 349
Sagle, IN 83860
208-265-5353
http://goldlinepercussion.com
email: embrown@televar.com

1724 The Guard Gear Company (flag and
weapon bags)
408-236-2093
Fax 707-248-2141
www.theguardgear.com.org
email: ThinkKarma@aol.com

1725 Hamilton Stands, Inc.
3415 Cincinnati-Dayton Rd.
Middletown, OH 45044

1726 Hite Clarinet and Saxophone Mouthpieces
P.O. Box 0332
Estero, FL 33928
www.jdhite.com/default.htm

1727 Humes and Berg (mutes)
4801 Railroad Avenue
East Chicago, IN 46312

1728 J. D'Addario & Company, Inc. (Vandoren mouthpieces, Gripmaster)
P.O. Box 290
Farmingdale, NY 11735
www.planet-waves.com
email: mail@planet-waves.com

1729 Jarvis Industries, Inc. (drum major
podiums, mallet and percussion
carts, gong and Hamilton Music
Stands)
23924 Lenze Road

Spring, TX 77389
800-548-4239
Fax 281-251-5443
www.jarvisonline.com
email: jenniferg@jarvisonline.com

1730 Jeffers Handbell Supply Inc.
455 Western Lane
Irmo, SC 29063-1728
800-547-2355
Fax 803-781-3020
www.handbellworld.com

1731 Jet-Tone, Inc. (mouthpieces)
P.O. Box 1462
Elkhart, IN 46515
219-288-1080
Fax 219-251-3527
www.jet-tone.com
email: info@jet-tone.com

1732 Johnny Rabb Drumsticks
3405 Highway 138
Toone, TN 38381
www.johnnyrabb.com

1733 Jo-Ral Mutes (distributed by the Selmer Company)
P.O. Box 597
Elkhart, IN 46515
219-288-1263
Fax 219-251-3559
www.jo-ral.com
email: info@jo-ral.com

1734 JTG of Nashville
1024-C 18th Avenue South
Nashville, TN 37212

1735 Kombo Cart International
P.O. Box 837
Orem, UT 84059
800-574-1095
Fax 801-226-2678
www.komboproducts.com

1736 Krishna Textiles (polyester China silk for flags)
795 Newark Avenue

Jersey City, NJ 07306
888-659-2700 or 201-659-2700
Fax 201-963-8719
http://colorguardfabrics.com
e-mail: sales@colorguardfabrics.com

1737 Légére Reeds
c/o Orpheus Music
13814 Lookout Road
San Antonio, TX 78233
800-821-9448
www.orpheusmusic.com
email: Legerereeds@aol.com

1738 L-S Music Innovations
250 H Street, Suite 8110
Department 718
Blaine, WA 98230

1739 McCormick's Entrprises, Inc. (carts, flags, gloves, headgear, mallets, podiums, shoes)
P.O. Box 577
Arlington Heights, IL 60006
800-323-5201
Fax 800-324-3884
www. mccormicksnet.com
email: sales@mccormicksnet.com

1740 McFarland Double Reed Shop (new and used oboes and English horns, accessories, repairs)
P.O. Box 13505
Atlanta, GA 30329
404-321-5356
Fax 404-634-3796
www.McFarlandDoubleReed.com

1741 Manhasset Specialty Company (music stands and accessories)
P.O. Box 2518
Yakima, WA 98907
509-248-3810
Fax 509-248-3834
www.manhasset-specialty.com

1742 Marlin Lesher Reed, Inc.
P.O. Box 1004
Port Townsend, WA 98368

1743 Mike Balter Mallets
      15 East Palatine Road, Suite 116
      Prospect Heights, IL 60070
      847-541-5777
      Fax 847-541-5785
      www.mikebalter.com / contact.html
      email: info@mikebalter.com

1744 Mitchell Lurie (mouthpiece)
      2277 Pelham Avenue
      Los Angeles, CA 90064

1745 MMB Music, Inc.
      10370 Page Industrial Blvd.
      St. Louis, MO 63132

1746 The Music Mart Inc. (manuscript paper,
      music, notation software, reeds,
      strings)
      3301 Carlisle Blvd. NE
      Albuquerque, NM 87110
      800-545-6204 / 505-889-9777
      Fax 505-889-9070
      www.musicmart.com
          also Phoenix and Prescott, AZ

1747 Neill Sanders Mouthpieces
      186 Podunk Lake Road
      Hastings, MI 49058

1748 Northwind Cases Inc.
      31 East Rillito Street
      Tucson, AZ 85705

1749 Olathe Band Instrument (flute bags)
      13260 Lakeshore Drive
      Olathe, KS 66061
      913-764-4159
      Fax 913-764-5967

1750 The Original Swab Company
      5280 Rockfish Road
      Raeford, NC 28376
      910-848-6916
      Fax 910-848-6917

1751 Peterson Electro-Musical Products,
      Inc. (strobe tuners, ear training de-
      vices)

11601 South Mayfield Avenue
Worth, IL 60482

1752 Ploeger Sound Mirror for Saxophone
      27003 Norcross
      Harrison Township, MI 48045

1753 Prestini Reed Corporation
      2020 N. Aurora Drive #5
      Nogales, AZ 85621

1754 Professional Brass Refinishing
      1860 West Davenport Street
      Rhinelander, WI 54501
      715-369-4050

1755 PRO MARK (drumsticks)
      10707 Craighead Drive
      Houston, TX 77025

1756 Protune Corporation (Drum Timp-
      Tuner)
      P.O. Box 1808
      Poughkeepsie, NY 12601
      845-462-6452 (Fax same)
      www.protune.com / welcome.htm
      email: protune@aol.com

1757 PureCussion, Inc.
      3611 Wooddale Avenue South
      Minneapolis, MN 55416
      612-927-2330

1758 Rammitt Percussion Company
      9510 Owensmouth Avenue #6
      Chatsworth, CA 91311
      818-709-5199
      Fax 818-709-2719
      email: Rammittco@aol.com

1759 Rascher Mouthpieces (saxophone)
      P.O. Box 761
      East Aurora, NY 14052

1760 Rhythm Tech Inc.
      29 Beechwood Avenue
      New Rochelle, NY 10801
      800-726-2279
      Fax 914-636-6947
      email: drumcorps@rhythmtech.com

1761 RIA (saxophone & clarinet mouth-
pieces)
P.O. Box 010359
Staten Island, NY 10301

1762 RICO International (reeds)
8484 San Fernando Road
Sun Valley, CA 91352
800-891-7426
Fax 818-504-9207
www.ricoreeds.com
email: marketing@ricoreeds.com

1763 Roland Corporation (tuners)
7200 Dominion Circle
Los Angeles, CA 90040

1764 S and H Manufacturing Co. (instrument racks)
316 W. Summit St.
Normal, IL 61761

1765 The Sabre Line (custom sabres)
J&S Associates
4756 NW 14th Street
Coconut Creek, FL 33063
954-974-7980
Fax 954-979-8501
http://sabreline.net
email: sabremaker@hotmail.com

1766 Seiko (tuners)
c/o Kaman Music Corporation
P.O. Box 507
Bloomfield, CT 06002

1767 Sherrard "Roll-Away" Musical Instrument Racks
316 West Summit Street
Normal, IL 61761-1258

1768 Shure Microphones
222 Hartrey Avenue
Evanston, IL 60202

1769 Sounds of Woodwinds
Box 91
Hancock, MA 01237

1770 Sto-cote Products, Inc. (floor covers)
888-WG-FLOOR
Fax 414-279-6744
e-mail: stocote@genevaonline.com

1771 Stork Custom Mouthpieces
Rt. 2, Box 1818
Maple Hill Road
Plainfield, VT 05667

1772 Sugarbushbags (garment bags)
P.O. Box 118
Barnesville, PA 18214
570-467-3193
Fax 570-467-2202
email: kevinconnors@sugarbushbags.
com

1773 Superslick Products (trombone slide
oil)
c/o American Way Marketing
4561 Pine Creek Road
Elkhart, IN 46516
219-295-6633
Fax 219-293-9888

1774 Tote Unlimited (banners, drum carriers, maces, plume carriers
P.O. Box 7875
Fort Worth, TX 76111
888-698-8300
Fax 817-698-8301
www.toteunlimited.com
email: tom@toteunlimited.com

Tru-Vu Transparent Mouthpieces *see* L-S
Music Innovations

Vandoren Paris (reeds, mouthpieces) *see*
J. D'Addario & Co., Inc.

1775 Wemsco Tuba Hangers
136 North 5th Street
Grand Junction, CO 81501

1776 Wenger Corporation (chairs, stands,
conducting equipment)
555 Park Drive
Owatonna, MN 55060

800-733-0393
Fax 507-455-4258
www.wengercorp.com

1777 Westamerica Custom Case Corporation
10-91 Golden Drive
Coquitlam, British Columbia V3K 6R2
Canada
877-668-2273

Fax 604-718-4184
email: sales@wccase.net

1778 XL Specialty Percussion, Inc.
16335-5 Lima Road
Huntertown, IN 46748
800-348-1012
Fax 260-637-6354
www.xlspec.com

Instrument Repair

1779 American Band Instrument Service
(flutes)
124 Shelley Drive
Tyler, TX 75701
903-593-3195
www.bandusa.com/Flute_Pages/Flute
Repair.Html

1780 The Brass Shop
459 Sun Hill Lane
Webster, NY 14580
716-671-7135
Fax 716-670-0323
www.thebrassshoponline.com
email: TheBrassShop@ATTGlobal.net

1781 Cincinnati Fluteworks
621 Clemmer Avenue, #13
Clifton Heights
Cincinnati, OH 45219

1782 Conn Band Instruments
c/o United Musical Instruments
P.O. Box 727
Elkhart, IN 46515
513-579-8294
Fax 513-579-8305
www.fluteworks.com
email: Pat@fluteworks.com

1783 The Drum Doctor
3021 Villa Drive
Orlando, FL 32810-4806

407-294-3786
Fax 407-678-5346
email: thedrumdoc@att.net

1784 Ferree's Tools, Inc.
1477 E. Michigan Avenue
Battle Creek, MI 49014
800-253-2261

1785 Flute Specialists, Inc.
120 W. 11 Mile Road, Suite 12
Royal Oak, MI 48067
888-590-5722
Fax 248-548-9407
www.flutespecialists.com
email: info@flutespecialists.com

1786 Renton Technical College Musical Instrument Technician Repair Program
3000 NE 4th Street
Renton, WA 98056
425-235-2453
email: dhickman@rtc.ctc.edu

1787 Take Care (video tapes on maintenance)
P.O. Box 73266
Puyallup, WA 98373-0266

1788 Woodwind Repair and Sales
3 Joda Road
West Allenhurst, NJ 0771

Uniform and Footwear
Manufacturers and Distributors

Note: The Instrumentalist *contains a classified section in which schools offer old uniforms for sale.*

1789 Artcraft Blazers
7502 Thomas Street
Pittsburgh, PA 15201

1790 Art Stone—Dept. MO
1795 Express Dr. N
P.O. Box 2505
Smithtown, NY 11787
800-522-8897
Fax 631-582-9541
www.artstonecostumes.com
e-mail: artstonedance@aol.com

1791 Ashley Company
10 Harold Street
Sylva, NC 28779

1792 The Band Hall (costumes, flags)
800-398-3064

1793 Band Mans Company
3328 Towerwood Drive
Dallas, TX 75234
800-527-2214
www.bandmans.com
email: sales@bandmans.com

1794 Band Shoppe
8900 Highway 65
P.O. Box 428
Cynthiana, IN 47612
800-457-3501
Fax 800-874-3635
www.bandshoppe.com
email: sales@bandshoppe.com

1795 Banners by Barbara, Inc. (flags, banners, embroidery)
735 Creekwood Bluffs Drive
Milford, OH 45150
513-722-3881
Fax 513-722-3660
www.bannersbybarbara.com
email: babsflag@iglou.com

1796 Bayly, Inc. (caps, helmets)
4151 N. 29th Ave.
Hollywood, FL 33020
800-882-0255
Fax 954-923-9596
www.baylyinc.com

1797 Blanche Simmons Enterprises
9480 Wilson Road
Elbrta, AL 36530
800-352-2987
Fax 334-987-5226
email: flashcat@ametro.net

1798 Body Wrappers
1350 Broadway
New York, NY 10018
www.bodywrappes.com

1799 The Burrows Company (gloves, pom-pom/dance/drill team supplies)
6918 Clarendon Street
Rowlett, TX 75089
972-412-6518
Fax 972-475-8638
www.route66streetrods.com/tbc/contactus.htm
email: burrows@route66streetrods.com

1800 Colorifics (auxiliary units)
8325 Green Meadow Drive North
Westerville, OH 43081-9443
800-322-1961

1801 Cote Inc.
74 W. Bridge Street
Morrisville, PA 19067

1802 TheCrownStore.com (fabric, shoes)
888-342-2345
Fax 803-547-2295
www.thecrownstore.com
email: info@thecrownstore.com

1803 Dance Fashions
800-747-0875
Fax 770-754-0470
www.dancefashions.com

1804 Dance Sophisticates
647 Virginia Avenue
Indianapolis, IN 46203
888-248-2090
Fax 317-634-7854
www.dancesoph.com
email: Dance@DanceSoph.com

1805 DeMoulin
1025 S. 4th Street
Greenville, IL 62246
800-228-8134
Fax 618-664-1647
www.demoulin.com
email: jpulley@demoulin.com

Dinkles Marching Shoe *see* Up-Front Footwear

1806 Director's Showcase (flags, poles, rainwear, gloves, rifles, mtxshoe.com
shoes, uniforms) [ok]
505 Sroufe Street
Ligonier, IN 46767-0229
800-893-8171
Fax 800-274-4953
www.dshowcase.com
email: info@dshowcase.com

1807 Discount Dance Supply
5065 East Hunter Avenue
Anaheim, CA 92807
800-328-7107
www.discdance.com
email: info@discountdance.com

1808 Drillmaster Corporation (shoes)
344 Ocean Boulevard
Atlantic Highlands, NJ 07716
201-794-7806
Fax 201-794-8197
www.drillmaster.com
email: info@drillmaster.com

Drillstar Company *see* Drillmasters

1809 Earl C. Benson & Associates (Fruhauf
uniforms, shoes)
25989 Gerlach Way
Cannon Falls, MN 55009
800-720-0304
Fax 507-263-9447
email: ecbenson@rconnect.com

1810 Ebert Sportswear Manufacturing
5000 Fernandina Road
Columbia, SC 29212

1811 Ed Jameson & Associates (shoes, flags,
gloves, etc.)
2127 N. Genesee Road
Burton, MI 48509

1812 En Garde (costumes, flags, props)
856-616-1989

1813 Express Band Products (fabric, flags,
footwear, gloves, guard outfits, maces,
rifles)
312 South Main Street
North Syracuse, NY 13212
315-458-0456
www.dxmarket.com/xpressband/dir
email: express@a-znet.com

1814 Fear Nothing Music Gear (brass instruments, caps,sweatshirts, t-shirts)
9550 Grove Road
Cordova, TN 38016
800-361-GEAR
Fax 901-937-8652
www.fearnothingmusicgear.com
email: fearnotgear@aol.com

1815 Fechheimer Sol Frank
4545 Malsbary Road
Cincinnati, OH 45242-5624
210-223-3018

1816 Flint Enterprises
812 E. Water Street
Lock Haven, PA 17745

570-893-4786
email: flintenterprises@yahoo.com

1817 Foxx Manufacturing (has Otterwear
    Rainwear)
    5199 E. Mahoning Ave.
    Warren, OH 44483

1818 Fred J. Miller Inc. (includes Caesario
    Collection, Millennia Line)
    118 Westpark Road
    Dayton, OH 45459
    800-444-FLAG
    Fax 937-434-0356
    www.fjminc.com
    email: fred@fjminc.com

1819 Fruhauf Uniforms Inc.
    800 E. Gilbert
    Wichita, KS 67211
    800-858-8050
    Fax 316-263-5550
    www.fruhauf.com
    email: fruhauf@fruhauf.com

1820 Galapagos Studios, Inc. (t-shirts)
    1791 South Murray Blvd.
    Colorado Springs, CO 80916
    800-932-5713
    Fax 800-772-3119
    www.galapagos-studios.com/index.
        html
    email: info@galapagos-studios.com

1821 Gateway Shoes
    910 Kehrs Mill Road, #112
    Ballwin, MO 63011
    800-539-6063
    Fax 636-527-3797
    www.gatewayshoes.com
    email: info@gatewayshoes.com

1822 Gotham Shoe Co. Inc.
    P.O. Box 1629
    Binghamton, NY 13902

1823 Hamburger Woolen Company
    P.O. Box 796
    23 Denton Avenue

New Hyde Park, NY 11040
516-352-7400
Fax 516-352-7704

1824 Happy Feet (footwear)
    10641 Hidden Mesa Place
    Monterey, CA 93940
    800-934-2668
    www.happyfeetboots.com

1825 Hayden School Supply
    P.O. Box 27777
    Tempe AZ 85285

1826 Ictus Ltd.
    Band Uniforms & Accessories (blaz-
    ers, shoes, fabric, flag poles, gloves,
    maces, pants, rainwear)
    13351 S. W. 49th Place
    Ocala, FL 34481-4189
    800-664-2887
    Fax 352-873-1991
    www.ictuslimited.com
    email: sales@ictuslimited.com

1827 Illinois Theatrical
    P.O. Box 34284
    Dept. DT
    Chicago, IL 60634-0284
    800-745-3777

1828 Indigo Graphics
    14225 Dayton Circle, Suite 14
    Omaha, NE 68137
    888-698-9550
    Fax 402-934-9220
    email: info@gearforschools.com

Insignia Band Uniforms *see* Band Shoppe

1829 In-Step International, Inc.
    917 Market
    Portland, TX 78374
    899-318-4798
    www.instepshoes.com

1830 Intermedia, Inc.
    85 Carver Avenue
    Westwood, NJ 07675

1831 Jarrand Associates
24 Wyckoff Avenue, Suite 2
Waldwick, NJ 07463
201-447-3131
Fax 201-794-2289
email: ZEEMIKE7@yahoo.com

1832 Kerr's Music World
911 Bigley Avenue
Charleston, WV 25302
800-642-3047
Fax 304-345-5043
www.kerrsmusic.com
email: kerrsmusic@kerrsmusic.com

1833 Krishna Textiles
795 Newark Avenue
Jersey City, NJ 07306
888-659-2700
Fax 201-963-8719
http://www.colorguardfabrics.com
e-mail: sales@colorguardfabrics.com

1834 K12 Outfitters
3630 South 144th Street
Omaha, NE 68144
800-235-9327
Fax 402-697-0241
email: info@k12outfitters.com

1835 Leo's Dancewear
Dept. DS
1900 N. Narragansett Avenue
Chicago, IL 60639
800-736-5367
www.leosdancewear.com
email: info@leosdancewear.com

1836 Liberts (shoes and dance attire, including Capezio)
4920 Northpark Loop
Colorado Springs, CA 80918
800-624-6480
Fax 719-592-1526
www.liberts.com

1837 Littwitz Investments, Inc. (ponchos)
10847 Britoak Lane
Houston, TX 77079-3628

800-658-1008
email: dlittwitz@houston.rr.com

1838 Marcéa (jazz pants and tops)
1374 South Flower Street
Los Angeles, CA 90015
800-821-7737
www.marcea.com

1839 Marching Concepts
c/o The Pageantry Group
423 Pine Ridge Road
Bluff City, TN 37618
540-523-5184
email: webmaster@marchingconcepts.com

1840 Marching Show Concepts (gloves, shoes, uniforms, rainwear)
829 Lawrence Drive
Fort Wayne, IN 46804
800-356-4381
Fax 260-459-0615
www.msconcepts.com
email: msc@msconcepts.com

1841 Merchants Uniform Manufacturing Inc.
7520 E. Colfax Avenue
Denver, CO 80203

1842 MTX Marching Shoe
www.mtxshoe.com
See also Director's Showcase

1843 Music-T's (t-shirts)
1031 Eastgate
Midlothian, TX 76065
800-587-4287
Fax 800-430-3226
www.music-ts.com
email: musict@flash.net

1844 Nicsinger Uniform Company (purchased by Band Man Company)

1845 Northeast Band Supply Company
201 S. Main Street
North Syracuse, NY 13212
800-458-6185

Fax 315-458-6189
email: ChuckTrout@att.net

1846 Opening Night Glitters (dance costumes)
9650 Strickland Road, Suite 103
PMB 251
Raleigh, NC 27615
919-846-0521
Fax 704-542-2359
www.openingnightglitters.com

1847 Orefice Ltd.
7520 Main Street
Jenison, MI 49428
616-457-9300
Fax 616-457-9453
email: service@oreficeltd.com

1848 Oriental Silk Co. Imports
8377 Beverly Blvd.
Los Angeles, CA 90048
323-651-2323
www.orientalsilk.com

1849 Palombo Uniforms, Inc.
123 Edgewood Avenue
Pittsburgh, PA 15218

1850 Peacock's Marching World
1251 N. Tustin Avenue
Anaheim, CA 92807-1603
714-630-7077
Fax 714-630-7241
email: peacocksmw@aol.com

1851 Pep Threads
1141 West Katella Avenue
Orange, CA 92667
800-367-8195

1852 Raeford Uniform Fabrics
1345 Avenue of the Americas
New York, NY 10105

1853 Satin Stitches Ltd.
11894 Reisling Blvd. NW
Minneapolis, MN 55433
800-48SATIN
www.satinstiches.com

Sefco Plumes *see* Kerr's Music World

Sol Frank Uniforms, Inc. *see* Fechheimer Sol Frank, Band Shoppe

1854 Spirit by Curtain Call
333 East Seventh Avenue
P.O. Box 709
York, PA 17405-0709
717-852-6910
Fax 717-852-6995; 800-839-1039

1855 Stanbury Uniforms
P.O. Box 100
Brookfield, MO 64628
800-826-2246
fax 660-258-5781
www.stanbury.com

1856 StarStyled
P.O. Box 119029
Hialeah, FL 33011-9029
800-5DANCER
www.starstyled.com

1857 Team Design
800-899-9941
310-323-2711

1858 Under the Sun Productions (flag and costume fabric, jackets, neck coolers)
882 South Matlack Street, Suite 202
West Chester, PA 19382
800-264-1121
Fax 610-431-6511
www.utsp.com
email: undersunpr@aol.com

1859 Up-Front Footwear
925 Scull Street
P.O. Box 718
Lebanon, PA 17042-0718
888-DINKLES
Fax 717-270-6695
www.dinkles.com

1860 Warren Creative Designs
223 Claremont Circle
P.O. Box 32
Brooklyn, MI 49230

800-947-5877
Fax 517-592-3997
www.warren-creative-design.com
email: ewarren@voyager.net

1861 Wear-A-Knit Corporation
1306 18th Street
Cloquet, MN 55720

1862 Weissman's
1600 Macklind Avenue

St. Louis, MO 63110
800-477-5410
Fax 800-777-8270

1863 WinterGarb
1089 Third Avenue, SW #108
Carmel, IN 46032
800-796-8732
www.wintergarb.com
email: estephenie@hotmail.com

Selected Bibliography

Articles

1864 Beckwith, Gene, and John Huth. "Cleaning Piston Valve Instruments." *Instrumentalist* (July 1988): 26–28, 30.

1865 Cristo, Jessica Rae. "Donations Expand Music's Talent Pool." *News Journal* [Wilmington, DE], August 23, 2001, pp. B1, B6.

1866 Fisher, Daniel, "Music Man." *Forbes*, September 15, 2003, p. 152 [instrument rental business].

1867 Fonder, Mark. "The Instrument Manufacturing Industry and the School Band Movement: A Look at the 'Holton School Band Plan'." *Journal of Band Research* (Fall 1988): 44–51.

1868 Harris, Wilbur C. "Ten Repairs Every Band Director Should Know." *School Musician, Director & Teacher* (April 1981): 16.

1869 Healy, Guinevere. "Tuba in the Tub: A Guide to Cleaning." *Instrumentalist* (November 1992): 38, 40, 42.

1870 Knight, Richart Arret. "Whiter Whites." *Bandworld* (August-October, 1987): 53. [cleaning fiberglass sousaphones, drum carriers, spats and shoes]

1871 McKinney, James. "Percussion Accessories You Can Make." *Instrumentalist* (April 1983): 46–48.

1872 Page, Nick. "Guide to Purchasing Band Uniforms." *Instrumentalist* (February 1988): 66, 68, 70–72.

1873 Sperl, Gary. "Woodwind Instrument Maintenance." *Music Educators Journal* (March 1980): 46.

1874 Von Bergen, Elizabeth F. "Careers in Manufacturing and Merchandising." *Instrumentalist* (August 1977): 44–48.

Books

1875 Brand, Erick D. *Selmer Band Instrument Repairing Manual*. 4th ed. Elkhart, IN: H. & A. Selmer, 1946.

1876 Brown, Ed. *Band Director's Percussion Repair Manual*. Van Nuys, CA: Alfred Publishing Company, 1996.

1877 Hart, Mickey, Fredric Lieberman, and D. A. Sonneborn. *Planet Drum: A Celebration of Percussion and Rhythm*. Petaluma, CA: Acid Test Productions, 1998.

1878 Meyer, R.F. *The Band Director's Guide to Instrument Repair*. Port Washington, NY: Alfred Publishing Company, 1973.

1879 Mueller, Kenneth A. *A Complete Guide to the Maintenance and Repair of Band Instruments*. West Nyack, NY: Parker Publishing Company, 1982.

1880 Springer, George H. *Maintenance and Repair of Wind and Percussion Instru-* ments. Boston, MA: Allyn and Bacon, 1976.

1881 Tiede, Clayton H. *The Practical Band Instrument Repair Manual*. Dubuque, IA: William C. Brown, 1976.

1882 York Band Instrument Company. *Care of Band Instruments*. Grand Rapids, MI, 1940.

Part 8
Music Selection

The following music has been used successfully by indoor color guards, marching bands, and twirling units.

Indoor Color Guard Performance Numbers

1883 "All Night Long" (Lionel Ritchie)

1884 "American Salute" (Morton Gould)

1885 "Another Cha-Cha" (Santa Esmeralda)

1886 "Babes in Toyland" (Victor Herbert; 1961 soundtrack)

1887 "Bacchanale from Samson and Delilah" (Saint-Saens)

1888 "Birdland" (Manhattan Transfer; arr. Zawinul/Lowden)

1889 "Bolero" (Ravel)

1890 "Breakfast at Tiffany's" (Deep Blue Something)

1891 "Breathe" (Willy Porter)

1892 "Bury My Lovely" (October Project)

1893 "Candide" (Leonard Bernstein)

1894 "Can't Fight the Moonlight" (LeAnn Rimes)

1895 "Captain from Castile" (soundtrack)

1896 "Carmen" (Bizet)

1897 "Carry On Wayward Son" (Kansas)

1898 "Casino Royale" (soundtrack)

1899 "Cat's in the Cradle" (Harry Chapin)

1900 "Celebration" (Kool and the Gang)

1901 "Center Field" (John Fogarty)

1902 "Cheeseburger in Paradise" (Jimmy Buffett)

1903 "Children of Eve" (Linda Eder)

1904 "Christmas Eve, Sarajevo" (Trans-Siberian Orchestra)

1905 "Circle Game" (Joni Mitchell)

1906 "Classical Gas" (Mason Williams)

1907 "Come Sail Away" (Styx)

1908 "Conga" (Miami Sound Machine)

1909 "Copacabana" (Barry Manilow)

1910 "Deep as You Go" (Mary Fahl)

1911 "Devil Went Down to Georgia" (Charlie Daniels Band)

1912 "Don't Cry" (Asia)

1913 "Don't Hold Back Your Love" (Daryl Hall)

1914 "Don't Let Me Be Misunderstood" (Santa Esmeralda)

1915 "Don't Stop Me Now" (Queen)

1916 "Dreamer" (Supertramp)

1917 "Dust in the Wind" (Kansas)

1918 "Ecstasy" (Rusted Root)

1919 "Everywhere" (Michelle Branch)

1920 "Fantasy and Fugue in C Minor" (Bach)

1921 "Fast Car" (Tracy Chapman)

1922 "Funeral for a Friend/Love Lies Bleeding" (Elton John)

1923 "Getaway" (Earth, Wind & Fire)

1924 "(Ghost) Riders in the Sky" (Vaughn Monroe or Sons of the Pioneers)

1925 "Hands Down" (Dan Hartman)

1926 "Here Comes the Sun" (George Harrison)

1927 "Hey, Man" (Nelly Furtado)

1928 "Hitman" (AB Logig)

1929 "Holding Out for a Hero" (Bonnie Tyler)

1930 "Hot, Hot, Hot/Ole, Ole" (Sam Wright)

1931 "The House" (*American Beauty* soundtrack)

1932 "How You Remind Me" (Nickelback)

1933 "Infernal Dance" (Stravinsky's *Firebird*)

1934 "In the Name of the Father" (Bono/*In the Name of the Father* soundtrack)

1935 "In the Stone" (Earth, Wind and Fire)

1936 "In Your Eyes" (Peter Gabriel)

1937 "Iris" (Goo Goo Dolls)

1938 "It's Raining Men" (Weather Girls)

1939 "Joy" (Switched on Bach)

1940 "Karma Slave" (Splashdown)

1941 "Karn Evil 9" (Emerson, Lake and Palmer)

1942 "Kashmir" (Led Zeppelin)

1943 "Kokomo" (Beach Boys)

1944 "Kyrie" (Mr. Mister)

1945 "Lady in Red" (Chris Deberg)

1946 "Late in the Evening" (Paul Simon)

1947 "Leader of the Band" (Dan Fogelberg)

1948 "Let the River Run" (Carly Simon)

1949 "Live and Let Die" (soundtrack)

1950 "Long Time" (Boston)

1951 "Lord of the Dance," aka "The Gift to Be Simple" (Aaron Copland, *Appalachian Spring*)

1952 "Lost Boys" (soundtrack)

1953 "Manhattan Skyline" (*Saturday Night Fever* soundtrack)

1954 "Me and Bobby McGee" (Janis Joplin)

1955 "Miss Saigon" (Broadway cast album)

1956 "More Than a Feeling" (Boston)

1957 "Mortal Kombat" (soundtrack)

1958 "Moulin Rouge" (2002 soundtrack selections)

1959 "Mountain Music" (Alabama)

1960 "Music Is My First Love" (Don Miles)

1961 "My Stronger Suit" (Spice Girls)

1962 "Night on Bald Mountain" (Mussorgsky)

1963 "One Voice" (Billy Gilman)

1964 "Paradise Theater" (Styx)

1965 "Peace of Mind" (Boston)

1966 "Peer Gynt Suite" (Grieg; Peer Gynt)

1967 "Piano Man" (Billy Joel)

1968 "Pressure" (Billy Joel)

1969 "Proud Mary" (Tina Turner)

1970 "Ride-O-Rocket" (Brothers Johnson)

1971 "Rocky" (soundtrack)

1972 "Run Like Hell" (David Palmer and Royal Philharmonic Orchestra)

1973 "Sailing" (N'Sync)

1974 "Shaft" (1971 soundtrack)

1975 "Ships That Pass in the Night" (Barry Manilow)

1976 "Short Skirt Long Jacket" (Cake)

1977 "Smooth" (Santana)

1978 "Starlight Express" (Broadway cast album)

1979 "Starry, Starry Night" (Josh Groban)

1980 "Star Wars" (soundtrack)

1981 "State of Independence (Jon Anderson/Vangelis)

1982 "Superman" (soundtrack)

1983 "This Woman's Work (Kate Bush)

1984 "A Thousand Miles (Vanessa Carlton)

1985 "Time to Say Goodbye" (Sarah Brightman, Andrea Bocelli)

1986 "Touched by the Rose of the Day" (Seal)

1987 "Tomorrow" (*Annie* soundtrack/Broadway cast album)

1988 "Tonight, Tonight" (Smashing Pumpkins)

1989 "Treasure of You" (Steven Curtis Chapman)

1990 "Trust" (Janet Jackson)

1991 "Turn It on Again" (Phil Collins & Genesis)

1992 "U.G.L.Y." (*Bring It On* soundtrack)

1993 "Under Pressure" (Queen/David Bowie)

1994 "Volare"/"That's Amore" (Dean Martin)

1995 "Walking in Memphis" (March Cohn)

1996 "Walt Disney Presents Millennium Celebration"

1997 "We're in the Money" (*Golddiggers of 1933* soundtrack)

1998 "Witches of Eastwick" (London cast album)

1999 "You Can Still Be Free" (Savage Garden)

Marching Band Field Show and Parade Numbers

2000 "Adagio for Strings" (Barber; arr. Jennings; G. Schirmer)

2001 "Alexander's Ragtime Band" (arr. Bocook; Jenson)

2002 "America the Beautiful" (arr. Jay Dawson; Arrangers Publishing Company)

2003 "An American in Paris" (arr. Snoeck; McCormick's)

2004 "Appalachian Spring" (Copland; arr. Jay Dawson; Arrangers Publishing Company)

2005 "Aquarius/Let the Sun Shine In" (arr. Brad Pearson; Arrangers Publishing Company)

2006 "Aztec Fire" (arr. Bocook; Jenson)

2007 "Bacchanale from Samson and Delilah" (Saint-Saens; J. W. Pepper or Warner Bros.; drumline version arr. Erik Johnson; Arrangers Publishing Co.)

2008 "Beauty and the Beast" (arr. Lavender; Jenson; arr. Bocook, Jenson)

2009 "Beethoven's Fifth" (arr. Tom Wallace; Arrangers Publishing Company)

2010 "Bellavia" (arr. Mangione/Holcombe; Warner Bros.)

2011 "Ben-Hur" (Miklos Rozsa; arr. Ralph Ford; Southern Music Co.)

2012 "Big Noise from Winnetka" (arr. Michael Sweeney and J.J. Jenkins; Warner Bros.; arr. Robert Smith, Warner Bros.)

2013 "Birdland" (arr. Snoeck; Barnhouse; Hal Leonard; arr. Wallace, Arrangers Publishing Company)

2014 "Bohemian Rhapsody" (Queen; Hal Leonard)

2015 "Boogie Woogie Bugle Boy" (arr. Bill Windham; Warner Bros.)

2016 "Brian's Song" (arr. Cotter; Columbia/Jenson)

2017 "Cantus—Song of Aeolus" (Jenkins/Wallace; J. W. Pepper)

2018 "Captain from Castille" (arr. Bocook; Jenson)

2019 "Carmen Medley" (Bizet; arr. Sharp, Major; Southern Music Co.)

2020 "Carmen Overture" (Bizet; arr. Ahronheim; Presser; arr. Dawson, J. W. Pepper)

2021 "Carmina Burana" (Orff; arr. Roberson; Warner Bros.; arr. Ford, J. W. Pepper)

2022 "Circle of Life" (*The Lion King* soundtrack; Hal Leonard)

2023 "Colonel Bogey March" (Maurice Jarré; arr. Michael Sweeney; Hal Leonard)

2024 "Come in from the Rain" (arr. Bocook; Jenson)

2025 "Copacabana" (arr. Vinson; Warner Bros.)

2026 "The Cowboys" (arr. Dye; Southern Music Co.)

2027 "Crown Imperial" (Walton; arr. Bocook; Hal Leonard)

2028 "Don't Cry for Me, Argentina" (arr. Edmondson; Leeds/MCA; arr. Michael Sweeney; Southern Music Co.; arr. Brian Scott; Warner Bros.)

2029 "Ease on Down the Road" (percussion; arr. Rapp; Jenson)

2030 "1812 Overture" (Tchaikovsky; arr. Jurrens; Jenson; arr. Henning; Southern Music Co.)

2031 "El Capitan" (John Philip Sousa; Presser)

2032 "El Gato Triste" (Mangione; arr. Kerchner/Tuthill; Hal Leonard; arr. Dawson, J. W. Pepper)

University of Delaware Fightin' Blue Hen Marching Band (Newark, DE)

2033 "Endless Love" (arr. Kerchner; Hal Leonard)

2034 "Fantasy" (arr. Jennings; Jenson)

2035 "Feels So Good" (arr. Mangione/Tkazyik/Holcombe; Warner Bros.)

2036 "Finale from Symphony No. 3 in C Minor, Op. 78" ["Organ Symphony"] (Saint-Saens; International Music Company)

2037 "Firebird Suite" (arr. Bocook; Jenson; arr. Richard Saucedo; Hal Leonard)

2038 "First Knight" (Jerry Goldsmith; arr. Richar Saucedo; Southern Music Co.)

2039 "Georgia on My Mind" (Hoagy Carmichael/Stuart Gorrell; arr. Michael Sweeney; Southern Music Co.)

2040 "Gettysburg" (Edelman; arr. Moss; Hal Leonard)

2041 "Gladiator" (Zimmer; arr. John Wasson; Hal Leonard)

2042 "God Bless the U.S.A." (Lee Greenwood; arr. Mike Story; Warner Bros.; arr. Robert W. Smith; Warner Bros.)

2043 "Goldfinger/James Bond Theme" (arr. Mike Story; Warner Bros.)

2044 "Gonna Fly Now (Theme from *Rocky*)" (Conti; arr. L. Clark; Southern Music Co.)

2045 "Great Gate of Kiev" (arr. Salzman; Columbia; arr. Dawson; Arrangers' Pub. Co.—corps style)

2046 "Harry Potter and the Sorcerer's Stone" (Williams; arr. Ford; J. W. Pepper)

2047 "Havendance" (David Holsinger; arr. Cauley; TRN Music Publisher)

2048 "Hawaii Five-O" (arr. Doug Adams; Warner Bros.)

2049 "The Hey Song" (arr. Mike Story; Warner Bros.)

2050 "House of the Rising Sun" (arr. Tom Wallace; Arrangers Publishing Company)

2051 "How the West Was Won" (Alfred Newman; arr. Clark; Southern Music Co.)

2052 "If You Believe" (arr. Smalls/Bocook; Columbia/Jenson)

2053 "I Got Rhythm" (Gershwin; arr. Victor Lopez; Warner Bros.)

2054 "In Caelum Fero" (Jenkins/Wallace; J. W. Pepper)

2055 "Independence Day (Themes)" (arr. Brian Scott; Southern Music Co.)

2056 "In the Midnight Hour" (arr. Waters; Hal Leonard)

2057 "In the Stone" (Earth, Wind & Fire; arr. Brian Scott; Warner Bros.; or Hal Leonard)

2058 "(I've Been Working on the) Railroad" (William Ballenger/Mid-America Music Publishers)

2059 "I Write the Songs" (arr. Higgins; Jenson)

2060 "James Bond Themes" (arr. Clark; Southern Music Co.)

2061 "King Cotton March" (John Philip Sousa; Presser)

2062 "Lady Marmalade" (arr. Michael Brown; Hal Leonard)

2063 "La Fiesta" (arr. Corea/Ahronheim; Warner Bros.)

2064 "Land of Make Believe" (Mangione; arr. Jay Dawson; J. W. Pepper; arr. Kercher; Southern Music Co.)

2065 "Lassus Trombone" (arr. Moffit; Hal Leonard)

2066 "Let It Be Me" (arr. Curtis, De Lanoe, Becaud/Ott, Cahill; Hal Leonard)

2067 "Long and Winding Road" (arr. Pegram; Hal Leonard)

2068 "Lord of the Rings" (Shore; arr. Victor Lopez; Warner Bros.)

2069 "MacArthur Park" (arr. Doug Adams; Warner Bros.)

2070 "The Magnificent Seven" (arr. Bullock; Belwin; arr. Dye; Southern Music Co.; arr. Doug Adams, Warner Bros.)

2071 "Malaguena" (arr. Higgins or Sweeney; Hal Leonard)

2072 "Marriage of Figaro" (arr. Balent; Jenson)

2073 "[Disney's] Millennium Celebration (Tapestry of Nations/Chaos, Reflections of Earth, We Go On)" (Gavin Greenaway; arr. Bocook/Rapp; Hal Leonard)

2074 "Miss Saigon (Heat Is on in Saigon, Sun and Moon, Kim's Nightmare)" (Schsnberg/Maltby/Boublil; arr. Bocook; Hal Leonard)

2075 "Moulin Rouge" (Hal Leonard)

2076 "The Muppet Show" (percussion; arr. Rapp; Jenson)

2077 "My Favorite Things" (Sound of Music soundtrack; arr. Lavender/Rapp; Hal Leonard)

2078 "New World Symphony" (Dvorak; arr. Bocook; Jenson; arr. Sweeney, Hal Leonard)

2079 "Night on Bald Mountain" (arr. Wanamaker; Alfred; arr. Bocook; Hal Leonard; arr. Chris Sharp/Carl Major; Southern Music Co.)

2080 "Noel" (Cal Danielson/Mid-America Music Publishers)

2081 "Ol' Man River" (arr. Moffit; Hal Leonard)

2082 "Olympic Fanfare and Theme" (arr. Lavender; Warner Bros.)

2083 "Olympic Fanfare and Theme" (John Williams; arr. Bocook; Southern Music Co.)

2084 "On Broadway" (arr. Lavender; Jenson; or Hal Leonard)

2085 "Over the Rainbow" (arr. Brian Scott; Southern Music Co.)

2086 "Overture from Candide" (arr. Grundmun; Boosey & Hawkes)

2087 "Pas de trois' from Ballet Sacra" (David Holsinger; arr. Cauley; TRN Music Publisher)

2088 "The Patriot" (John Williams; Hal Leonard)

2089 "Peg" (arr. Higgins; Jenson)

2090 "Phantom of the Opera" (arr. Vinson; Hal Leonard; arr. Paul Lavender; Southern Music Co.)

2091 "Pictures at an Exhibition" (arr. Bocook; Jenson or Southern Music Co.; also Hal Leonard)

2092 "The Planets" (Holst; arr. Michael Sto-
      pry; Warner Bros.)

2093 "Ready to Take a Chance Again" (arr.
      Bocook; Jenson)

2094 "Rhapsody in Blue" (Gershwin; arr.
      Larry Clark; Warner Bros.)

2095 "Ride Like the Wind" (arr. Tim Wa-
      ters; Hal Leonard)

2096 "Riverdance" (Bill Whelan; arr. Tom
      Wallace; Southern Music Co.)

2097 "Robin Hood: Prince of Thieves" ["Sym-
      phonic Movies Show"] (Kamen; arr.
      Brian Scott; Warner Bros.)

2098 "Russian Christmas Music" (arr. Hop-
      per; Barnhouse)

2099 "Russian Sailor's Dance" (arr. Walters;
      William Allen; arr. Fabrizio; South-
      ern Music Co.)

2100 "Saints [Go Marching In]." (arr. Wal-
      ters; Hal Leonard; arr. Steve Pfaff-
      man; Band Music Press)

2101 "Salute to Sousa!" (Neil Boumpani/
      Mid-America Music Publishers)

2102 "Semper Fi" (arr. Bocook; Jenson)

2103 "Send in the Clowns" (arr. Sondheim/
      Higgins; Jenson; arr. Mike Story;
      Southern Music Co.)

2104 "Seventy-Fix Trombones" (Hal Leo-
      nard)

2105 "Shaker Hymn" (arr. Taylor; Columbia)

2106 "Shenandoah" (arr. Downey/Rapp;
      Jenson)

2107 "Sinfonia Voci" (David Holsinger; arr.
      Cauley; TRN Music Publisher)

2108 "Sing, Sing, Sing" (arr. Moffitt; Hal
      Leonard; arr. Nick Baratta; Warner
      Bros.)

2109 "Slaughter on Tenth Avenue" (arr.
      Rodgers/Kerchner; Hal Leonard)

2110 "Smooth" (Santana; arr. Ralph Ford;
      Warner Bros.; arr. Richard Saucedo;
      Hal Leonard)

2111 "Softly as I Leave You" (arr. DeVita/
      Kerchner, Cahill; Hal Leonard; arr.
      Mike Story; Warner Bros.)

2112 "Somewhere Out There" [Theme
      from *An American Tail*] (arr. Bocook;
      Warner Bros.)

2113 "The Sorcerer's Apprentice" (arr. Rich-
      ard Saucedo; Hal Leonard)

2114 "Sousa Classics" ["El Capitan, Liberty
      Bell, Stars and Stripes Forever"] (arr.
      Victor Lopez; Warner Bros.)

2115 "Spartacus" (Khachaturian; concert;
      Edwin F. Kalmus and Hal Leonard)

2116 "Sport" (Cal Danielson/Mid-America
      Music Publishers)

2117 "Star" (arr. Cotter; Jenson)

2118 "StarDate" (arr. Brinkman; Mid-Amer-
      ica Music Publishers)

2119 "The Stars and Stripes Forever" (arr.
      Smith; Jenson; also Presser; arr.
      Chris Sharp; Southern Music Co.)

2120 "Star Wars" (John Williams; arr. Victor
      Lopez; Southern Music Co.)

2121 "Star Wars Themes" (John Williams;
      arr. Larry Clark; Southern Music
      Co.)

2122 "Strike Up the Band" (Gershwin; arr.
      Higgins; Jenson; arr. Ralph Ford;
      Warner Bros.)

2123 "Superman Theme" (arr. Cotter; Jenson/Warner Bros.)

2124 "Swamp Boogie" (David Brinkman/Mid-America Music Publishers)

2125 "Swanee River/Camptown Races" (David Brinkman/Mid-America Music Publishers)

2126 "Swan Lake" (arr. Pegram; Hal Leonard)

2127 "Sweet Georgia Brown" (arr. Will Rapp and Paul Jennings; Jenson)

2128 "Take the 'A' Train" (arr. Higgins; Jenson)

2129 "Tempered Steel" (Charles Young; concert, Southern Music Co.)

2130 "Temptation" (arr. Bocook; Jenson)

2131 "Tequila" (Chuck Rio; arr. Paul Lavender; Hal Leonard)

2132 "Terminator 2" (arr. Michael Sweeney; Hal Leonard)

2133 "They're Playing Our Song" (arr. Nowak; Hal Leonard)

2134 "Thriller" (Michael Jackson; arr. Bocook; Hal Leonard)

2135 "Through the Eyes of Love" [Theme from *Ice Castles*] (arr. Hamlisch/Cotter; Jenson/Columbia; arr. Doug Adams, Warner Bros.)

2136 "T J" (David Brinkman/Mid-America Music Publishers)

2137 "Tomorrow" (from *Annie*) (arr. Jennings; Jenson)

2138 "Tusk" (Fleetwood Mac; arr. Brian Scott; Warner Bros.)

2139 "Twelfth Street Rag" (arr. Higgins; Jenson)

2140 "Twilight Zone" (arr. Higgins; Jenson)

2141 "Under the Sea" (ar. Will Rapp; Jenson)

2142 "Veracruz" (arr. Bocook; Jenson)

2143 "Victors" (Jeff James/Mid-America Music Publishers)

2144 "Washington Post March" (John Philip Sousa; Hal Leonard)

2145 "The Way We Were" (arr. McCullough; Columbia)

2146 "Weekend in New England" (arr. Edelman/Scott; Warner Bros.)

2147 "What I Did for Love" (arr. Edmonson; Hal Leonard)

2148 "The Wiz" (arr. Victor Lopez; Southern Music Co.)

2149 "Wizard of Oz" (arr. Michael Story; Warner Bros.)

2150 "Yankee Doodle Dandy" (Cal Danielson/Mid-America Music Publishers)

2151 "You'll Never Walk Alone" (arr. Kerchner; Hal Leonard)

2152 "You're a Grand Old Flag" (arr. Moffitt; Hal Leonard)

2153 "You've Lost That Lovin' Feelin'" (arr. Cotter; Jenson)

2154 "Zarabanda—Palladio" (Jenkins/Wallace; J. W. Pepper)

Twirling Selections
(Corps/Ensemble/Group Dance-Twirl)

Entrance/Exit Numbers

2155 "Alive Again" (Chicago)

2156 "Girls Just Want to Have Fun" (Cyndi Lauper)

2157 "Had Enough" (The Who)

2158 "I Love Rock and Roll" (Joan Jett & the Blackhearts)

2159 "Jet Airliner" (Steve Miller)

2160 "Long Time" (Boston)

2161 "Music Box Dancer" (Frank Mills)

2162 "On Broadway" (George Benson)

2163 "Rise" (Herb Alpert)

2164 "Stony End" (Barbra Streisand)

2165 "What I Did for Love" (*A Chorus Line* cast album)

Performance Numbers

2166 "Alegria" (René Dupéré/Cirque du Soleil; RCA Victor)

2167 "All That Jazz" (Chicago)

2168 "Beat It" (Michael Jackson)

2169 "Best of My Love" (Emotions)

2170 "Brand New Day" (The Wiz)

2171 "Breaking Away" (Balance)

2172 "Bye Bye Birdie" (soundtrack)

2173 "Can-Can" (arr. Wanamaker; Alfred)

2174 "Cats" (Broadway cast album)

2175 "Celebration" (Kool and the Gang)

2176 "Changes" (Yes)

2177 "City Lights" (Liza Minnelli)

2178 "Danger Zone" (Kenny Loggins)

2179 "Desdemona" (*Fame* soundtrack)

2180 "Don't Stop Till You Got Enough" (Michael Jackson)

2181 "Dreams" (Van Halen)

2182 "Ease on Down the Road" (*The Wiz* soundtrack/Broadway cast album)

2183 "Every Little Thing She Does Is Magic" (Police)

2184 "Fame" (soundtrack; Irene Cara)

2185 "Fragile" (Sting)

2186 "Hands Down" (Dan Hartman)

2187 "Hawaii 5-0" (TV theme; Ventures)

2188 "The Heat Is On" (Kenny Loggins)

2189 "Hip to Be Square" (Huey Lewis and the News)

2190 "Hit Me with Your Best Shot" (Pat Benatar)

2191 "House of the Rising Sun" (Eric Burdon and the Animals)

2192 "I'm Coming Out" (Diana Ross)

2193 "Jailhouse Rock" (Elvis Presley)

2194 "Jump" (Van Halen)

2195 "Jump" (Pointer Sisters)

2196 "Jump Shout Boogie" (Barry Manilow)

2197 "Knock on Wood" (Aretha Franklin)

2198 "Kokomo" (Beach Boys)

2199 "(Theme from) *Ladyhawke*" (soundtrack)

2200 "Let's Hear It for Me" (Barbra Streisand)

2201 "MacArthur Park" (Donna Summer)

2202 "The Main Event" (soundtrack; Barbra Streisand)

2203 "Makin' It" (*Meatballs* soundtrack; David Naughton)

2204 "Manhattan Skyline" (*Saturday Night Fever* soundtrack)

2205 "The Music and the Mirror" (*A Chorus Line* cast album)

2206 "New York City Rhythm" (Barry Manilow)

2207 "Once Upon a Time" (Donna Summer)

2208 "Perry Mason" (Ozzy Osbourne)

2209 "Ring My Bell" (Anita Ward)

2210 "Rio" (Peter Allen)

2211 "Rootbeer Rag" (Billy Joel)

2212 "Scarborough Fair" (Sarah Brightman)

2213 "Scotch Machine" (Marlin "Voyage" album; T.K. Productions, Hialeah, FL)

2214 "Son of Man" (Phil Collins; Disney *Tarzan* soundtrack)

2215 "Spies in the Night" (Manhattan Transfer)

2216 "Surfin' U.S.A." (Beach Boys)

2217 "That Thing You Do" (soundtrack)

2218 "They're Playing Our Song" (Broadway cast album)

2219 "Time to Say Goodbye" (Sarah Brightman, Andrea Bocelli)

2220 "Unchained Melody" (Al Hibbler or Righteous Brothers or Les Baxter instrumental)

2221 "A View to a Kill / Dance Into the Fire" (*View to a Kill* soundtrack / Duran Duran)

2222 "Viva Las Vegas" (Elvis Presley)

2223 "Walk Him Up the Stairs" (*Purlie* cast album)

2224 "We Are Young" (Pat Benatar)

2225 "We Can Get There" (Mary Griffin)

2226 "Why" (Annie Lennox)

2227 "Working for the Weekend" (Loverboy)

2228 "Yankee Doodle Boy" (DCA Experience, Bicentennial Gold Album; Private Stock Records)

2229 "You're the One That I Want" (*Grease* soundtrack)

2230 "You Should Be Dancing" (*Saturday Night Fever* soundtrack)

Music Libraries and Research Centers

2231 American Bandmasters Association
Research Center
University Libraries
University of Maryland
College Park, MD 20742-7011
301-405-0800
www.lib.umd.edu/MUSIC/ABA/Col-
lections.html

2232 American Music Center
30 W. 26th Street, Suite 1001
New York, NY 10010-2011
212-366-5260
www.amc.net

2233 Chatfield Brass Band Music Lending
Library
81 Library Lane
Chatfield, MN 55923
507-867-3275
www.rochestermn.com/community/
chatfieldbrass

2234 The Mummers Museum
1100 S. Second Street
Philadelphia, PA 19147
215-336-3050
Fax 215-389-5630
http://riverfrontmummers.com/mu
seum.html
email: mummersmus@aol.com

2235 Sousa Archives for Band Research
236 Harding Band Building
1103 South Sixth Street
University of Illinois at Urbana-Champaign
Champaign, IL 61820
217-244-9309
Fax 217-244-8695
www.library.uiuc.edu/sousa
email: cressman@uiuc.edu

Music Publishers and Distributors

2236 Alfred Australia
P.O. Box 2355
Taren Point, NSW 2229
Australia
Fax 61-2-9524-0033
email: promo@alfredpub.com.au

2237 Alfred Germany
Max-Planck-Str 4
53577 Neustadt-Fernthal
Germany
49-268-3939346
Fax 49-268-3939348
email: sales@alfredverlag.de

2238 Alfred Los Angeles (Alfred Publishing
Company, Inc. main office)
P.O. Box 10003
Van Nuys, CA 91410-0003
818-891-5999

Fax 818-891-2369
www.alfred.com
email: customerservice@alfred.com

2239 Alfred Singapore
15 Queen Street #03-09
Tan Chong Tower
Singapore 188537
65-3371629
Fax 65-3376319
email: alfredco@pacific.net.sg

2240 Alfred UK
Burnt Mill Elizabeth Way
Harlow, Essex CM20 2HX
England
44-1279-828960
Fax 44-1279-828961
email: Music@alfredpublishing.demon.
co.uk

Manchester Township High School Marching Hawks Band (Manchester Township, NJ)

2241 All Star Records
c/o Star Line Baton Company
P.O. Box 5490
Pompano Beach, FL 33074-5490

2242 Altissimo Recordings
1830 Air Lane Drive, Suite 3-B

Nashville, TN 37210
800-999-9911

2243 Arrangers Publishing Company
200 Hill Avenue, Suite 4
Nashville, TN 37210
800-331-6806

Fax 615-726-3691
www.arrpubco.com

Associated Music Publishers, Inc. *see* G.
Schirmer Inc.

2244 Band Music Press
P.O. Box 600
Wilmette, IL 60091
847-251-3000
Fax 847-251-1199
email: bmuspress@aol.com

Belwin Mills Publishing Corporation *see*
CPP/Belwin Music

2245 Boosey and Hawkes, Inc.
52 Cooper Square
New York, NY 10003
212-979-1090
Fax 212-358-5303
www.boosey.com
email: sales.us@boosey.com

2246 Brodt Music Company, Inc.
1906 Commonwealth Avenue
Charlotte, NC 28299
800-438-4129
Fax 800-446-0812
www.brodtmusic.com
email: orders@brodtmusic.com

2247 Broude Brothers, Ltd.
170 Varick Street
New York, NY 10013

C.F. Peters Corporation *see* Edition Peters
Ltd.

2248 C.L. Barnhouse Company
205 Cowan Avenue West
Oskaloosa, IA 52577

2249 Carl Fischer LLC (also distributed by
music dealers nationwide)
65 Bleecker Street
New York, NY 10012
212-777-0900
Fax 212-477-6996

www.carlfischer.com
email: cf-info@carlfischer.com

Chappell & Company *see* Hal Leonard Publishing Corporation

Colfranc Music Publishing Corporation *see*
CPP/Belwin, Inc.

2250 Cherry Lane Music Publishing
6 East 32nd Street, 11th Floor
New York, NY 10016
212-561-3000
www.cherrylane.com
and: 5757 Wilshire Blvd., Suite 401
Los Angeles, CA 90036
323-904-4510

Columbia Pictures Publications *see* CPP/
Belwin, Inc.

2251 CPP/Belwin, Inc.
15800 N.W. 48th Avenue
Miami, FL 33014
305-620-1500
Fax 305-625-3480

2252 Edition Peters Ltd.
Hinrichsen House
10-12 Baches Street
London N1 6DN
United Kingdom
+44 (0) 20 7553 4000
Fax +44 (0) 20 7490 4921
www.edition-peters.com
email: sales@uk.edition-peters.com

2253 Educational Programs Publications
1784 West Schuylkill Road
Douglassville, PA 19518
800-323-0974
Fax 610-327-4786
www.educationalprogams.com
email: info@edprog.com

Edward B. Marks Music Corporation *see* Hal
Leonard Publishing Corporation

2254 Edwin F. Kalmus & Company, Inc.
P.O. Box 5011

Boca Raton, FL 33431
800-434-6340
Fax 561-241-6347
www.kalmus-music.com

2255 800-SheetMusic.com
27475 Ynez Road, #310
Temecula, CA 92591-4612
Fax 909-693-2840
www.800sheetmusic.com
email: customerservice@800sheetmu
sic.com

2256 Elkan-Vogel, Inc.
Presser Place & Lancaster Avenue
Bryn Mawr, PA 19010

2257 G. Schirmer, Inc.
257 Park Avenue South, 20th Floor
New York, NY 10010
212-254-2100
Fax 212-254-2013
www.schirmer.com
e-mail: schirmer@schirmer.com
    See also Hal Leonard Publishing
    Corporation

2258 GIA Publications, Inc.
7404 S. Mason Avenue
Chicago, IL 60638
800-442-1358
Fax 708-496-3828
www.giamusic.com
email: custserv@giamusic.com

2259 Hal Leonard Publishing Corporation
7777 W. Bluemound Road
Milwaukee, WI 53213
414-774-3630
Fax 414-774-3259
www.halleonard.com
email: halinfo@halleonard.com
    Distributes catalogs of Associated
    Music Publishers, Chappell & Co.,
    G. Schirmer, Jenson Publications,
    Edward B. Marks

2260 HaMaR Percussion Publications
333 Spring Road

Huntington, NY 11743
631-427-7194
Fax 631-732-5007
email: HaMaRPERC@aol.com

Highland/Etling Publishing Company *see*
Alfred Publishing Company

2261 The Hindsley Transcriptions, Ltd.
18559 Carpenter Street
Homewood, IL 60430-3533
708-799-6491
Fax 708-799-9696
www.hindsleytranscriptions.com
email: robert@hindsleytranscriptions.
    com

2262 International Music Company
5 West 37th Street
New York, NY 10018
212-391-4200
Fax 212-391-4306
www.internationalmusic.com
email: info@internationalmusic.com

2263 J.W. Pepper and Son, Inc.
P.O. Box 850
Valley Forge, PA 19482
800-345-6296
Fax 800-260-1482
www.jwpepper.com
email: satisfaction@jwpepper.com
    Also located in Atlanta; Dallas;
    Detroit; Los Angeles; Paiges, IN;
    Winston-Salem, NC

2264 James F. Chapin
14 Elizabeth Street
Sag Harbor, NY 11963
516-725-2221

2265 Jenson Publications
c/o Hal Leonard Corporation
7777 W. Bluemound Road
Milwaukee, WI 43213
414-774-3630
Fax 414-774-3259
www.halleonard.com
email: halinfo@halleonard.com

Ridley High School Raider Marching Band (Folsom, PA)

2266 Kendor Music, Inc.
P.O. Box 278
Delevan, NY 14042-0278
716-492-1254
Fax 716-492-5124
www.kendormusic.com
email: kendor@wycol.com

2267 Ludwig Music Publishing Company, Inc.
557 East 140th Street
Cleveland, OH 44110-1999
216-851-1150
Fax 216-851-1958
www.ludwigmusic.com
email: ludwig_accounts@ameritech.net

2268 M.M. Cole Publishing Company
251 East Grand Avenue
Chicago, IL 60611

M. Witmark and Sons *see* Warner Brothers Publications, Inc.

2269 Magnamusic-Baton
10370 Page Industrial Blvd.
St. Louis, MO 63132

2270 Manhattan Beach Music (specializes in concert band music)
1595 East 46th Street
Brooklyn, NY 11234
718-338-4137
Fax 718-338-1151
http://members.aol.com/mbmband/index.html
email: mbmband@aol.com

2271 Manhattan Music Publications, Inc. (acquired by CPP/Belwin, Inc.)

Marching Percussion Northwest *see* Matrix Publishing Company

2272 Matrix Publishing Company
2510 Debra Drive
Springfield, OR 97477
541-747-6903

Fax 541-746-7718
www.matrixmusic.com

Mercury Music Corporation *see* Theodore Presser Company

2273 Meredith Music Publications (distributed by Hal Leonard)
P.O. Box 344
Galesville, MD 20765
800-637-2852
Fax 301-261-5015
www.meredithmusic.com
email: garwoodw@aol.com (editorial), sales@halleonard.com (dealers)

2274 Mid-America Music Publishers
3541 N. 2nd Street
Lincoln, NE 68521
404-474-4023
www.midamericamusic.com

2275 Midland CD Club (brass and military band CD specialists)
www.midland-cd-club.co.uk/cgi-bin/index-mid.pl

2276 MilitaryMusic.com (CDs and cassettes)
www.militarymusic.com

2277 The Music Mart Inc.
3301 Carlisle Blvd., NE
Albuquerque, NM 87110
800-545-6204/505-889-9777
Fax 505-889-9070
www.musicmart.com

2278 The Music Mart Inc.
5070 N. Central Avenue
Phoenix, AZ 85012
602-263-4039
Fax 602-263-4085
www.musicmart.com

2279 Neil A. Kjos Music Company
P.O. Box 178270
San Diego, CA 92117-8270

858-270-9800
Fax 858-270-3507
www.kjos.com
email: email@kjos.com

2280 Norman Lee Publishing, Inc.
Box 528
Oskaloosa, IA 52577
515-673-7459
Fax 515-673-4718
www.mpa.org/agency/224p.html

2281 Oxford University Press, Inc.
Music Department
198 Madison Avenue
New York, NY 10016
212-726-6000
Fax 212-726-6440
www.oup-usa.org

2282 Pecknel Music Company
1660 Sam Rittenberg Blvd.
Charleston, SC 29407
843-766-7660
Fax 843-766-7662
www.pecknelmusic.com
email: info@pecknelmusic.com
        also in Columbia and Greenville, SC

Peer International Corporation *see* Southern
Music Company

2283 Per-Mus Percussion Publications Inc.
P.O. Box 21833
Columbus, OH 43221
614-529-0085
email: permus@aol.com

2284 Publishers Outlet
P.O. Box 40772
Nashville, TN 37204

2285 RBC Music Company, Inc.
P.O. Box 29128
San Antonio, TX 78229
800-548-0917
Fax 210-736-2919
www.rbcmusic.com
sales@rbcmusic.com

2286 Shattinger Music Inc.
1810 South Broadway
St. Louis, MO 63104-4051
www.shattingermusic.com

2287 sheetmusicplus.com

2288 Solid Brass Music Company
71 Mt. Rainier Drive
San Rafael, CA 94903
800-873-9798
Fax 415-472-0603
www.sldbrass.com
email: dick@sldbrass.com

2289 Songo Music
7188 Cradlerock Way, Suite 138
Columbia, MD 21045

2290 Southern Music Company
P.O. Box 329
San Antonio, TX 78292
800-284-5443
Fax 210-223-4537
www.southernmusic.com
email: info@southernmusic.com

2291 Southern Music Company of Houston
9189 Winkler, Suite E
P.O. Box 12687
Houston, TX 77217
713-941-5500

2292 Stanton's Sheet Music
330 South 4th Street
Columbus, OH 43215
614-224-4257
Fax 614-224-5929
www.stantons.com

2293 Studio P/R
15800 Northwest 48th Avenue
P.O. Box 4340
Miami, FL 33126
2294 Sunhawk.com Digital Music
www.sunhawk.com/print

2295 Theodore Presser Company
588 North Gulph Road

King of Prussia, PA 19406
610-525-3636
Fax 610-527-7841
www.presser.com
email: presser@presser.com

2296 TRN Music Publisher, Inc.
P.O. Box 1076—119 Torreon Loop
Ruidoso, NM 88355
505-258-4325
Fax 505-258-3129
www.trnmusic.com
email: maillist@trnmusic.com

2297 Warner Bros. Publications, Inc.
15800 N.W. 48th Avenue
Miami, FL 33014
305-620-1500
Fax 305-621-4869
www.warnerbrospublications.com
email: wbpsales@warnerchappell.com

2298 Warner/Chappell Music, Inc.
10585 Santa Monica Blvd.
Los Angeles, CA 90025-4950
310-441-8600
Fax 310-470-1587
www.warnerchappell.com
email: webmaster@warnerchappell.
com

2299 William Allen Music, Inc.
P.O. Box 790
Newington, VA 22122
703-550-2500
Fax 703-550-2503

2300 Wingert-Jones Music, Inc.
11225 Colorado
Kansas City, MO 64137-2502
800-258-WJMO
Fax 800-382-8250
www.wjmusic.com

Associations

2301 American Music Conference
5790 Armada Drive
Carlsbad, CA 92008-4372
760-431-9124
Fax 760-438-7327
www.amc-music.org
email: info@amc-music.org

2302 American Musicians Union
8 Tobin Court
Dumont, NJ 07628
201-384-5378

2303 American Society of Music Arrangers
& Composers
P.O. Box 17840
Encino, CA 91416
818-994-4661
Fax 818-994-6181
www.asmac.org

2304 International Horn Society
8180 Thunder Street
Juneau, AK 99801

907-789-5477
Fax 907-790-4066
www.hornsociety.org

2305 Music Distributors Association
262 West 38th Street, Room 1506
New York, NY 10018-5808
212-302-0801
Fax 212-302-0783
http://musicdistributors.org
email: assnhdqs@aol.com

2306 Music Library Association
8551 Research Way, Suite 180
Middleton, WI 53562
703-556-8780
Fax 703-556-9301
www.musiclibraryassoc.org

2307 Music Publishers' Association of the
United States
1562 First Avenue, PMB 246
New York, NY 10028
212-327-4044

Jackson Memorial High School Jaguar Marching Band (Jackson, NJ)

www.mpa.org
email: mpa-admin@mpa.org

2308 National Association of School Music
       Dealers
13140 Coit Road, Suite 320/LB-120
Dallas, TX 75240-5737

972-233-9107, x204
Fax 972-490-4219
www.nasmd.com

2309 National Music Council
425 Park Street
Upper Montclair, NJ 07043

973-655-7974
Fax 973-655-5432
www.musiccouncil.org

2310 National Music Publishers Association
711 Third Avenue, 8th Floor
New York, NY 10017-4014
212-370-5330
Fax 212-953-2384
www.nmpa.org

2311 Retail Print Music Dealers Association
13140 Coit Road,
Suite 320, LB 120
Dallas, TX 75240-5737
972-233-9107, x204
Fax 972-490-4219
www.printmusic.org
email: office@printmusic.org

Selected Bibliography

Articles

2312 Baker, Richard. "Finding That Old Familiar Tune." *Instrumentalist* (September 1987): 84.

2313 Higgins, John. "How to Buy (and Repair) Marching Band Arrangements." *Instrumentalist* (Sepember 1977): 39–44.

2314 Jenson, Art. "Careers in Educational Music Publishing." *Instrumentalist* (August 1977): 48–50.

2315 "Marching Band Music: Comments from Our New Music Reviewers." *Instrumentalist* (June 1980): 8–10.

2316 Mendyk, Lee A. "The Chatfield Brass Band Free Music Lending Library." *Library Journal* (October 1982): 21.

Books

2317 Benton, Rita, comp. *Directory of Music Libraries. Part 1: Canada and the United States.* Iowa City, IA: University of Iowa, 1967.

2318 Instrumentalist Company. *Band Music Guide: Alphabetical Listing of Titles and Composers of All Band Music.* 10th ed. Northfield, IL, 1996.

2319 *Music Article Guide.* Philadelphia, PA: Information Services. Quarterly, 1969–1996.

2320 *Music Index.* A Subject-Author Guide to Over 300 Current Periodicals from the U.S., England, Canada & Australia and 19 Non-English Language Countries. Warren, MI: Harmonie Park Press (Information Coordinators, Inc.) Monthly.

2321 Rehrig, William H. *The Heritage Encyclopedia of Band Music: Composers and Their Music.* Edited by Paul E. Bierley. Westerville, OH: Integrity Press, 1991.

2322 Smith, Norman, and Albert Stoutamire. *Band Music Notes.* San Diego, CA: Neil A. Kjos Music Company, 1979.

Part 9
Parades

Some high school marching bands eschew competitions in favor of halftime show and parades and may gear up for trips to the Rose Bowl Parade or Miss America Parade.

Directory

Parades listed here are annual, the biggest of the big, nationally known, or street competitions exclusive of a field show.

AAA Michigan Heritage Parade *see* National Cherry Festival Parades

2324 ABC/Boscov's Philadelphia Thanksgiving Day Parade
c/o Todd Marcocci
Under the Sun Productions
882 South Matlack Street, Suite 202
West Chester, PA 19382
800-264-1121

2325 Albert Lea Festival of Bands
Albert Lea Convention and Visitor's Bureau
Albert Lea, MN
507-373-3938
www.festivalofbands.org
email: alcvb@smig.net

2326 Albertson's Conquistadors Grand Fiesta Parade
P.O. Box 1943
Pensacola, FL 32589
850-433-6512
Fax 850-438-5572
www.fiestaoffiveflags.org/parade.htm
email: info@FiestaofFiveFlags.org

America's Thanksgiving Parade (site: Detroit, MI) *see* Bowl Games of America

2327 Appletime Grand Parade
Murphysboro Apple Festival
203 South 13th Street
Murphysboro, IL 62966
Fax 618-684-2010
www.murphysboro.com/events/AppleFest/parade.html
email: executive@GlobalEyes.net

2328 Azalea Festival Parade (April)
North Carolina Azalea Festival
P.O. Box 51
Wilmington, NC 28402
910-794-4650
Fax 910-794-4651
email: info@ncazaleafestival.org
www.ncazaleafestival.org

Bank United Thanksgiving Parade (site: Houston, TX) *see* Bowl Games of America

2329 Blockbuster Hollywood Spectacular (December)
Hollywood, CA
www.hollywoodspectacular.com

2330 Bowl Games of America
292 West 5400 South, Suite 100
P.O. Box 571187
Salt Lake City, UT 84157-1187
801-263-3445
Fax 801-288-9310
www.bgaskys.com
email: mail@bgaskys.com

Brach's Christmas Parade (Chicago, IL) *see* Bowl Games of America

2331 Bristol 4th of July Parade
Addison County Chamber of Commerce
2 Court Street
Middlebury, VT 05753
email: info@midvermont.com
www.midvermont.com/towns/bristol.html

2332 Bristol Music Festival (site: Bristol, England)

c/o Gateway Music Festivals & Tours
P.O. Box 1165
Monticello, MN 55362
800-331-8579
www.musicfestivals.com

Capital One Bowl Parade *see* Florida Power
Super Holiday Parade

2333 Cedarburg July 4th Parade
      Cedarburg Chamber of Commerce
      General Store Museum and Visitors
        Center
      W61 N480 Washington Avenue
      Cedarburg, WI 53012
      800-237-2874
      Fax 262-377-6470
      www.cedarburg.org/chamber.asp
      email: festivals@cedarburg.org

CenturyTel Cherry Royale Parade *see* National
Cherry Festival Parades

2334 Chinese New Year Festival & Parade
        (San Francisco)
      c/o Southwest Airlines
      www.chineseparade.com

Citrus Bowl Parade *see* Florida Power Super
Holiday Parade

Clearwater Fun 'N Sun (Clearwater, FL) *see*
Bowl Games of America

2335 Cloverdale Rodeo Parade
      Cloverdale Rodeo & Exhibition Association
        ciation
      6050A-176th Street
      Surrey, British Columbia V35 4E7
      Canada
      604-576-9461
      Fax 604-576-0216
      www.cloverdalerodeo.com
      email: info@cloverdalerodeo.com

Conquistador Festival (Albuquerque Founders' Day Parade, April) *see* Performance
Connection

2336 Daffodil Festival Parade
      c/o Susan Clements, Parade Chairperson
        person
      P.O. Box 2096
      Gloucester, VA 23016
      804-693-5907
      www.gloucesterva.info/pr/events/df/
        parade.htm

2337 Dairy Day/Rodeo Parade
      Richland Area Chamber of Commerce
      Box 128, 397 West Seminary Street
      Richland Center, WI 53581
      800-422-1318
      Fax 608-647-5449
      www.richlandchamber.com
      email: info@richlandchamber.com

2338 Dakota Days Parade
      University of South Dakota
      414 East Clark Street
      Vermillion, SD 57069
      877-COYOTES
      http://usd.edu

2339 Daytona 500 Parade & Festival
      c/o Music Tours Unlimited, Inc.
      P.O. Box 533
      321 North Furnace Street, Suite 90
      Birdsboro, PA 19508
      800-545-0935
      www.musfestivals.com/mtctc.htm

2340 Disney Magic Music Days
      866-752-0429 (Walt Disney World)
      800-854-8671 (Disneyland)
      www.magicmusicdays.com

Dogwood Arts Festival *see* Festival of Nations Parade
tions Parade

2341 Downey Holiday Lane Parade (site:
        Downey, CA)
      c/o Pageantry Productions
      11904 Long Beach Blvd.
      Lynwood, CA 90262
      310-537-4240
      Fax 310-631-1134
      www.pageantryproductions.com

Haddon Heights High School Marching Unit (Haddon Heights, NJ)

2342 Edinburgh Military Tattoo
The Tattoo Office
32 Market Street
Edinburgh, Scotlant EH1 1QB
+44 (0) 131 225 1188
Fax +44 (0) 131 225 8627
www.edinburgh-tattoo.co.uk
email: edintattoo@edintattoo.co.uk

Edison Festival of Light Grand Parade *see*
Suntrust Edison Festival of Light Grand Parade

2343 Egleston Children's Christmas Parade
3312 Piedmont Road, Suite 506
Atlanta, GA 30305
404-264-9348, x107
www.choa.org/festival/parade.shtml

2344 Englewood Holiday Parade
Greater Englewood Chamber of Com-
merce
Colonial Bank Building

3501 South Broadway
Englewood, CO 80110
303-789-4473
Fax 303-789-0098
http://greaterenglewoodchamber.com

Everglades Festival (Ft. Lauderdale-Broward
County St. Patrick's Day Parade, March)
see Performance Connection

2345 Festival of Champions
8317 Front Beach Road, Suite 27
Panama City Beach, FL 32407
www.festivalofchampions.com

2346 Festival of Nations Parade (site: Dolly-
wood theme park)
Knoxville, TN
www.dogwoodarts.com/calendar.html

2347 Festival of States
P.O. Box 1731
St. Petersburg, FL 33731

727-898-3654
www.festivalofstates.com
email: festivalofstates@ij.net

Field's Jingle Elf Parade (site: Chicago, IL) *see* Bowl Games of America

2348 Fiesta Bowl Parade (site: Phoenix, AZ)
c/o International Travel, Inc.
4004 Hillsboro Road, Suite 214B
Nashville, TN 37215
615-385-1222
Fax 615-385-5704
http://fiestabands.com

500 Festival Parade (site: Indianapolis, IN; May) *see* Bowl Games of America

2349 Florida Power Super Holiday Parade (site: Orlando, FL)
800-327-2116
http://fcsports.com/events/parade/news/parade-information.shtml

Foley's Thanksgiving Day Parade (Houston, TX) *see* Bowl Games of America

Gasparilla Pirate Fest *see* Southwest Airlines Gasparilla Pirate Fest

2350 Gaspee Days Celebration
c/o Karleen Wrath
Box 1772
Pilgrim Station, Warwick, RI 02888
401-781-1772
Fax 401-463-5465
www.gaspee.com

2351 Germanfest
8229 West Capitol Drive
Milwaukee, WI 53222
414-464-9444
www.germanfest.com
email: info@germanfest.com

2352 Grand Floral Parade
c/o Portland Rose Festival Association
5603 SW Hood Ave.
Portland, OR 97201

503-227-2681
Fax 503-227-6603
www.rosefestival.org/contact.htm
email: info@rosefestival.org

2353 The Great American Brass Band Festival
c/o Kay Berggren, Executive Director
Danville-Boyle Convention & Visitors Bureau
304 S. Fourth Street
Danville, KY 40422
800-755-0076
Fax 859-236-3197
www.danville-ky.com
email: tourism@searnet.com

2354 Great Circus Parade (site: Milwaukee, WI; circus band, fife & drum, military)
c/o Circus World Museum
550 Water Street
Baraboo, WI 53913-2597
608-355-9450
Fax 608-356-1800
www.circusparade.com
email: ringmaster@circusworldmuseum.com

2355 Gypsy Day Parade
Northern State University
Box 861
1200 S. Jay Street
Aberdeen, SD 57401
605-626-2534
Fax 605-626-2559
http://science.northern.edu/exponent/top_bar/contact.htm
email: stupub@northern.edu

Hollywood Christmas Parade *see* Blockbuster Hollywood Spectacular

2356 Hyack Parade (site: Vancouver, British Columbia)
c/o Heritage Festivals
P.O. Box 571187
Salt Lake City, UT 84157-1187
800-223-4367
www.heritagefestivals.com

2357 Kenosha Civic Veterans Parade
c/o Fran Puidokas, Chairman
5920—82nd Street
Kenosha, WI 53142
262-694-3111
www.marching.com/events/kenosha.
html
email: kparade@execpc.com

2358 Kentucky Derby Festival Pegasus Parade
Kentucky Derby Festival
Band Committee
1001 South Third Street
Louisville, KY 40203
800-928-3378
www.kdf.org/applications/Bands.asp

2359 King Frost Parade
c/o Hamburg Jaycees
P.O. Box 171
Hamburg, PA 19526
610-562-3632
www.hamburgboro.com/king_frost_
parade.htm

Klondike Days (site: Edmonton, Alberta, Canada) *see* Bowl Games of America

2360 La Habra Host Lions Corn Festival Parade
c/o Pageantry Productions
11904 Long Beach Blvd.
Lynwod, CA 90262
site: La Habra, CA
310-537-4240
Fax 310-631-1134
www.pageantryproductions.com

2361 Lake Waconia Band Festival
c/o Don Schultz, Waconia High School
Band Director
Waconia, MN 55387
952-442-6785
www.waconiaband.com/1wbf
email: dschultz@waconia.k12.mn.us

2362 Limerick International Parade, Band
and Choir Festival

Gateway Music Festivals & Tours
P.O. Box 1165
Monticello, MN 55362
800-331-8579
Fax 763-295-6029
www.musicfestivals.com
email: gmf@musicfestivals.com

2363 Long Beach Veterans Day Parade (site:
Long Beach, CA)
c/o Pageantry Productions
11904 Long Beach Blvd.
Lynwood, CA 90262
310-537-4240
Fax 310-631-1134
www.pageantryproductions.com

2364 (Macy's) Thanksgiving Day Parade
Attn: Band Committee
151 West 34th Street
New York, NY 10001
212-494-4495
www.ny.com/holiday/thanksgiving/
parade.html

2365 Maid of the Mist Blossom Festival Parade
Spring Festival
Niagara Falls Parks Commission
877-642-7275
Fax 905-356-8448
www.niagaraparks.com/index/html/
DYNS/spring_festival/PS/329
email: npinfo@niagaraparks.com

2366 Mardi Gras! Galveston
c/o Justin Turner
Group Tour Sales Manager
2504 Church Street
Galveston, TX 77550
888-425-4753
Fax 409-765-8611
www.mardigrasgalveston.com
email: jturner@-galvestoncvb.com

Michigan Thanksgiving Parade (Detroit) *see*
Bowl Games of America

2367 Miss America Pageant Parade
c/o Sally Romonowski

Miss America Organization
#2 Miss America Way, Suite 1000
Atlantic City, NJ 08401
609-345-7571, x26

2368 Music in the Parks
1784 West Schuylkill Road
Douglassville, PA 19518
800-305-7565 (West Coast), 800-
323-0974 (East Coast)
www.musicintheparks.com (and/
or www.educationalprograms.
com)
email: info@ed.prog.com
Locations: Kings Dominion,
Doswell, WV; Valleyfair,
Shakopee, MN; Astroworld,
Houston, TX; Old Country
Bush Gardens, Williamsburg,
VA; Canada's Wonderland,
Toronto, Canada; Cedar Point,
Sandusky, OH; Dorney Park,
Allentown, PA; Six Flags Great
Adventure, Jackson, NJ; Six
Flags Great America, Gurnee,
IL; Great America, Santa Clara,
CA; HersheyPark, Hershey,
PA; Opryland, Nashville, TN;
Six Flags Over Georgia, Atlanta,
GA; Six Flags Magic Mountain, Los
Angeles, CA; Six Flags Over Mid-
America, St. Louis, MO; Six Flags
Over Texas, Arlington, TX.

Muziekparade *see* Tulip Time Festival

2369 National Cherry Blossom Festival Parade (April)
c/o Downtown Jaycees
P.O. Box 4985
Washington, DC 20008
800-699-2466
Fax 781-459-0541
www.nationalcherryblossomfestival.
org
email: dcjaycees@yahoo.com

2370 National Cherry Festival Parades (AAA
Michigan Heritage Parade, Touch-
stone Energy Junior Royale Parade,
CenturyTel Cherry Royale Parade)

Bensalem High School Indoor Guard (Bensalem, PA)

108 W. Grandview Parkway
Traverse City, MI 49684
231-947-4230
Fax 231-947-7435
www.cherryfestival.org/events/pa
rades.php

2371 New Orleans Mardi Gras Parade
c/o Florida Festival Tours
7548 Municipal Drive
Orlando, FL 32819
800-443-2120
www.floridafestivaltours.com/tv/ind
ex.htm
email: fftours@aol.com

2372 The New Year's Day Parade
Research House
Fraser Road
Greenford, Middlesex UB6 7AQ
United Kingdom
+44 20 8566 8586

Brou-Ha-Ha Indoor Guard (Southern Chester County, PA)

www.londonparade.co.uk
email: markp@londonparade.co.uk

North Carolina Azalea Festival Parade *see*
Azalea Festival Parade

2373 Pageant Parade of the Rockies (August)
Pikes Peak or Bust Rodeo
P.O. Box 2016
Colorado Springs, CO 80901
719-635-3547
www.pikespeakorbustrodeo.org
email: info@pikespeakorbustrodeo.
org

Pegasus Parade *see* Kentucky Derby Festival
Pegasus Parade

Philadelphia Thanksgiving Parade *see* ABC/
Boscov's Philadelphia Thanksgiving Parade

2374 Pioneerland Band Festival (June)
Benson Area Chamber of Commerce
203 14th Street South
Benson, MN 56215
320-843-3618
www.marching.com/events/benson.
html
email: bensoncc@willmar.com

2375 Pittsfield 4th of July Parade
Fourth of July Parade Committee
City Hall
Allen Street
Pittsfield, MA 01201
www.berkshireweb.com/plexus/pa
rade/music.html

2376 Preble County Pork Festival
P.O. Box 818
Eaton, OH 45320
937-456-7273
www.porkfestival.com
email: info@porkfestival.org

Queen City Festival Findlay Market Opening
Day Parade (Cincinnati; April) *see* Performance Connection

2377 Riviera Parade
Nice, France
c/o Gateway Music Festivals & Tours
P.O. Box 1165
Monticello, MN 55362
800-331-8579
Fax 763-295-6029
www.musicfestivals.com
email: gmf@musicfestivals.com

2378 Rome New Years Festival & Parade
c/o Music Tours Unlimited, Inc.
P.O. Box 533
321 North Furnace Street, Suite 90
Birdsboro, PA 19508
800-545-0935
www.musfestivals.com/Ro.../Rome
%20New%20Years%20Festival%20
&%20Parrade.ht

2379 St. Patrick's Day Parade (New York
City)
www.saintpatricksdayparade.com/NYC
/newyorkcity.htm

2380 St. Patrick's Day Parade
Sydney, N.S.W. 2219
Australia

2381 St. Patrick's Day Parade & Festival
North Myrtle Beach, SC 29582
843-361-0038
www.stpatnmb.com
email: stpatnmb@aol.com

2382 St. Patrick's Festival Parade
Gateway Music Festivals & Tours
P.O. Box 1165
Monticello, MN 55362
800-331-8579
Fax 763-295-6029
www.musicfestivals.com/internation
al/europe/ireland.htm
email: gmf@musicfestivals.com

2383 St. Patrick's Week
St. Stephen's Green House
Earlsfort Terrace
Dublin 2

Ireland
+353 (0) 1 676 3205
Fax +353 (0) 676 3208
www.stpatricksday.ie
email: info@stpatricksday.ie

Shamrock Festival (San Diego St. Patrick's Day Parade, March) *see* Performance Connection

Shannon Development Company, Ltd. *see* St. Patrick's Week

2384 Shenandoah Apple Blossom Festival Grand Feature Parade
135 N. Cameron Street
Winchester, VA 22601
800-230-2139
www.sabf.org/parades.htm

2385 Shrewsbury International Music Festival
c/o Nichola Stokes, Festival Director
P.O. Box 264
Northwich Cheshire CW8 1FB
England
+44 1606 872633
Fax +44 1606 872926
www.shoppingshropshire.com
email: info@iftm.co.uk

2386 Southwest Airlines Gasparilla Pirate Fest
EventMakers Corporation
Attn: Gasparilla Entertainment
3701 W. Azeele Street
Tampa, FL 33609
813-353-8070
Fax 813-353-8075
www.gasparillapiratefest.com
email: events@eventmakers-fl.com

2387 Spectacle of Bands Parade (site: New Holland, PA)
c/o Mitch Dissinger
email: mdbikes@epix.net

2388 Sun Fun Festival Band Competition (May)

Myrtle Beach Area Chamber of Commerce
P.O. Box 2115
Myrtle Beach, SC 29578
800-356-3016
www.myrtlebeachinfo.com/chamber
or www.mbchamber.com/cvb/events/sunfun/sf-parade.htm

2389 Suntrust Edison Festival of Light Grand Parade (February)
Ft. Myers, FL 33901
www.edisonfestival.org/grand.htm

2390 Target Thanksgiving Parade
Chicago Festival Association
111 North State Street, 11th Floor
Chicago, IL 60602
312-781-5681
Fax 312-781-5407
www.chicagofestivals.org/site/epage/2501_211.htm
email: info@chicagofestivals.org

2391 Tater Daze Parade
Brooklyn Park, MN 55443
763-493-8122
www.marching.com/events/brooklyn park.html
email: AnnetteH@ci.brooklyn-park.mn.us

2392 Tipp City Mum Festival
Tipp City, OH 45371
937-667-8631
www.tippcity.org

2393 Toronto St. Patrick's Day Parade
www.gitcheegumee.ws/topatrick/index.htm

Touchstone Energy Junior Royale Parade *see* National Cherry Festival Parades

2394 Tournament of Roses Parade
Pasadena Tournament of Roses Association
391 S. Orange Grove Blvd.
Pasadena, CA 91184
626-449-4100

Fax 626-449-9066
email: rosepr@earthlink.net

2395 Tulip Festival
Chamber of Commerce
P.O. Box 36
Orange City, IA 51041
712-707-4510
Fax 712-707-4523
www.orangecityiowa.com
email: Tulip@orangecitycomm.net

2396 Tulip Time
Pella Historical Village
507 Franklin Street
Pella, IA 50219
641-628-4311
Fax 641-628-9192
http://homepages.kdsi.net/~pellatt/
tulipt.html
email: pellatt@kdsi.net

2397 Tulip Time Festival Inc.
171 Lincoln Avenue
Holland, MI 49423
800-822-2770
www.tuliptime.org/contact/index.html
email: tulip@tuliptime.org

2398 Vikingland Band Festival (June)
Alexandria Lakes Area Chamber of
Commerce
206 Broadway
Alexandria, MN 56308
800-235-9441
www.marching.com/events/vbf
email: drydberg@alexandriamn.org

2399 V.P. Parade
P.O. Box 1903
St. Louis, MO 63118

2400 Waikiki Holiday Parade
Gateway Festivals & Tours

P.O. Box 1165
Monticello, MN 55362
800-331-8579
Fax 763-295-6029
www.musicfestivals.com
email: gmf@musicfestivals.com

2401 Wakefield Independence Day Parade
Wakefield Independence Day Committee
28 Yale Avenue
Wakefield, MA 01880
781-246-1291
www.marching.com/events/wakefield.
html
email: america704@aol.com

Washington Mutual Thanksgiving Day Parade (site: Houston, TX) *see* Bowl Games
of America

2402 Wells Fargo Sun Bowl Music Festival
Parade of Bands
c/o Music Tours Unlimited, Inc.
P.O. Box 533
321 North Furnace Street, Suite 90
Birdsboro, PA 19508
800-545-0935
www.musfestivals.com/Wells%20Far
go%20Sun.../wells_fargo_sun_bo
wl_festival.hi.ht

2403 Westminster Lord Mayor's Parade and
Albert Hall Performance
c/o Super Holiday Companies, Inc.
DBA Citrus Sports Travel
1 Citrus Bowl Place
Orlando, FL 32805
(800) 932-6440

Your Hometown America Parade *see* Pittsfield 4th of July Parade

Springfield High School Indoor Guard (Springfield, Delaware County, PA)

Selected Bibliography

Articles

2404 Casavant, A. R. "Alternative Parade Turns." *Instrumentalist* (September 1997): 102–103.

2405 "Community Action: They Parade and Perform Just for Fun … Theirs Every Bit as Much as Yours." *Sunset* (January 1978): 60–61.

2406 Darnall, Josiah. "Rosy Success Stories." *Instrumentalist* (March 1988): 45–46, 48.

2407 Dart, Leslie. "'Music of America' in Rose Bowl Parade." *School Musician, Director & Teacher* (December 1979): 6–7, 15.

2408 Fahrlander, Phil. "I Love a Parade: Phil Fahrlander Just Loves Parades." *Nebraska Music Educator* (1997), Vol. 56, No. 1, p. 28.

2409 Haney, Ray B. "McDonald's All-American High School Band: They Do It All for Us!" *School Musician, Director & Teacher* (March 1979): 54–55.

2410 "Hometown Parades." *Good Old Days* (2000), Vol. 37, No. 8, p. 42.

2411 Howard, Karol. "Exercises for the Parade Band." *Instrumentalist* (August 1984): 23–25.

2412 Kenney, Edward L. "A.I. [du Pont] Band Steps Off to Another 1st." *News Journal* [Wilmington, DE], December 31, 1991, pp. D1, last page.

2413 ____. "Rose Parade: Walk on the Weary Side." *News Journal* [Wilmington, DE], January 2, 1990, pp. D1, D2.

2414 Lavelle, Mariane P. "One Band's Run for the Roses." *Philadelphia Inquirer Today Magazine*, December 30, 1979, pp. 1, 8–12.

2415 Miller, Jennifer Marie. "A.I. [du Pont] Band Opens British Queen's 50th Jubilee: Group Selected to Lead the New Year's Parade." *News Journal* [Wilmington, DE], January 10, 2002, p. RC4.

2416 Mundi, Joseph T., and R. Bruce Bradshaw. "St. Patrick's Week in Ireland: A Band Goes There and Back Again." *Instrumentalist* (December 1981): 14–16.

2417 Pappas, Peter M. "Bowl Parades Again, Again, and Again." *School Musician, Director & Teacher* (August/September 1979): 12–13.

2418 Riordan, Kevin. "CR [Caesar Rodney] Band Struts Stuff in London." *News Journal* [Wilmington, DE], January 2, 1990, p. D1.

2419 Roth, Edith B. "A Band, A Community, An Event." *American Education* (October 1981): 23–26.

2420 Wright, Al G. "Band Parade Procedures." *Instrumentalist* (March 1965): 82–85.

Books

2421 Bennett, George T. *Street Routines for Marching Band Contests and Public Exhibitions*. Marching Maneuver Series, Vol. V. Chicago, IL: Gamble Hinged Music Company, 1938.

2422 Casavant, Albert R. *Street Parade Drills*. San Antonio, TX: Southern Music Company.

2423 Dvorak, Raymond F. *The Band on Parade*. New York, NY: Carl Fischer, 1937.

2424 Hackney, C.R., and Hugh H. Emerson. *Parade Stunts*. Marching Maneuver Series, Vol. X. Chicago, IL: Gamble Hinged Music Company, 1941.

2425 Johnston, Laurence. *Parade Techniques*. Rockville Centre, NY: Belwin, 1944.

2426 Lagauskas, Valerie. *Parades: How to Plan, Promote & Stage Them*. New York: Sterling Publishing, 1982. [includes marching bands chapter]

Museum

2427 The Mummers Museum
1100 S. Second Street
Philadelphia, PA 19147
215-336-3050
Fax 215-389-5630
http://riverfrontmummers.com/museum.html
email: mummersmus@aol.com

Part 10
Publicity and Public Relations

The marching activity frequently receives little publicity. Newspapers may not consider music news. There are few funds for promotion. Add to this what seems to be either an insularity or lack of concern for the captive audience of parents and friends. Announcers frequently fail to tell spectators a competing unit's hometown and often do not list upcoming contests. Some organizations forbid videotaping of units other than those in which a parent has a competing child.

A publicity chairperson for a high school band boosters' organization will learn through trial and error what will and what will not work to get one's band noticed in the community. Remember, the budget may be minuscule and not cover stamps, envelopes, and other mundane but necessary items.

In theory, a monthly general boosters meeting will be covered in the local newspapers. "County Events" sections usually will list one's activities. Letters to the editor regarding a particular musical event or letters from boosters praising the school and students might be printed.

Weekly newspapers are likely to print notices and, nine times out of ten, the 5" × 7" black and white photograph submitted. Photos should be submitted for significant events; take and submit photos of band parents repainting a refreshment stand at the stadium, students on a trip, area marching band championships, the last practice before a halftime show, benefit performances for injured class members.

It is difficult to tell if newspaper notices attract people to boosters meetings because phone chains and mailing are also used. Labor under the theory that every little bit counts.

Television stations will occasionally cover a marching activity, and it certainly does no harm to contact them. Marching band and indoor competitions are a rather well-kept secret in most communities and a TV reporter may find them novel and newsworthy.

The band director can obtain publicity by forming brass choirs for Christmas "caroling" around town and by taking senior high band members to the middle schools for recruiting purposes. Slide presentations and videotapes of a band's field show will also generate enthusiasm. Even an average band can look good from the grandstand on a television monitor.

In-house publicity can be achieved by means of band scrapbooks, photo albums, videos or DVD screening of performances. Displayed at all boosters meetings, the scrapbook can be held by the publicity chairperson or located in the school library or band director's office. The scrapbook should include photos, newspaper clippings, programs, and any other items relating to the band or its members.

Lest we forget, in the Internet age band members can create exciting websites. Remember to include unit or instructor addresses.

Catalogs

2428 Best Impressions (candy, lanyards, magnets, mugs, pens, stress balloons)
The Best Impressions Catalog Company
345 N. Lewis Avenue
Oglesby, IL 61348
800-635-2378
Fax 815-883-8346
www.bestimpressions.com

2429 Campus Marketing Specialists, Inc. (keytags, lanyards, mousepads, mugs, pens, posters, sportswear)
P.O. Box 2130

Brandywine High School Marching Wind and Percussion Ensemble (Wilmington, DE)

Ft. Lauderdale, FL 33303-2130
800-795-4267
Fax 954-627-3887
www.campusmarketing.com
email: info@campusmarketing.com

2430 4imprint (balloons, beach balls, caps,
lanyards, mugs)
101 Commerce Street
P.O. Box 320
Oshkosh, WI 54903-0320
877-446-7746

Fax 800-355-5043
email: 4care@4imprint.com

2431 Promo Unlimited (balloons, caps,
mugs, t-shirts, umbrellas)
2291 W. 205th Street, #201
Torrance, CA 90501
800-748-6150
Fax 800-748-3326
www.4imprint.com
www.promounlimited.com

Photography and Videography Services

2432 Bateman Photographic Services, Inc.
P.O. Box 55167
Indianapolis, IN 46205
800-359-3686

2433 BVP Marching Videos
790 W. Main Street
Newark, OH 43055

800-252-8433
www.bandvideos.com
email: BVP@alink.com

2434 Champion Photo
2502 SW 3rd Avenue
Box 21398
Ft. Lauderdale, FL 33315

Archbishop Wood High School Indoor Guard (Warminster, PA)

954-523-2880
www.championphoto.net

2435 Impact Digital Media Services
1918B Northwood Drive
Salisbury, MD 21801
888-554-3383

2436 Jolesch Photography
2771 104th Street, Suite E
Des Moines, IA 50322
515-278-6500
www.jolesch.com

Selected Bibliography

Articles

2437 Abdoo, Frank B. "A Portable Video Tape Recording System for Your Program." *Instrumentalist* (September 1982): 22–25.

2438 Clayton, Nancy. "Television Coverage for High School Bands?" *School Musician, Director & Teacher* (August/September 1979): 16–18.

2439 Ellis, Roger C. "Views from the Sidelines Through the Eye of a Camera." *Drum Corps News*. 7 parts. Oct. 21–Nov. 4, 1981, p. 19; Nov. 25, 1981, p. 4; Dec. 16, 1981, p. 9; Jan. 13, 1982, p. 11; Mar. 17, 1982, p. 10; Mar. 31, 1982, p. 5; Apr. 21, 1982, p. 11.

2440 Gretick, Tony. "Bryan Music Boosters—An Organization That Works." *Instrumentalist* (May 1983): 21–23.

2441 Lautzenheiser, Tim. "Family Affair." *Booster* (November 1982): 5.

2442 Michaels, Arthur J. "Hop Aboard the Music Education Magazine Bandwagon." *Writer's Digest* (April 1981): 39–43.

2443 _____. "Yes, You Too Can Be a Music Director-Photographer." *School Musician, Director & Teacher* (March 1981): 18–19.

2444 Perkins, Charlene A. "Drum Corps Is Worth the Parental Effort." *Drum Corps News*, June 16, 1982, p. 9.

2445 _____. "Now Is a Good Time to Contact the Pillars of the Community." *Drum Corps News*, June 16, 1982, p. 8.

2446 Wenner, Gene C. "Promoting Our School Music Program." *School Musician, Director & Teacher* (October 1980): 12–14.

2447 Wright, Al. "Public Relations." *Bandworld* (November-December 1990).

Books

2448 Ask, Carolyn, comp. *How to Tell Your Story: A Guide to Public Relations.* Columbus, OH: Ohio Arts Council (727 E. Main St., 43205).

2449 Gillespie, Lester. *The Use of Publicity in the Public Relations Program of the High-School Instrumental Music Department.* Fullerton, CA: F.E. Olds & Son, 1960.

2450 Leibert, Edwin R., and Bernice E. Sheldon. *Handbook of Special Events for Non-Profit Organizations: Tested Ideas for Fund Raising and Public Relations.* New York, NY: Association Press, 1976.

2451 Levine, Michael, and George Gendron. *Guerilla PR Wired: Waging a Successful Publicity Campaign On-Line, Offline, and Everywhere in Between.* New York: McGraw-Hill, 2001.

2452 Lewis, H.G. *How to Handle Your Own Public Relations.* Chicago, IL: Nelson-Hall, 1976.

2453 McIntyre, Catherine. *Writing Effective News Releases...: How to Get Free Publicity for Yourself, Your Business, or Your Organization.* Colorado Springs, CO: Piccadilly Books, 1992.

2454 O'Brien, Richard. *Publicity: How to Get It.* New York, NY: Barnes & Noble, 1977.

2455 Selmer, H. & A., Inc. *How to Promote Your Band—A Manual of Public Relations for the Band Director*. Elkhart, IN, 1957.

2456 Smith, Bud, and Arthur Bebak. *Creating Web Pages for Dummies*. 6th ed. New York: Hungrey minds, 2002.

2457 Yale, David R., and Andrew J. Carothers. *The Publicity Handbook*. 2nd ed. New York: McGraw-Hill, 2001.

2458 Yaverbaum, Eric, and Robert Bly. *Public Relations Kit for Dummies*. New York: Hungry Minds, 2001.

Part 11
Travel Arrangements

Directory

All American Music Festival *see* American
Tours & Travel

2459   American Tours & Travel, Inc.
8651 Commodity Circle
Orlando, FL 32819
800-243-4365
Fax 407-352-2962
www.travelgroups.com

2460   America's Travel Centre
291 W. 5400 S.
Salt Lake City, UT 84157
801-266-8100
www.americastravelcentre.com

2461   Anne Cottrell Tours and Travel
45 Tecunseth Street
Toronto, Ontario M5V 2X6
Canada
416-364-5235
email: annecott@sympatico.ca

2462   Associate Consultants for Education
Abroad
1567 Fourth Street
San Rafael, CA 94901
800-886-2055
www.acfea.com

2463   AWOL Travel, Inc.
7836 Wicklow Circle
Orlando, FL 32817
800-992-2965
www.disneyexperts.com
email: info@disneyexperts.com

2464   Bob Rogers Travel, Inc.
P.O. Box 673
Warrenville, IL 60555
630-393-4343
Fax 630-393-4674
www.bobrogerstravel.com
email: brtravel@ameritech.net

2465   Bowl Games of America
292 West 5400 South, Suite 100

Salt Lake City, UT 84157-1187
801-263-3445
Fax 801-288-9310
www.bgaskys.com
email: mail@bgaskys.com

2466   Busch Gardens Special Events Department
P.O. Box 290377
Tampa, FL 33687

2467   Coastline Travel (for "Hawaii Invitational")
642 South Brookhurst
Anaheim, CA 92804
800-448-2374
www.coastlinetravel.com
email: jerry@deltanet.com

2468   C-S Travel
10031 South Roberts Road
Palos Hills, IL 60465
708-599-0083

2469   Disney Magic Music Days
P.O. Box 3232
Anaheim, CA 92803
800-833-9806
Fax 407-566-7688
www.magicmusicdays.com
and: P.O. Box 10020
Lake Buena Vista, FL 32830-0020
800-854-8671
Fax 714-781-1351

2470   Dixie Classic Festivals
3811 Cottrell Road
Richmond, VA 23234
800-422-8445
Fax 804-743-8290
www.bandfest.com/festivals.html

2471   Educational Programs Network
1784 W. Schuylkill Road
Douglassville, PA 19518-9100
800-323-0974 (East Coast)
800-305-7565 (West Coast)

Lancaster-Catholic High School Marching Band (Lancaster, PA)

www.educationalprograms.com
email: info@edprog.com

2472 Educational Travel Consultants
P.O. Box 1580
Hendersonville, NC 28793-1580
800-247-7969
www.educationaltravel.net
email: info@edtvl.com

2473 Festivals of Music
1784 W. Schuylkill Road
Douglassville, PA 19518
800-323-0974
Fax 610-327-4786
www.festivalsofmusic.com
email: info@edprog.com

2474 Festivals with Creative Arts Workshop
Showcase (CAWS)
800-445-2297
Fax 973-492-5572
www.festivalswcaws.org

2475 Fiesta-Val Invitational Music Festivals
6223 Lakeside Avenue
Richmond, VA 23228
800-222-6862
Fax 804-264-6302
www.fiestaval.com

2476 Florida Festival Tours
7548 Municipal Drive
Orlando, FL 32819
includes arrangements for Macy's
Thanksgiving Day Parade (NY),
Philadelphia Thanksgiving Day Parade, Rose Bowl Parade, New Orleans Mardi Gras Parade
800-443-2120
www.floridafestivaltours.com/contact.
htm
email: fftours@aol.com

2477 Friendship Ambassadors Foundation
110 Mamaroneck Avenue, Suites 7 & 8
White Plains, NY 10601
800-526-2908

www.faf.org
email: friendly@aol.com

2478 Gateway Music Festivals & Tours
      P.O. Box 1165
      Monticello, MN 55362
      800-331-8579
      Fax 763-295-6029
      www.musicfestivals.com
      email: gmf@musicfestivals.com

2479 Hawaii Music Festivals
      P.O. Box 6479
      Honolulu, HI 96818
      800-366-7486
      Fax 808-837-0008
      www.himusicfest.com
      email: bands@himusicfest.com

2480 Heritage Festivals
      P.O. Box 571187
      Salt Lake City, UT 84157-1187
      800-223-4367
      www.heritagefestivals.com

2481 Homestead Travel
      7 West Main Street
      P.O. Box 304
      Hummelstown, PA 17036-0304
      800-635-8749
      www.homesteadtravel.vacation.com
      email: book@homesteadtravel.com

2482 International Travel, Inc.
      4004 Hillsboro Road, Suite 214B
      Nashville, TN 37215
      615-385-1222
      Fax 615-385-5704
      email: travel@itbna.com

2483 Intropa Tours
      4950 Bissonnet Road, Suite 201
      Bellaire, TX 77401
      800-INTROPA
      Fax 713-772-4527
      email: info@intropa.com

2484 Irish Tourist Board
      757 Third Avenue
      New York, NY 10017

2485 Kaleidoscope Adventures
      7021 Grand National Drive, Suite 104
      Orlando, FL 32819
      800-774-7337
      Fax 407-345-2890
      www.kaleidoscopeadventures.com
      email: info@kaleidoscopeadventures.
      com

2486 Mike Miller & Associates (includes
      Macy's Thanksgiving Day Parade)
      P.O. Box 25276
      Dallas, TX 75225
      800-692-5596
      www.mmaspecialevents.com

2487 Millennium Travel & Cruise
      Diane Heller, Performing Events Co-
      ordinator
      10937 Poppleton Avenue
      Omaha, NE 68144
      800-350-9570 pin 13
      Fax 402-397-2631 (D. Heller)
      http://performingevents.com/who.htm

Music Festivals see Music Tours Unlimited

2488 Music Tours Unlimited, Inc.
      P.O. Box 533
      321 North Furnace Street, Suite 90
      Birdsboro, PA 19508
      800-545-0935
      www.musfestivals.com/mtctc.htm

MusicFest Orlando see Gateway Music Festivals & Tours

2489 National Events (includes continental
      U.S. locations, Hawaii, Mexico City,
      and Bahamas cruise)
      9672 South 700 East, Suite 200
      Sandy, UT 84070
      800-333-4700

New Horizons Tour & Travel, Inc. see Performing Arts Consultants

2490 Norman Travel International
      1146 E. Alosta Avenue
      Glendora, CA 91740

Desire Indoor Guard (Coatesville, PA)

West Chester University Golden Ram Marching Band (West Chester, PA)

626-914-2768
Fax 626-335-6803
email: normantravel@earthlink.net

2491 North American Music Festivals &
Custom Tours
P.O. Box 36
50 Brookwood Drive, Suite 1
Carlisle, PA 17013
800-533-6263
Fax 717-245-9060
ww.greatfestivals.com
email: Info@greatfestivals.com
Sites include: New York City; To-
ronto, Canada; Myrtle Beach, SC;
Virginia Beach, VA

2492 Pacific Basin Music Festival
World Projects
P.O. Box 7365
Berkeley, CA 94707
800-922-3976
Fax 510-525-0502
www.wpintl.com/festivals
email: bobl@wpintl.com

2493 Peak Performance Tours
105 Bridgewater Drive
New Hope, PA 18938
800-220-0165
Fax 215-862-8096
www.peakperformancetours.com
email: br@peakperformancetours.com
and: 2439 Durham Place
Jeffersonton, VA 22724
800-937-9251
Fax 240-282-4281
email: tm@peakperformancetours.com

2494 Performing Arts Abroad, Inc.
P.O. Box 50844
Kalamazoo, MI 49005
800-952-0643
www.paa-net.com/performing/p_
index.html

2495 Performing Arts Consultants Music
Festivals (festivals and cruises)

88 West Front Street
Keyport, NJ 07735
800-872-3378
www.usafest.org
Sites include Anaheim, CA; San
Francisco, CA; Breckenridge, CO;
Washington, DC; Orlando, FL; At-
lanta, GA; Honolulu, HI; Chicago,
IL; Wildwood, NJ; Branson, MO; St.
Louis, MO; Boston, MA; New Or-
leans, LA; Minneapolis, MN; New
York, NY; Corpus Christi, TX; Dal-
las, TX; Houston, TX; San Antonio,
TX; Norfolk, VA (Azalea Festival);
Toronto, Canada

2496 Star Travel Services, Inc.
P.O. Box 1270
301 North Morton Street
Bloomington, IN 47402-1270
www.startravelservices.com

2497 Super Holiday Tours, Inc.
116 Gatlin Avenue
Orlando, FL 32806
800-327-2116
Fax 407-851-0071

2498 Vanguard Tour Service, Inc.
P.O. Box 5377
Lansing, IL 60438
800-383-0061
Fax 708-895-0067

2499 Wells Cargo (trailers)
P.O. Box 728-1011
Elkhart, IN 46515

2500 World of Music Festivals
3651 Mt. Ashmun Court
San Diego, CA 92111
800-748-5579
Fax 858-292-9951
Sites include: Anaheim, CA; Chi-
cago, IL; Denver, CO; Las Vegas,
NV; Minneapolis, MN; San Diego,
CA; San Jose, CA

Blessed Sacrament World Guard (Cambridge, MA)

Insurance

2501 Global Music High School Exchange
(Accident & Sickness Insurance
Plan)

Marketed by:
CMI Insurance Specialists
1447 York Road, Suite 400

Lutherville, MD 21093
410-583-2595
Fax 410-583-8244
www.studyabroadinsurance.com
www.psafinancial.com

Underwritten by:
ACE American Insurance Company
1601 Chestnut Street
Philadelphia, PA 19103

Selected Bibliography

Articles

2502 Blahnik, Joel. "The Case Against Travel." *Music Educators Journal* (January 1982): 43–45.

2503 "Festivals and Travel: Music Travel Rebounds in 2002." *School Band and Orchestra* (June 2002): 42–43.

2504 Gerardi, J.L. "The Legal Aspects of an Out-of-State Trip." *Instrumentalist* (May 1983): 12–14.

2505 Haas, Lance. "Take Your Band Camping." *School Musician, Director & Teacher* (November 1977): 70.

2506 Neidig, Kenneth L. "Travel Tips from the Professionals." *Instrumentalist* (May 1983): 8–12.

2507 Prentice, Barbara. "On the Road Again." *Instrumentalist* (January 1990): 27–30, 88–90.

2508 Ritter, Sara. "T[win] V[alley] Band Struts Down Main St., Disney World." *Tri County Record* [Berks, Chester, Lancaster, PA], April 20, 1993, pp. 1, 23.

2509 Stevens, Mark. "The Unexpected Problems Begin When the Band Bus Pulls Out." *Instrumentalist* (June 2002): 48, 50, 52.

2510 Thoms, Paul E. "Is This Trip Really Necessary?" *School Musician, Director & Teacher* (October 1982): 6–7.

2511 Wood, Roy. "Big Tour ... on a Small Budget." *School Musician, Director & Teacher* (October 1982): 8–10.

Part 12
Trophies, Awards, Gifts, Medals, and Plaques

Directory

2512 Ampros Trophies
      4830 N. Front St.
      Philadelphia, PA 19120
      215-324-5566
      Fax 215-324-0417

2513 Bandribbons
      7200 Corvallis Road
      Independence, OR 97351
      800-487-9747
      Fax 503-838-5331
      www.Bandribbons.com

2514 Best Impressions (calendars, clocks,
      pens, pins, mugs, stadium cushions)
      345 North Lewis Ave.
      Oglesby, IL 61348
      800-635-2378
      Fax 815-883-8346
      www.bestimpressions.com

2515 Charms for the Arts
      7701 SW 10th Avenue
      Gainesville, FL 32607
      352-331-1617
      email: sales@barbare.cc

2516 Crown Awards (trophies, plaques, rib-
      bons)
      800-227-1557
      www.crownawards.com

2517 DrumBum.com (t-shirts, gifts, lessons)
      P.O. Box 6564
      Glen Allen, VA 23058
      804-273-1353
      Fax 804-273-6003
      email: tshirts@drumbum.com

2518 Friendship House (medals, ornaments,
      pens, pins, plaques)
      P.O. Box 450978
      Cleveland, OH 44145-0623
      800-791-9876
      Fax 440-871-0858
      www.friendshiphouse.com

2519 Guard Jewels of Florida (bracelets,
      pins, rings, chains)
      321-951-3420
      http://guardjewels.hypermart.net
      email: ILEANAT@worldnet.att.net

2520 John Philip Sousa Band Award
      c/o Instrumentalist Company
      200 Northfield Road
      Northfield, IL 60093
      847-446-8550
      Fax 847-446-6263

2521 Medals & Awards International
      434 E. Ackard Place
      San Antonio, TX 78221
      210-927-6373

2522 The Music Stand (hair clips, t-shirts,
      caps, drumstick bags)
      2921 Peak Ave.
      Longmont, CO 80504-6221
      877-275-0966
      Fax 303-682-7139
      www.themusicstand.com

2523 Pageantry Productions (trophies,
      plaques, custom awards)
      (Division, World Wide Spectaculars,
      Inc.)
      www.pageantryproductions.com

Patrick S. Gilmore Band Award see John
Philip Sousa Band Award

2524 Sales Guides, International (balloons,
      key chains, lanyards, lollipops, mugs,
      pens, pins, snow brushes, vinyl ban-
      ners)
      P.O. Box 64784
      St. Paul, MN 55164-0784
      800-352-9899
      Fax 800-352-9501
      www.sales-guides.com

2525 Southwest Emblem Company (med-
      als, patches, pins)
      P.O. Box 350

Middle Township High School Panther Marching Band (Cape May Court House, NJ)

Henderson High School Warrior Marching Band (West Chester, PA)

Cisco, TX 76437
888-442-2514
Fax 254-442-2514
www.southwestemblem.com
email: swinfo@southwestemblem.com

2526 Trophyland USA, Inc. (medals, plaques,
trophies)
Dept. DM
7001 W. 20th Avenue
Hialeah, FL 33014
800-327-5820
Fax 305-823-4836
www.trophyland.com

2527 United Musical Instruments (sells
Super Star Twirling Batons)
(subsidiary Steinway Musical Instruments)
1000 Industrial Parkway
P.O. Box 727
Elkhart, IN 46516-5581
www.unitedmusical.com
email: info@unitedmusical.com

World Wide Spectaculars, Inc. *see* Pageantry
Productions

Part 13
Twirling

The nation's largest baton twirling organizations are the United States Twirling Association (USTA) and the National Baton Twirling Association (NBTA). Both publish magazines. Twirl and Drum Major contain ads, rule changes, readers' comments, champion profiles—male and female—and contest schedules.

Like band competitions, many twirling contests (held indoors, the TV movie Twirl notwithstanding) are won by the best people who show up. USTA holds annual championships at different locations, while the NBTA's "America's Youth on Parade" annual championship is always held at Notre Dame University. USTA has endeavored to have baton twirling recognized as a sport and discontinued the modeling portion of its contests.

Individual contest twirling has many categories, e.g., novice, intermediate, and advanced, which are further broken down by age and sometimes state. Group twirling, known as dance-twirl, parade corps, or corps, is usually performed to music selected by the unit's director.

In addition to the national twirling associations, group twirling is done by junior and senior high school squads in such organizations as the Tournament Indoor Association (TIA) and Cavalcade Indoor Association (CIA), which feature twirlers in addition to color guards and percussion units. These contests are geared for the spectators and judges in the bleachers, whereas in NBTA and USTA competitions the soloists and small dance-twirl squads perform for a judge whose table is sometimes in the middle of the gym floor, obstructing the spectators' view.

A great deal of twirling is done on football fields each autumn by high school majorettes. "Majorette" is a term frowned upon by contest—and increasingly by most—twirlers, but to a novice spectator only a hazy line separates the twirler from the majorette. Suffice it to say that all majorettes (not drum majorettes) are twirlers but not all twirlers are majorettes.

On occasion Twirl lists the colleges and universities that have twirlers. Times change and the popularity of twirling is cyclical. College bands frequently have "golden girls." But a corps-style high school band generally will eschew twirlers. It depends on geography and culture—some areas are more "twirler-oriented" than others. Expertise counts, too, and that may be dependent on having a local twirling school or dance school that features twirling instruction. On the World Wide Web check www.angelfire.com/in2/geminibaton/linkteamsusa2.html to see a list of twirling and majorette teams in the United States. It's not complete but is constantly being updated.

Associations

2528 Alberta Baton Twirling Association
11759 Groat Road
Edmonton, Alberta T5M 3K6
Canada
780-415-0144
Fax 780-415-0170
www.telusplanet.net/public/abta/fr
main.htm
email: abta@telusplanet.net

2529 The British Baton Twirling Sports Association
www.bbtsa.co.uk

2530 California Baton Council (affiliated with USTA)
c/o Angela Martens, Director
67 Essanay Avenue
Fremont, CA 94536

Salisbury High School Twirlers (Allentown, PA)

Brandywine Heights High School Twirlers (Topton, PA)

510-790-8938
www.ca-baton-twirling.org/officers_
and_board_of_directors.htm

2531 Cavalcade Indoor Association
c/o Bill Powers
www.cavalcadeofbands.com
email: bill_powers@hempfield.K12.
pa.us

2532 College Majorette Headquarters
www.collegemajorette.com (has map
with regions to be clicked on to
find twirling squads by state)

2533 Drum Majorettes of America
c/o Doris Faber, Executive Director
P.O. Box 19028
Charlotte, NC 28219
704-392-5472
Fax 704-394-5611
www.homestead.com/DrumMajor
ettesOfAmerica/DMAhistory~ns4.
html
email: dfaber2520@aol.com

2534 International Academy of Twirling
Teachers
300 S. Wright Road
Janesville, WI 53545

2535 Manitoba Baton Twirling Association
200 Main Street
Winnipeg, Manitoba R3C 4M2
Canada
925-5682
Fax 925-5703
www.sport.mb.ca/baton
email: Baton Twirl Manitoba

2536 Maryland Baton Council
c/o Terry Stewart, President
13202 11th Street
Bowie, MD 20715
301-805-2204
www.geocities.com/mdbatoncouncil/
email: TStwirl@aol.com

2537 National Baton Twirling Association
(NBTA)
Box 266
Janesville, WI 53545
email: baton@americanbaton.com

2538 National Baton Twirling Association
[United Kingdom]
Twirl Inn
24, Cargate Terrace
Aldershot, Hants. GU11 3EL
United Kingdom
www.nbta.org.uk/membership.htm

2539 NBTA Europe
Case postale 215
CH-2501 Biel-Bienne

2540 Tournament Indoor Association
Liz Barnhart, Majorette/Drill Team
Chairperson
215-657-4978
www.tob.org
email: lbarnhartl@aol.com

2541 Twirling Unlimited
700 Ghent Road
Akron, OH 44333
330-666-1163
Fax 330-665-1862
www.geocities.com/twirlingunlimited/
contact.htm

2542 United States Twirling Association
(USTA)
USTA Director of Operations
46 Caldwell Street
Huntington Station, NY 11746
631-427-2876
Fax 208-474-9067
www.us-twirlingassoc.org
email: twirlusta@sprintmail.com

2543 World Federation of Baton Twirling
and Majorette Associations
P.O. Box 266
Janesville, WI 53547

Baton Manufacturers and Distributors

2544 American Baton Company
P.O. Box 266
Janesville, WI 53545
608-754-2238
Fax 608-754-1986
www.drummajor.com
email: baton@americanbaton.com

2545 Dancer's Dream (batons, shoes, costumes)
330-493-0957
www.angelfire.com/oh/jazzdolls/Da
ncersDream.html
email: jazzdoll@neo.lrun.com

2546 The Jemm Company
3306 Blake Street
Denver, CO 80205
303-296-1660
Fax 303-292-3638
http://practapal.com
email: Jemmcompany@IPWS.com

2547 Kraskin Batons
12475 Xenwood Avenue So.
Savage, MN 55378
952-890-5153
http://home.att.net/~kraskin
email: kraskin@worldnet.att.net

2548 Sharp Baton
2445 Decamp Avenue
Elkhart, IN 46516
574-293-1360
Fax 574-522-2172
www.sharp-baton.com/cart

2549 Starline Baton Company, Inc.
P.O. Box 839
Monterey, TN 38574
931-839-7654
Fax 931-839-7827
www.starlinebaton.com
email: sales@starlinebaton.com

2550 United Musical Instruments (Super
Star Twirling Batons)
100 Industrial Parkway
P.O. Box 727
Elkhart, IN 46516-5581
www.unitedmusical.com
email: info@unitedmusical.com

2551 World Twirling, Inc. (batons, apparel,
charms, flag shafts, videos)
P.O. Box 8721
Deerfield Beach, FL 33443-8721
866-468-9475
Fax 561-394-6749
www.worldtwirling.com

Costumes and Accessories

2552 Algy Costumes & Uniforms
P.O. Box 090490
440 N.E. 1st Avenue
Hallandale, FL 33009
800-458-2549/305-457-8100
www.algy-dance.com

2553 Baums Inc.
106 South 11th Street, Dept. DS
Philadelphia, PA 19107
800-8-DANCIN
Fax 215-592-4194

www.baumsdancewear.com
email: info@baumsdancewear.com

2554 Colorifics
8325 Green Meadow Drive North
Westerville, OH 43081-9443
800-322-1961

2555 Costume Gallery
1604 S. Rte. 130
Burlington, NJ 08016
609-386-6601

Kutztown High School Twirlers (Kutztown, PA)

Fax 609-386-0677
www.costumegallery.net
email: CG456@aol.com

2556 Cote, Inc. (American flags, appliqués,
batons and cases, gloves, shoes)
74 W. Bridge Street
Morrisville, PA 19067
215-295-8156
www.cote-inc.com

2557 Dansco
30 Frank Mossberg Drive
Attleboro, MA 02703
800-326-7365
Fax 508-431-1865
www.dansco.com

2558 Fred Frankel & Sons, Inc. (rhinestone
and beaded trimmings)
Jeweltrim Inc.
Jewel Fastener Corp.
19 West 38th Street
New York, NY 10018

212-840-0810
Fax 212-391-1214
www.fredfrankel.com
email: info@fredfrankel.com

2559 Galaxy Enterprises, Inc. (fringe, rhinestone jewelry, appliqués)
2421 Crofton Lane #14
Crofton, MD 21114-2228
410-721-0040
Fax 410-721-6423
www.galaxytrim.com
email: galaxytrim@erols.com

2560 Lebo's
2321 Crown Centre Drive
Charlotte, NC 28227
Fax 704-321-5100

2561 Leo's Dancewear Inc.
1900 N. Narragansett Avenue, Dept.
DS
Chicago, IL 60639
800-736-LEOS

Allstars Twirlers (Coatesville, PA)

www.leosdancewear.com
email: info@leosdancewear.com

2562 Satin Stitches Ltd.
11894 Rond Lake Blvd. NW
Minneapolis, MN 55433
800-48SATIN

2563 Spandex House, Inc.
263 West 38th Street, 2nd Floor
New York, NY 10018
212-354-6711
Fax 212-354-7432
spandexhouse.com
email: sales@spandexhouse.com

2564 Taffy's Capezio
200D Linden Street
Wellesley, MA 02482

781-237-5526
Fax 781-239-0544
and: Taffy's Capezio
1633 Golden Gate Blvd.
Mayfield Heights, OH 44124
800-982-3397

2565 Thompson Costume Trim and Fabric
1232 SW 59th Street
Oklahoma City, OK 73109
405-631-8850

2566 Varsity Spirit (dance costumes)
800-533-8022
www.varsityspirit.com

2567 Watercolour Dancewear
800-767-9523
www.watercolordancewear.com

Selected Bibliography

Articles

2568 Barbian, Kathy. "Stretch Yourself to a Better Strutting Routine." Twirl (June/July/August 1978): 21.

2569 Bauers, Sandy. "Nothing but the Sky for Twirlers: Up They Go! Batons Are Back, If They Were Even Gone." *Philadelphia Inquirer*, November 30, 2003, p. B1, B4.

2570 Campbell, Sharon. "Let's Talk About … Knee Injuries." *Twirl* (September/October 1981): 10.

2571 Cass, Julia. "Pity the Poor Twirling Girl." *Philadelphia Inquirer Today Magazine*, October 22, 1978, pp. 10–11.

2572 Coberley, Ron. "Twirling with the Band." *Twirl* (November 1980): 16.

2573 Elliott, Joseph E. "Tips on Buying Uniforms." *Instrumentalist* (August 1979): 39–41.

2574 Ewoldt, Karen. "Advice from a Graduate." *Drum Major* (July 1982): 9.

2575 Follett, Richard J. "What About the Majorettes?" *Instrumentalist* (October 1977): 57–59.

2576 Groome, Ginnette. "Try Twirling Three Batons." *Juggler's World*, Vol. 39, No. 1. www.juggling.org/w/87/1/baton.html

2577 Howard, Diane. "Tips for School Twirlers." *Drum Major* (December 1980): 7.

2578 Humphrey, Elizabeth. "Baton Twirling: Discipline, Responsibility, Commitment." *Daily Local News* [West Chester, PA], July 12, 1987, p. A3.

2579 Kirkpatrick, Curry. "Calvin [Murphy] Discovers Murphy's Law." *Sports Illustrated* (August 15, 1977): 14–15.

2580 McCormack, Patricia. "Baton Twirling: An Unusual Route to College Scholarships." *Twirl* (November 1980): 13.

2581 March, Barbara M.; Nazario, Beth G.; and Moors, Susan D. "A Tribute to Terry Hopple." *Daily Local News* [West Chester, PA], November 20, 1987, p. 4.

2582 Moncure, Sue Swyrs. "U.D. Junior Becomes America's 'No.1' Twirl Girl." *University of Delaware Update* (September 21, 1989): 3.

2583 National Association of Uniform Manufacturers. "How to Buy School Band Uniforms." New York, NY.

2584 Page, Nick. "Guide to Purchasing Band Uniforms." *Instrumentalist* (February 1988): 66, 68, 70–72.

2585 Pogue, Jan. "Lost in a Spin, A World Turns." *Philadelphia Inquirer*, October 18, 1981, pp. 1B, 5B.

2586 Portner, Robert. "How to Buy Band Uniforms." *American School and University* (July 1978): 44–47.

2587 Shields, Mike. "Twirling: Combination of Sport and Art Skills." *West Chester Citizen*, November 25, 1981, pp. 1, 10.

2588 Verhulst, Jacob. "A Twirling Program." *Twirl* (February 1981): 21.

2589 Wareham, Duane E. "A Case for Majorettes." *Instrumentalist* (September 1959): 75–77, 91.

2590 Wolfe, Howard A. "Developing Trends in Band Uniforms." *School Musician, Director & Teacher* (November 1977): 48–49.

2591 Wurmstedt, Bob. "In Texas: Twirling to Beat the Band." *Time*, December 11, 1978, pp. 12, 16.

Books (Fiction)

2592 Clarke, Michael. *Whenever He Saw a Marching Band*. Lincoln, NE: iUniverse.com, 2000. [a majorette is one of the main characters in this book set mostly in the 1950s]

2593 Lowry, Beverly. *Come Back, Lolly Ray*. Garden City, NY: Doubleday, 1977.

Books (Nonfiction)

2594 Atwater, Constance. *Baton Twirling: The Fundamentals of an Art and a Skill*. Rutland, VT and Tokyo, Japan: Charles E. Tuttle Company, 1964.

2595 *Cheerleading and Baton Twirling*. New York, NY: Tempo Books, 1972. "Cheerleading" by Roberta Davis; "Baton Twirling" by Harriette Behringer and Doris Wheelus. New York: Ace Books 1982 reissue.

2596 Finney, Shan. *Cheerleading and Baton Twirling: A First Book*. Danbury, CT: Franklin Watts, 1982.

2597 Frazier. *Complete Book of Baton Twirling*. New York: Hill & Wang, 1979.

2598 Hawkins, Jim W. *Baton Twirling is for Me*. Minneapolis, MN: Lerner Publications, 1982.

2599 Hindsley, Mark H. *How to Twirl a Baton*. Chicago, IL: Ludwig and Ludwig, 1928. (drum major baton/mace)

2600 Lee, Roger L. *The Baton: Twirling Made Easy!* New York, NY: Boosey and Hawkes, 1949.

2601 Miller, Fred, Gloria Smith, and Perri Ardman. *The Complete Book of Baton Twirling*. Garden City, NY: Doubleday, 1978.

2602 Orr, Susan Daily. *Baton Twirling Unlimited*. Indianapolis, IN: Carl Hungness Publishing, 1981.

2603 Roberts, Bob. *The Twirler and the Twirling Corps*. New York, NY: Carl Fischer, 1954.

2604 Robison, Nancy. *Baton Twirling*. New York: Harvey House, 1980.

2605 *Who's Who in Baton Twirling*. Janesville, WI: National Baton Twirling Association. annual.

Film

2606 *Twirl*. NBC TV movie first broadcast 10/25/1981.

Play

2607 Martin, Jane. *Twirler*. in *Esquire* (November 1982): 156–158.

Part 14
General Bibliography

Articles

2608 Anderson, Robert. "Woodwind Crisis in Corps-Style Bands." *The Instrumentalist* (November 1982): 13.

2609 Bachman, Harold B. "The Case for the Marching Band." *Instrumentalist* (September 1959): 50–53.

2610 Bencriscutto, Frank A. "Let's Put It All Together." *The School Musician, Director & Teacher* (November 1979): 8–9.

2611 Bierley, Paul. "More Band History Needed." *Instrumentalist* (September 1992): 12.

2612 Blackford, R. Winston. "The Marching Band as a Musical Entity." *School Musician, Director & Teacher* (June/July 1978): 50–51.

2613 Bocook, Jay. "Performing Corps-Style Music." *Instrumentalist* (June 1978): 32–33.

2614 Boullion, James L. "A Study of Music Performances at Athletic Contests." *School Musician, Director & Teacher* (March 1979): 46–48.

2615 Bouth, Thomas. "Four Views [Richard Lorenzen, Terry Martinez, David Morrison, Michael Wilson] on Developing an Outstanding Marching Band." *Instrumentalist* (September 2002): 13–17.

2616 Brammer, George. "A Primer on Sportslighting." *American School & University* (June 1987): 25–26, 30, 32.

2617 Branson, Branley A. "The Great Highland Pipes." *Instrumentalist* (October 1979): 23–25.

2618 "Brass Bands at Centre College." *Chronicle of Higher Education*, June 12, 1991, p. B5.

2619 Brazaukas, Paul. "Tips for Good Cymbal Playing." *Instrumentalist* (August 1982): 56, 58–59.

2620 Brion, Keith. "The 'Alternative' Marching Band." *Instrumentalist* (October 1977): 60–61.

2621 Cass, Julia. "High Stepping and Not for Half-Time Only." *Philadelphia Inquirer*, October 15, 1978, pp. 1-A, 8-B.

2622 Castronovo, Albert J. "New Marching Sounds of the 80s." *School Musician, Director & Teacher* (August/September 1980): 8–9.

2623 Clayton, Nancy. "Battle of Flowers: Corps Style." *School Musician, Director & Teacher* (August/September 1981): 24–25.

2624 Clyne, Robert. "Memories of Marching on Liberty Weekend." *Instrumentalist* (January 1987): 71–74.

2625 Covert, Bob. "Easing the Transition from Traditional to Corps Style Marching." *Instrumentalist* (June 1981): 8–9.

2626 Cowherd, Ron. "Sousa Marches: The Arranged Versions." *Instrumentalist* (December 1977): 44–47.

2627 Davis, Oscar B. "Those Magnificent Marches." *School Musician, Director & Teacher* (June/July 1980): 10–11, 45.

2628 Day, Kingsley. "Music at the White House." *Instrumentalist* (August 1992): 38–40, 42, 60–61.

2629 De Leon, Erlinda A. "Letter: Support Our Bands." *Wilmington News-Journal* [DE], January 11, 1988, p. A11.

2630 Dubois, John. "The Great Band Boom Marches On." *Philadelphia Bulletin*, October 10, 1978, pp. 1, 5.

2631 Elliott, Robert. "The History of Bands from Jericho to Goldman." *Instrumentalist* (August 1992): 70–71.

2632 Evenson, E. Orville. "The March Style of Sousa." *Instrumentalist* (November 1954): 13–15, 48–50.

2633 "Everything's Fair Dinkum Down Under." *Instrumentalist* (August 1987): 54, 56, 58.

2634 Flor, Gloria J. "The 'Frumpet' and Other Marching Band Oddities." *School Musician, Director & Teacher* (August/September 1979): 24–25.

2635 Floyd, Robert. "No Pass/No Play—How is Texas Faring?" *Instrumentalist* (April 1987): 33–34, 36.

2636 Gagliardi, Melissa. "Marching Bands Drum Up Respect." *Courier-Journal* [Louisville, KY], October 30, 2002.

2637 Garrison, Paul. "The Value of Marching Band." *Music Educators Journal* (January 1986): 48–52.

2638 Gasser, J.R., and B.G. Fred. "Bibliography of Marching Band, Baton Twirling, Flag Swinging, Gun Spinning, Drum and Bugle Corps." *Instrumentalist* Vol. I, No. 1 (September-October 1946): 15–17.

2639 Gerardi, J.L. "No Longer Football's Stepchild." *Instrumentalist* (June 1978): 28–29.

2640 Green, Don. "Fifty Steps to a Better Marching Band." *School Band and Orchestra* (August 2002).

2641 Greene, Kelly, and Rick Brooks. "Bored by Oom-Pah, High-School Bands March to Hip-Hop." *The Wall Street Journal*, April 18, 2003, pp. A1, A3.

2642 Hartsough, Jeff, and Derrick Logozzio. "Timeline of Marching and Field Percussion: Part I." *Percussive Notes* (August 1994).

2643 _____, and _____. "Timeline of Marching and Field Percussion: Part II." *Percussive Notes* (October 1994).

2644 _____, and _____. "Timeline of Marching and Field Percussion, Part III." *Percussive Notes* (December 1994).

2645 "A High School Band with Bagpipes." *Instrumentalist* (October 1979): 25.

2646 Holmes, Kristin E. "A Grim Lesson and Sad Farewell: Victim [designer Bobby Hoffman] Reveals His AIDS for Students' Sake." *Philadelphia Inquirer*, October 24, 1990 [?], pp. 1, 7-A.

2647 Hoover, J. Douglas. "New Drums on an Old Budget." *School Musician, Director & Teacher* (August/September 1980): 10.

2648 Hoover, Jerry. "A Flip of the Coin." *Instrumentalist* (August 1982): 41.

2649 Houston, Bob. "Multiple Percussion on the March." *Instrumentalist* (May 1978): 32–35.

2650 "How Willingly We March: Directors Survey." *Instrumentalist* (December 1990): 18–23.

2651 Iero, Cheech. "The Drums and Drummers of the Civil War." *Modern Drummer* (February 1994).

2652 "Is Marching Band in Step with Music Education?" *Music Educators Journal* (May 1985): 28–32.

2653 Jacobsen, James A. "The Responsibility of Music to Sports." *School Musician, Director & Teacher* (August/September 1981): 20–21.

2654 Johnson, William V. "Corps Style—Fad or Revolution?" *Instrumentalist* (June 1977): 22.

2655 Kastens, L. Kevin. "Achieving Musical Marching Band Performance." *Music Educators Journal* (September 1981): 26–29.

2656 Kilcup, Jodi. "The Element of Surprise: How Marching Bands, Nerf Balls, and Water Pistols Can Wake Up Alumni Volunteers." *Currents* [Council for Advancement and Support of Education] (1998): 26. [vol. 24, no. 4]

2657 Kohn, Jim. "'The Play' Just Won't Go Away." [Stanford, 1982] *Sports Illustrated*, November 21, 1988, p. 10.

2658 Lautzenheiser, Tim. "I Feel It!" *Instrumentalist* (October 1982): 30.

2659 Leckrone, Michael. "Simply Great—A Better Marching Band." *Music Educators Journal* (November 1987): 55–59.

2660 Lesinsky, Adam P. "Give the Girls a Chance." *School Musician, Director & Teacher* (August/September 1978): 60–61. (reprint from February 1930)

2661 Ludwig, W. F., Sr. "Sousa Had Rhythm." *School Musician, Director & Teacher* (October 1978): 78–79. (reprint from October 1935)

2662 Ludwig, William. "A History of American Drumming." *Instrumentalist* (November 1990): 22–26.

2663 McAllister, Robert L. "World's Largest Massed Band." *School Musician, Director & Teacher* (February 1979): 51–53. (reprint from November 1958)

2664 McMinn, Bill. "Small Marching Bands to the 'Fore." *Instrumentalist* (May 1988): 28–30, 33–34.

2665 "Making a List." [college marching bands] *Sports Illustrated*, October 7, 1991, p. 14.

2666 "Marching Bands at the Middle School Level?" *Music Educators Journal* (October 1990): 46–48.

2667 Mark, Michael, and Ansel Patten. "Emergence of the Modern Marching Band (1950–1970)." *Instrumentalist* (June 1976): 33–36.

2668 Middendorf, J. William. "The Drums Go 'Bang' and the Cymbals 'Clang.'" *Saturday Evening Post* (October 1976): 64–65, 78.

2669 Milbank, Dana. "Marching Bands Clean Up Their Acts Or Just Pretend To." *Wall Street Journal*, December 26, 1991, pp. 1, A4.

2670 Mitchell, Dave. "Corps vs. Traditional: A Comparison of Marching Styles and Values." *School Musician, Director & Teacher* (August/September 1980): 6–7.

2671 Moore, Daryl T. "The Music Comes Before the Marching." [interview with Florida A & M Director Julian White] *Instrumentalist* (July 2002): 12–16.

2672 Mufson, Steve. "Ivy League Bands Keep on Marching to X-Rated Tunes." *Wall Street Journal*, September 25, 1981, pp. 1, 19.

2673 Neilson, James. "The High School Marching Band." *School Musician,*

Director & Teacher (April 1981): 12–13.

2674 Nelson, Judy Ruppel. "Gene Thrailkill—Guiding the Pride." [University of Oklahoma] *Instrumentalist* (September 1987): 17–19.

2675 Paynter, John P. "Morale in the Marching Band." *Instrumentalist* (October 1959): 44–45, 102–103. [reprinted in September 2002 issue]

2676 Pedigo, Dwayne L. "Electronics in the Marching Band—A Sound New Sound Dimension." *Instrumentalist* (June 1980): 10–11.

2677 Peterson, Stephen G. "Creativity and the Marching Band." *Music Educators Journal* (November 1993): 29–32.

2678 Poe, Gerald. "The Marching Band: More Than 'Just Music.'" *School Musician, Director & Teacher* (August/September 1978): 70.

2679 Rapp, Willis. "The Evolution of Multi-Toms." *Percussionist* (Spring/Summer 1980): 132–139.

2680 Reisberg, Leo. "Colleges Struggle to Keep Would-Be Dropouts Enrolled: Institutions Try a Variety of New Methods to Raise Their Retention Rates." *Chronicle of Higher Education*, October 8, 1999, pp. A54–A56. [indicates that marching band, among other activities, keeps students in college]

2681 Revelli, William D. "Marching is an Educational Plus." *School Musician, Director & Teacher* (August/September 1979): 8–9, 60–61.

2682 Rideout, Roger R. "Summer Tasks for the First-Year Band Director." *Instrumentalist* (July 1987): 50, 52, 54.

2683 Rushin, Steve. "Remember the Tubas." *Sports Illustrated*, January 13, 2003.

2684 Salatto, Art. "Great Valley's Music Parents Assn. Drums Up Support for Band Students." *Suburban Advertiser* [PA], September 17, 1987, p. 19.

2685 Salzman, Tom. "A Marching Wind Ensemble." *Instrumentalist* (May 1985): 88, 90.

2686 "Saving the Program: UTA [University of Texas at Arlington] Tackles Marching Band—Without a Football Team." *School Band and Orchestra* (August 2002).

2687 Skilton, John M. "Some Items to Consider When Selecting a Music School Next Year." *Drum Corps News*, March 25, 1983, p. 15.

2688 Smith, Jack W. "An Alternative to the Marching Band." *School Musician, Director & Teacher* (January 1980): 8–9, 47.

2689 Snupp, Kenneth. "Corps Style Marching: A Blessing or a Curse?" *School Musician, Director & Teacher* (May 1980): 6, 13.

2690 "Steppin' Out at Stanford." *Oui* (November 1978): 94(5).

2691 Stock, Robert. "Bands on the March." *New York Times Magazine* (July 4, 1982): 12–15, 27, 33.

2692 Suggs, Welch. "For Black Americans, Better Than a Bowl Game: 'Classic' Events Feature College Fairs, Greek Reunions, Networking, and, Oh Yes, a Football Game." *Chronicle of Higher Education*, October 20, 2000, pp. A52–A53. [re black college football games; includes comments on bands]

2693 Sullivan, Robert. "Pianissimo, but Con Gusto." [Columbia University] *Sports Illustrated*, October 13, 1986, p. 17.

2694 Tuttle, David R. "Band—Take the Field." [University of Michigan in Rose Bowl] *Instrumentalist* (March 1965): 51–53.

2695 Wanamaker, Jay. "George H. Tuthill: A Pioneer in Marching Percussion." *School Musician, Director & Teacher* (August / September 1981): 22–23.

2696 _____. "The Olympic All-American Marching Band." *Instrumentalist* (January 1985): 37–40.

2697 _____. "Survey of Marching Percussion Materials." *Instrumentalist* (September 1980): 84, 86–89.

2698 Warnick, Jennifer. "Music and Bonding." [Sultan High School] *Herald* [Everett, WA] August 20, 2003.

2699 Waybright, David. "Brass Playing in the Marching Band." *Instrumentalist* (June 1984): 12–13.

2700 White, Jack W. "Corps-Style Rehearsals." *Instrumentalist* (June 1978): 30–31.

Books

Nonfiction

2702 Bierley, Paul E. *John Philip Sousa, American Phenomenon*. rev. ed. Westerville, OH: Integrity Press, 1992.

2703 Binion, T., Jr. *High School Marching Band*. Englewood Cliffs, NJ: Prentice-Hall, 1973.

2704 Blades, James. *Percussion Instruments and Their History*. New York: F. A. Praeger, 1970.

2705 Bollinger, Donald E. *Band Directors Complete Handbook*. Englewood Cliffs, NJ: Prentice-Hall, 1979.

2706 Chase, Gilbert. *America's Music: From the Pilgrims to the Present*. 3rd ed. Champaign: University of Illinois Press, 1987.

2707 Colwell, Richard, and Carol Richardson, eds. *The New Handbook of Research on Music Teaching and Learning: A Project of the Music Educators National Conference*. Cary, NC: Oxford University Press, 2002.

2708 Colwell, Richard, and Thomas W. Goolsby. *The Teaching of Instrumental Music*. 3rd ed. Upper Saddle River, NJ: Prentice Hall, 2001.

2709 Combs, F. Michael. *Percussion Manual*. Belmont, CA: Wadsworth Publishing Company, 1977.

2710 Duvall, W. Clyde. *The High School Band Director's Handbook*. Englewood Cliffs, NJ: Prentice-Hall, 1960.

2711 Foster, Robert E. *Multiple-Option Marching Band Techniques*. 3rd ed. Port Washington, NY: Alfred Publishing Company, 1992. Includes history of marching bands.

2712 Gibson, John G. *Old and New World Highland Bagpiping*. Montreal, Quebec: McGill-Queens, 2002.

2713 Goldman, Edwin Franko. *Band Betterment: Suggestions and Advice to Bands, Bandmasters, and Band-Players*. New York, NY: Carl Fischer, 1934.

2714   Hawkins, Holly Blue. *The Heart of the Circle: A Guide to Drumming*. Santa Cruz, CA: Crossing Press, 1999.

2715   Hazen, Margaret Hindle and Robert M. Hazen. *The Music Men: An Illustrated History of Brass Bands in America, 1800–1920*. Washington, D.C.: Smithsonian Institution Press, 1987.

2716   Herbert, T., ed. *Bands: The Brass Band Movement in the 19th and 20th Centuries*. Buckingham, England: Open University Press, 1991.

2717   Hertz, Wayne S., ed. *Music in the Senior High School*. MENC Music in American Life Commission VI. Washington, D.C.: Music Educators National Corporation, 1959.

2718   Hjelmervik, Kenneth, and Richard Berg. *Marching Bands*. New York, NY: A.S. Barnes and Company, 1953.

2719   Hong, Sherman, and Jim Hamilton. *Percussion Section: Developing the Corps Style*. Petal, MS: Band Shed, 1978.

2720   Instrumentalist Company. *Percussion Anthology*. 4th ed. Northfield, IL, 1988.

2721   Jones, Jay. *New Director Resource Guide*. Kansas City, MO. jonesj@pcriii.k12. mo.us [email for date, etc.]

2722   Kraus, David. *A Visible Feast*. Lawrence, KS: University of Kansas, 1980.

2723   Loken, Newt, and Otis Dypwick. *Cheerleading & Marching Bands*. New York, NY: A.S. Barnes and Company, 1945.

2724   Mercer, R. Jack. *The Band Director's Brain Bank*. Evanston, IL: Instrumentalist Company, 1970.

2725   Navarre, Randy. *Instrumental Music Teacher's Survival: Ready-To-Use Guidelines, Lessons & Exercises for Teaching Beginning Band Instruments*. West Nyack, NY: Parker Publishing Company, 2001.

2726   Neidig, Kenneth L. *The Band Director's Guide*. Englewood Cliffs, NJ: Prentice-Hall, 1964.

2727   Pavlakis, Christopher. *The American Music Handbook*. New York, NY: Free Press, 1974.

2728   Probasco, Jim. *A Parent's Guide to Band and Orchestra*. Foreword by Tom Batiuk. White Hall and Crozet, VA: Betterway Publications, 1991.

2729   Righter, Charles B. *Gridiron Pageantry: The Story of the Marching Band for Bandsmen, Directors and Football Fans*. Cooper Square, NY: Carl Fischer, 1941.

2730   Scott, Willard. *America is My Neighborhood*. New York: Simon & Schuster, 1987. includes section on Dr. William P. Foster of Florida A&M University and author of *Band Pageantry*.

2731   Sousa, John Philip. *Marching Along*. Boston, MA: Hale, Cushman and Flint, 1928.

2732   Shellahamer, Bentley, James Swearingen, and Jon Woods. *The Marching Band Program: Principles and Practices*. Oskaloosa, IA: C.L. Barnhouse, 1986.

2733   Wells, James R. *The Marching Band in Contemporary Music Education*. New York, NY; Interland Publishing, 1976.

2734   Whitwell, David. *A New History of Wind Music*. Evanston, IL: Instrumentalist, 1972.

Fiction

2735 Clarke, Michael A. *Whenever He Saw a Marching Band.* Lincoln, NE: iUniverse.com, 2000. [one major character was a high school and college majorette]

2736 Flowers, Arthur. *Cleveland Lee's Beale Street Band.* Illustrated by Anna Rich. Memphis, TN: Bridgewater Books/Troll Associates, 1996. [juvenile; ages 4–8]

2737 Francis, David "Panama," and Bob Reiser. *David Gets His Drum.* Tarrytown, NY: Marshall Cavendish, 2002. [juvenile, ages 5–8]

2738 Giff, Patricia Reilly. *Yankee Doodle Drumsticks.* Illustrated by Emily Arnold McCully. New York: Young Yearling/Dell, 1992. [juvenile]

2739 Moss, Lloyd. *Our Marching Band.* Illustrated by Diana Cain Bluthenthal. New York: Putnam Publishing Group, 2001. [juvenile; ages 4–8]

2740 Peters, Sharon. *The Marching Band Mystery.* Illustrated by Irene Trivas. Memphis, TN: Troll Associates, 1985. [juvenile]

Films

2741 *Drumline.* 20th Century Fox, 2002.

2742 *Mr. Holland's Opus.* Hollywood Pictures, 1995.

2743 *Pay the Price.* 2000 independent film produced and directed by Darryl Lassiter released on video 2002.

Periodicals

An attempt has been made to include only those magazines relevant to marching activities.

2744 *Accent on Music* (formerly *Accent*)
Accent Publications
12100 W. 6th Avenue
Box 15337
Denver, CO 80215

2745 *American Music*
University of Illinois Press
54 E. Gregory Drive
Champaign, IL 61820

2746 *The American Music Teacher*
Music Teachers National Association
617 Vine Street, Suite 1432
Cincinnati, OH 45202–2434

2747 *Bandworld*
407 Terrace Street

Ashland, OR 97520
published January, March, May, August, November by Western International Band Clinic

2748 *BDGuide*
Village Press, Inc.
2779 Aero Park Drive
Traverse City, MI 49684
published bimonthly during school year

2749 *The Brass Player*
New York Brass Conference for Scholarships
315 West 53rd Street
New York, NY 10019
212–581–1480

Fax 212–489–5186
www.charlescolin.com/nybc/bp.htm
email: webmaster@charlescolin.com

2750 Brass Quarterly (published 1957–1964)

2751 CBDNA Journal
College Band Directors National Association
Box 8028
Austin, TX 78767

2752 The Clarinet
P.O. Box 450622
Atlanta, GA 30345–0622

2753 Dance Spirit
P.O. Box 2041
Marion, OH 43306–2141
www.dancespirit.com

2754 Dance Spirit's InMotion (quarterly)
Lifestyle Ventures
250 W. 57th St., Suite 420
New York, NY 10107
212–265–8890
Fax 212–265–8908
www.dancespirit.com/inmotion/index.
shtml

2755 DCI Today
(Drum Corps International)
P.O. Box 548
Lombard, IL 60148–0548
www.dci.org/news/dci.today

2756 Drum Corps News (ceased publication)

2757 Drum Corps World
P.O. Box 8052
Madison, WI 53708–8052
800–554–9630 (subscriptions
Fax 608–241–4974
www.drumcorpsworld.com
email: publisher@drumcorpsworld.
com

2758 Drum Major Magazine
Box 266
Janesville, WI 53545

2759 Electronic Music Educator
200 Northfield Road
Northfield, IL 60093

2760 Field & Floor: An Online Pageantry Journal
http://fieldandfloor.homestead.com/
Home1.html

2761 Flute Talk
Instrumentalist Company
200 Northfield Road
Northfield, IL 60093

2762 High Fidelity (ceased publication after 1988)

2763 The Horn Call
International Horn Society
School of Arts and Letters
Southeast Oklahoma State University
Durant, OK 74701

2764 Insights Magazine (Drill Team Directors of America)
PMB 115
1645 Pat Booker Road #103
Universal City, TX 78148
800–695–6910, x15
www.dtda.org/insights
email: insights@dtda.org

2765 Instrumentalist
200 Northfield Road
Northfield, IL 60093

2766 Journal of Band Research
Troy State University Press
Troy, AL 36082

2767 Marching Bands & Corps (ceased publication)
River City Publications
P.O. Box 8341
Jacksonville, FL 32211

2768 *Modern Drummer*
Modern Drummer Publications
870 Pompton Avenue
Cedar Grove, NJ 07009

2769 *Modern Percussionist*
P.O. Box 469
Cedar Grove, NJ 07009

2770 *Music & Pageantry Journal* (one issue; ceased publication)

2771 *Music Educators Journal*
Music Educators National Conference
1902 Association Drive
Reston, VA 22091

2772 *Music Journal* (ceased publication 1985)

2773 *On Parade*
All American Association of Contest Judges
1627 Lay Boulevard
Kalamazoo, MI 49001

2774 *Percussive Notes*
Percussive Arts Society
214 West Main St.
P.O. Box 697
Urbana, IL 61801–0697
includes ongoing section, "Percussion on the March"

2775 *School Band & Orchestra Magazine*
50 Brook Road
Needham, MA 02494
781–453–9310, x24

www.sbomagazine.com/sbosubscribe.html
email: mprescott@larkinpublications.com

2776 *School Musician, Director & Teacher* (ceased publication 1987)
Ammark Publishing Company
4049 W. Peterson
Chicago, IL 60646

2777 *Sound & Vision*
Hachette Filipacchi Magazines, Inc.
1633 Broadway
New York, NY 10019
212–767–6000
Fax 212–767–5615
www.soundandvisionmag.com

Stereo Review see *Sound & Vision*

2778 *Today's Music Educator*
P.O. Box 8052
Madison, WI 53708
published February and September by Drum Corps Sights & Sounds, Inc.

2779 *Twirl Magazine*
U.S. Twirling Association
P.O. Box 24488
Seattle, WA 98124

2780 *World of Pageantry* (West Coast orientation)
Band & Drill Team News
P.O. Box 2961
Anaheim, CA 92804

Website

2781 www.bandparenting.net

Index

References are to entry numbers

253